Blacks of Tunis in al-Timbuktāwī's *Hatk al-Sitr*

Modern Intellectual Trends

THE MIDDLE EAST, AFRICA AND ASIA

Editorial Board

Elizabeth Kassab
Majid Daneshgar
Zeynep Direk
SherAli Tareen

VOLUME 2

The titles published in this series are listed at *brill.com/mit*

Blacks of Tunis in al-Timbuktāwī's *Hatk al-Sitr*

A West African Jihadist's Perspectives on Bori, Religious Deviance, and Race and Enslavement in Ottoman Tunisia
With Translation and Critical Edition

By

Ismael M. Montana

BRILL

LEIDEN | BOSTON

Cover illustration: Bash Aga, also known as *al-Ḥākim fī al-Qishra al-Sawdā'* (the Governor over the Black-Skinned). Postcard in possession of the author.

The Library of Congress Cataloging-in-Publication Data is available online at https://catalog.loc.gov
LC record available at https://lccn.loc.gov/2023054020

Typeface for the Latin, Greek, and Cyrillic scripts: "Brill". See and download: brill.com/brill-typeface.

ISSN 2773-1022
ISBN 978-90-04-51616-8 (hardback)
ISBN 978-90-04-51617-5 (e-book)
DOI 10.1163/9789004516175

Copyright 2024 by Koninklijke Brill NV, Leiden, The Netherlands.
Koninklijke Brill NV incorporates the imprints Brill, Brill Nijhoff, Brill Schöningh, Brill Fink, Brill mentis, Brill Wageningen Academic, Vandenhoeck & Ruprecht, Böhlau and V&R unipress.
All rights reserved. No part of this publication may be reproduced, translated, stored in a retrieval system, or transmitted in any form or by any means, electronic, mechanical, photocopying, recording or otherwise, without prior written permission from the publisher. Requests for re-use and/or translations must be addressed to Koninklijke Brill NV via brill.com or copyright.com.

This book is printed on acid-free paper and produced in a sustainable manner.

To the memory
of my brother, Olu (a.k.a. Haj Omar Sharif).
June 1969–August 17, 2021

يا أيّها العبيد علام تشركون باللّه

O you slaves, how on earth can you ascribe partners to Allah

Contents

Foreword IX
Acknowledgements XI
List of Maps and Figures XIV
Note on Transliteration XV

PART 1
Introduction and Historical Setting

Introduction 3

1 Religious and Intellectual Milieu 28

2 Defining al-Timbuktāwī's Infidel Blacks of Tunis (*Sūdān Tūnis*) 50

3 *Sūdān Tūnis* and Their Imprint on Urban Space 80

Epilogue 95

PART 2
Hatk al-Sitr*: Text and Translation*

Prologue 105

Introduction 109

1 An Account Establishing the Polytheism (*Shirk*) of the Slaves 111

2 The Names of Some of Their Deities 113

3 Describing Their Worship 129

Conclusion 139

Glossary 151
Bibliography 155
Index 167

Foreword

This astonishing document exposes the extremism of political thought in West Africa in the early nineteenth century, when jihād was transforming the political geography from Senegambia to Lake Chad from 1807–1808. In *Hatk al-Sitr ʿammā ʿalayhi sūdān Tūnis min al-kufr* ("Piercing the Veil: Being an Account of the Infidel Religion of the Blacks of Tunis"), Aḥmad b. al-Qāḍī b. Yūsuf b. Ibrāhīm al-Fulānī al-Timbuktāwī wrote a treatise for the pasha of Tunis which condemned what he considered to be deviant religious practice among the Black population, most of which was enslaved or had been enslaved and had been brought across the desert. According to al-Timbuktāwī, the idolatrous religious practices had been brought from south of the Sahara, which is a clear reference to *bori* spirit possession and similar practices found not only in Hausa society but throughout a broad belt across the savannah and sahel where Islam was well established. The condemnation that al-Timbuktāwī heaped upon the practice was consistent with the complaints of those who were promoting jihād in West Africa.

Although *Hatk al-Sitr* has been known to specialists for some time, Professor Montana provides the first detailed, annotated translation of the text, along with the original Arabic manuscript. It is often thought that sources for African history rely exclusively on European documentation, but al-Timbuktāwī demonstrates the inaccuracy of a focus solely on European observations. Indeed, the text more accurately represents a great flourishing in Arabic writing in the late eighteenth century and continuing through the nineteenth century, at least in Muslim regions of Africa. Indeed, Timbuktu, where he was from, was a center of Islamic scholarship for centuries. The text demonstrates the extent of literacy among the Muslim elite south of the Sahara. Moreover, he identified as Fulbe, based on the reference in his name to Fulani, which was the term Fulbe were known in the Hausa speaking regions south of the Sahara. He was also the son of an al-Qāḍī, that is, a judge, almost certainly at Timbuktu.

It is interesting that al-Timbuktāwī wrote his appeal to the pasha of Tunis on his return from pilgrimage to Mecca. His journey took him back across the Maghreb first to Tunis and then to Morocco, before returning to Timbuktu. His background is unclear other than his genealogical assertions. His time on the *ḥajj* brought him into contact with Muslims from various parts of the world. It is clear from his text that unbelief was a preoccupation of those with whom he came in contact. After leaving Tunis, he continued to Morocco, not exactly the shortest distance back to Timbuktu. He remained in Morocco for some time and where he interacted with its religious scholars (*ulamā*) before returning to his homeland in the western Sūdān. In Morocco, he composed a second treatise titled *Shikāyat al-Dīn al-Muḥammadī ʾilā Riʿayat al-muwakkalīn bihī*, which had as its primary concern the same problem that he had perceived in Tunisia, although in Morocco the possession cult was known as *gnaoua* (*gnawa*). The text of al-Timbuktāwī expressed intolerance to religious innovation (*bidʿa*), a fundamental justification for jihād.

The late eighteenth and early nineteenth centuries was a period of turmoil and transformation within the Islamic world of the Ottoman Empire, Morocco, and sub-Saharan Africa. The Mediterranean lands of Islam and the Sahara to the south faced mounting pressure from a European world beset with revolution and rapid economic expansion, often referred to as the Age of Revolutions. As is clear from Montana's analysis of al-Timbuktawi's *Hatk al-Sitr*, any analysis of the period that does not take into account the radical jihad movement and the subsequent efforts at reform in the Ottoman Empire and its domains seriously underestimates the vibrancy of the Islamic world and the efforts among Muslims, as centered on the pilgrimage, to exchange ideas, promote Islamic ideals, and study. The texts of al-Timbuktāwī, both the one analyzed here by Montana and the related treatise composed in Morocco demonstrate that Muslim scholars were concerned with internal dissension within the Muslim community as reflected in the perceived deviance of *bori* and similar practices in 1807–1808. Confrontation with non-Muslim Europe was thought to depend upon internal harmony among Muslims and the responsibility of governments to enforce the strictures of Islam.

Montana's rendition of al-Timbuktāwī should be placed in context. The outpouring of written texts at the time was phenomenal. The documentation is housed in numerous archives, not only the enormous collections in Timbuktu, but also in Sokoto, Morocco, and elsewhere. Undoubtedly, additional texts will come to light in French, Italian, Turkish, and other archives. Increasingly, texts written in Arabic or *ajami* are being examined critically and will require scrutiny to flesh out their significance. This volume can serve as a model for the presentation and discussion of such materials.

Paul E. Lovejoy

Acknowledgements

Every scholarly endeavor that culminates in a book accrues debts of gratitude. Such is the case with this book. I want to begin by thanking Abdurraouf Oueslati, Acquisitions Editor, Middle Eastern and Islamic Studies, under whose editorship this project came to fruition. In the Fall of 2018, when Abdurraouf contacted me and asked if I would be interested in contributing an entry on Ahmad b. al-Qādī b. Yusūf al-Timbuktāwī to the *Encyclopedia of Islam Three*, having written and published widely on al-Timbuktāwī, I immediately welcomed the opportunity. Thereafter, I proposed, and Abdurraouf saw the potential of a first complete English translation and a critical edition of the text of *al-Hatk al-Sitr* suitable for publication in the Brill series on Modern Intellectual Trends. While that exchange resulted in the publication of this book, my interest in this project goes back to my earlier years in graduate school at York University. I am deeply indebted to Paul Lovejoy and the late John Hunwick for introducing me to *Hatk al-Sitr* and encouraging me to look beyond al-Timbuktāwī's approach exemplified in this treatise. Studying this text as an intellectual pursuit brought nothing but joy and immeasurable fulfillment over the years. It is my hope that this complete English translation of the text will help broaden our understanding of the depth and implications of the displacement of Sūdānic West Africans outside their homelands and hence the birth of their diasporic experiences during the era of the slave trade.

Ultimately, the publication of this book would not have been possible without the support of many individuals and institutions who have given their time and support throughout the various stages of this project. I am grateful to the History Department, the College of Arts and Liberal Arts of Science and the United Faculty Alliance (UFA) at Northern Illinois University for the travel grants and financial support for the numerous research trips and conference travels associated with this project. I thank the staff of the Archives du Government Tunisienne and Bibliotheque Nationale de Tunisie. Special thanks are due to Rachida Smine, Head of the Manuscripts Department at the Bibliothéque Nationale de Tunis. I am admirably thankful to Chouki El Hamel for providing me with a copy of the treatise found in the King's Library in Rabat, Morocco. Alex Khaleeli offered helpful feedback in matters of style and transliteration of Arabic textual studies, and while Aisha Mousa did a fantastic job in reviewing the Arabic Text and polishing my translation, Kate Kingsford provided meticulously copyediting and editorial support. I wish to thank Glen Pawelski for producing some of the maps in this book. I am indebted to the two anonymous readers of the book manuscript for their constructive comments and feedback.

Portions of this book previously appeared in my previous works. Chapter 2 draws and expands on earlier argument expressed in "Enslavable Infidels: Sudan-Tunis as a classificatory categorization for a new wave of Enslaved Africans in the Regency of Tunis," in *The Maghreb Review*, 29, no. 1–4 (2004), while some of the ideas in chapter 4 can be found in "The Developments of Bori Diyar (Compounds) in the City of Tunis, 1738–1880s" in *Saharan Crossroads: Exploring Historical, Cultural, and Artistic Linkages between North and West Africa*, edited by Tara F. Deubel et al., (Cambridge Scholars Publishing, 2014). I am grateful to the publishers for the permission to reproduce some of this material here.

I have benefitted from several opportunities to present portions of this book in numerous conferences and colloquia. I am very grateful to the Center for Maghrib Studies (University of Arizona), Centre d'Etudes Maghrébines à Tunis (CEMAT), The Ifriqiyya Colloquium (Columbia University), The Harriet Tubman Institute (York University), the Trans-African Slaveries Network (Columbia University), African Abolitionism: The Rise and Transformations of Anti-Slavery in Africa (*AFRAB*), ERC Advanced Grant, Horizon 2020, (University College London) and Trajectories of Slavery in Islamicate Societies, (TrasSIS), University of Bern. The feedback I received at these venues has shaped and continued to inform the ideas articulated in this project.

Over the years, conversations with colleagues, friends, graduate students, and the descendants of Sūdān Tūnis have also deepened my interest in this project. To this end, I wish to thank the following individuals: Paul Lovejoy, the late Sydney Kanya-Forstner, Martin Klein, Mohammed Bashir Salau, Ehud Toledano, Ghislaine Lydon, Bruce Hall, Manuel Barcia, Damian Pargas, Mohamed Diaketé, Paul Naylor, Sahbi Kaddachi, Houda Mzioudet, Yacine Daddi-Addoun, Mariana Candido, Ibrahim Hamza, Sophie Ferchiou, Richard Jankowsky, Kalifa Chater, Chouki El Hamel, Nora Lafi, Marta Scaglioni, Abdelhamid Larguèche, Murray Last, Abdeljelil Temimi, Sean Farrell, Aaron Fogleman, Brian Sandberg, Valerie Garver, Beatrix Hoffman, Henry Lovejoy, Boubacar Mahamane, Ali Diaketé, Mamadou Diallo, M'hamed Oualdi, Chouki El Hamel, Catey Boyles, Vaffi F. Sharif, Mauro Nobili, Wendy Wilson Fall, Abu Bah, Benedetta Rossi, Bruno Veras, Abiodun Ademidun Ademiluwa, Justin Riner, Anna Henderson, Justin Iverson, Sheila Bombaare, Adiza Mohammed, Matilda Ansah, El-Cheikh Hammadi el-Bidalī, Abdelmejid Bournaouis, and Zohra Trabelsī.

My deepest and greatest debt are, of course, personal and are reserved for my loving and beautiful family. First and foremost, I am eternally grateful to Dzifa A. Hosi-Montana, my wife and partner, for much more than I could ever express in writing. Jilma (my daughter) and Bilsi (my son) have endured my frequent research and conference travels yet always comfort me with the warmest giggles and hugs when I need them the most. Dzifa, Jilma, and Bilsi, I am forever grateful for your unwavering support and unconditional love. You are my source of inspiration. Finally, my brother, Olu, to whom this book is dedicated, did not live to see it come to fruition. Olu, I will forever remember you as the kindest, loving, creative, and the most supportive brother I could have ever wished for.

I.M. Montana
Cortland, Illinois
October, 2023

Maps and Figures

Maps

1 Jihad and Muslim States in the early nineteenth-century Bilād al-Sūdān XVI
2 The Caravan Slave Trade across Tunisia and the Western and Central Sūdān XVII
3 Al-Timbuktāwī's Itinerary to Hajj, 1808–1809 18
4 Distribution of Bori Religious and Communal *Diyar* (Households) in Tunis 84

Figures

1 Ratio of the Bori households to gender and the volume of the slave trade 91

Note on Transliteration

Transliteration of Arabic when dealing with a broad and expansive geographical scope encompassing Ottoman North Africa and the *bilād al-sūdān* (Land of the Blacks), the latter with its own *ajami* variation of Arabic, if not standardized, can posed a challenge. In Tunisia as in other parts of North Africa, this problem is exacerbated by the adoption of French transliterations, which often reflect the local colloquial parlance. Hence, terms and names such as Stembālī and el-Ḥachā'ichī reflect the colloquial transliterations in French than the standardized Arabic form of transliteration.

To achieve a consistency, throughout the study, I have used the simplified system for translating Arabic words followed by the *International Journal of Middle East Studies* (IJMES). This informed choice also allows me to avoid unnecessary use of diacritics in Arabic terms or names, words such as jihad, Ramadan and other words that are commonly employed in English dictionaries without transliteration and are used in this study as such. Similarly, Arabic words that have been localized in the context of the *bilād al-sūdān* such as emir has also been used without transliteration.

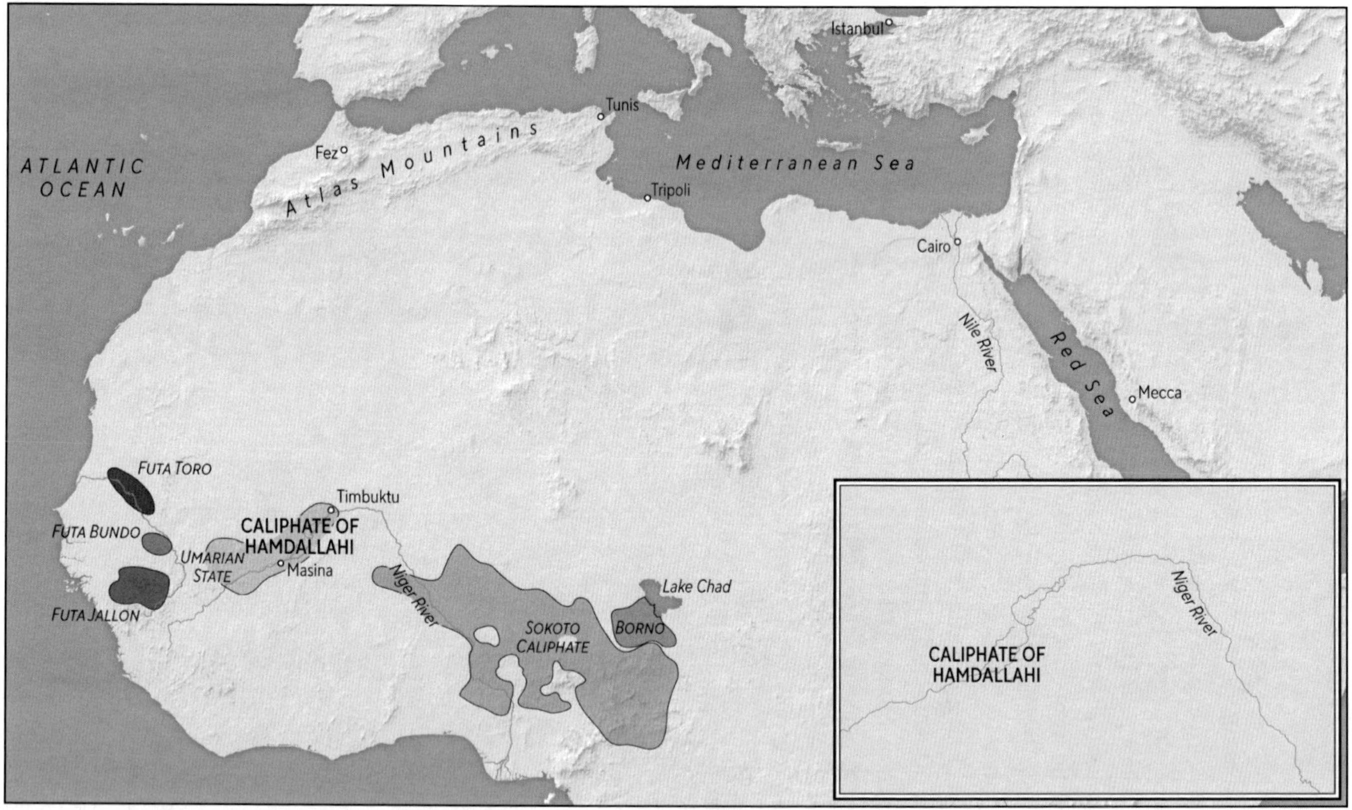

MAP 1 Jihad and Muslim States in the early nineteenth-century Bilād al-Sūdān
ADAPTED FROM HENRY B. LOVEJOY, AFRICAN DIASPORA MAPS LTD

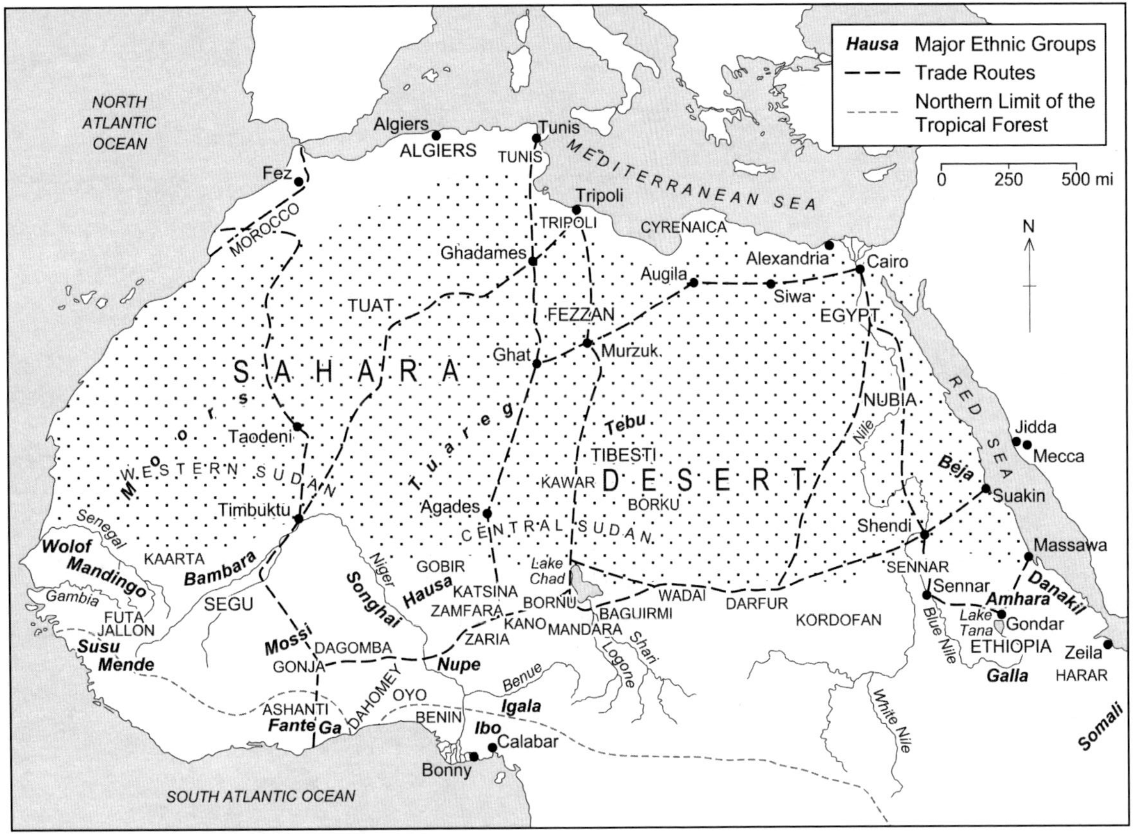

MAP 2 The Caravan Slave Trade across Tunisia and the Western and Central Sūdān

PART 1

Introduction and Historical Setting

Introduction

This book is about a distinct class of the enslaved Sūdānic West African community in the early nineteenth-century Regency of Tunis, who came under attack from a Timbuktu cleric, jurist (*qāḍī*) and a religious puritan, Aḥmad b. al-Qāḍī b. Yūsuf b. Ibrāhīm al-Fulānī al-Timbuktāwī, who labeled them infidels (*kuffār*). An Islamic religious scholar from the highly prestigious center of Islamic learning in Timbuktu in the western Sūdān,[1] al-Timbuktāwī came into contact with the Sūdānic community in the Maghrib on his way to perform the pilgrimage (*ḥajj*) in Mecca around 1808. His sojourn in the Maghrib coincided with two major historical developments: religious polemics triggered by a Wahhābi proclamation denouncing Sufism in the Maghrib and all over the Islamic World as a religious innovation (*bidʿa*), and an increased presence of enslaved Sūdānic West Africans as a result of the expansion of the trans-Saharan slave trade. While in Tunis on his way to *ḥajj*, he was confronted with the humming scenes of the Hausa-trance possession cult of Bori practiced by Sūdānic West Africans.[2] Convinced that Tunisian religious and political authorities did not know about the Bori cult practices in the beylic, upon his return from his pilgrimage he authored *Hatk al-Sitr ʿammā ʿalayhi sūdān Tūnis min al-kufr* ("Piercing the Veil: Being an Account of the Infidel Religion of the Blacks of Tunis"), which he dedicated to the Husaynid ruler Ḥammūda Pāsha (r. 1782–1814) while entreating the bey to ban the Bori cult and imprison its adherents or re-enslave them if they refused to disavow the cult.[3] In Morocco, where he

1 Throughout this book, "Sūdān" will refer not to the Islamic Republic of Sudan but the trans-continental savannah belt region lying south of the Greater Sahara. This region was historically described by classical and medieval Islamic geographers in Arabic as *bilād al-Sūdān* (meaning "land of the Blacks"). For more on this region, see Humphrey Fisher, "The Western and Central Sudan," in P.M. Holt, Ann K.S. Lambton, and Bernard Lewis (eds.), *The Cambridge History of Islam*, Vol. 2: *The Further Islamic Lands, Islamic Society and Civilization* (Cambridge: Cambridge University Press, 1970), 345.

2 See Ismael M. Montana, "Al-Timbuktāwī, Aḥmad b. al-Qāḍī," in Kate Fleet et al. (eds.), *The Encyclopedia of Islam Three* (Leiden & Boston: Brill, 2022), 148–150; Abdeljelil Temimi, "Pour une histoire sociale de la minorité africaine noire en Tunisie: Sources et perspectives," in Abdeljelil Temimi (ed.), *Études d'histoire arabo-africaine* (Zaghouan: Cermodi, 1994), 49–56; Fatima Harrak and Mohamed El-Mansour, *A Fulani Jihadist in the Maghreb: Admonition of Aḥmad Ibn Al-Qādī at-Timbuktī to the Rulers of Tunisia and Morocco* (Rabat: Institute of African Studies, 2000).

3 See Ismael M. Montana, "Bori Colonies in Tunis," in *Slavery, Islam and Diaspora*, eds. Behnaz Mirzai Asl, Ismael M. Montana and Paul E. Lovejoy (Trenton NJ: Africa World Press, 2009), 155–167; Ismael M. Montana, "Bori practice among enslaved West Africans of Ottoman Tunis:

© KONINKLIJKE BRILL NV, LEIDEN, 2024 | DOI:10.1163/9789004516175_002

stayed and interacted with its religious scholars (*ʿulamāʾ*) on his way back to his homeland in the western Sūdān, he composed a similar treatise titled *Shikāyat al-Dīn al-Muḥammadī ʾilā Riʿayat al-muwakkalīn bihī*, urging its religious authorities to suppress the Sūdānic indigenous religious practices, which he equally condemned as *kufr*.[4]

Both treatises, *Hatk al-Sitr* and *Shikāyat al-Dīn*, reveal the degree of al-Timbuktāwī's intolerance to religious innovation (*bidʿa*), which motivated him to influence the political and religious authorities in Tunisia and Morocco to stamp out the Bori cult throughout their lands. In so doing, al-Timbuktāwī displayed an attitude towards the Bori cult that was similar to those of the Fulfulde leadership of the jihad in the western and central Sūdān, specifically the leadership of the emergent Sokoto Caliphate and those in Māsina, south of Timbuktu, who sympathized with the Sokoto leadership. This book focuses solely on the *Risālat al-Hatk al-Sitr* in which al-Timbuktāwī provides a vivid account of aspects of religious practices associated with the Hausa Bori cult in the Regency of Tunis. In this treatise, al-Timbuktāwī issued a series of recommendations urging Ḥammūda Pāsha to ban the Bori cult and to adopt strict measures against its members, whom he specifically isolated from a heterogenous Black (*Wusfān*) population and categorized as *Sūdān Tūnis*,[5] as stated in the title of the treatise. Likewise, he condemned what he described as *al-musāḥaqa* or religiously induced lesbianism among some fully-fledged members of the Bori cult, which he decried as immoral and *fitna* (dissension). However, al-Timbuktāwī saved his worst criticism for the Bori chief priestesses—invariably called *ʿajāʾiz* (sing. *ʿajūz*), meaning old ladies, *ʿarāʾif* (sing. *ʿarīfa*, the wise women), or *sarauniyyas* (queens) by the cult's adepts—who acted as custodians of the Bori cult and exercised enormous authority over the Sūdānic West African community.[6]

This book presents for the first time a complete English translation and a critical edition of *Hatk al-Sitr*. It places the treatise in its historical contexts and

Unbelief (*Kufr*) or another dimension of the African diaspora?," *History of the Family: An International Quarterly* 16 (2011): 152–159; Richard C. Jankowsky, *Stambeli: Music, Trance, and Alterity in Tunisia* (Chicago: University of Chicago Press, 2010).

4 Harrak and El-Mansour, *A Fulani Jihadist in the Maghreb*, Montana, 12–13; Montana, "Al-Timbuktāwī, Aḥmad b. al-Qāḍī," 148.

5 Aḥmad b. al-Qāḍī b. Yūsuf b. Ibrāhīm al-Fulānī al-Timbuktāwī *Hatk al-Sitr ʿAmmā ʿAlayhi Sūdān Tūnis min al-Kufr* (Tunis: MS No. 21183, Bibliotheque Nationale de Tunisie, 1813) p. 3, Folio A; Ismael M. Montana, "Aḥmad Ibn al-Qāḍī al-Timbuktāwī on the Bori Ceremonies of Sūdān-Tūnis," in Paul E. Lovejoy (ed.), *Slavery on the Frontiers of Islam* (New Jersey: Marcus Weiner Publishers, 2004), 188.

6 Montana, "Bori Colonies in Tunis," 162–163.

intellectual environments of Islamic reformism in the Maghrib and in the western and central Sūdān, both of which informed and shaped al-Timbuktāwī's attitude towards the Bori cult's practitioners in the Maghrib. The book also maps out the ethnographic, demographic and other defining characteristics of the portion of the Blacks of Tunis (*Wusfān*) associated with the Bori cult. Additionally, it explores the intellectual background of the author of *Hatk al-Sitr* by examining his viewpoints concerning the central issues of religious innovation (*bidaʿ*), polytheism (*shirk*), anathematization (*takfīr*), intercession (*tawassul*), and enslavement, all of which dominated intellectual discourse at the time, particularly during the two decades prior to his pilgrimage, and argues that his perspectives on these issues reflected the sentiments of those who advocated jihad in his western Sūdānic homeland. Although the importance of *Hatk al-Sitr* as a useful text in illustrating our understanding of the scope of indigenous African religious practices beyond the trans-Saharan and Islamic Mediterranean contexts has been well recognized,[7] in this book I argue that *Hatk al-Sitr* should equally be considered significant as a previously unrecognized reverberation of the late eighteenth- and early nineteenth-century jihad movements in the frontiers of the Islamic world.

In his book *Jihad in West Africa During the Age of Revolutions*, historian Paul Lovejoy critiqued the canonical works on the Age of Revolutions for remaining geographically focused on events in Europe and the Americas while omitting those engendered by the jihad movements in West Africa, a region that was integrally interconnected with *Dār al-Islām* (the abode of Islam) and had been crucially important in shaping some of the pivotal events associated with the Age of Revolutions in Europe and the Americas. Thus, Lovejoy rightly called attention to the overlooked dimensions of the West African jihad movements in the Revolutions. According to him, not only were these Islamic jihad movements pivotal in shaping the events of the Age of Revolutions, but also they had

---

7 See for example, Montana, "Aḥmad Ibn al-Qāḍī al-Timbuktāwī on the Bori Ceremonies of Sūdān-Tūnis,"; Montana, "Bori practice among enslaved West Africans of Ottoman Tunis: Unbelief (Kufr) or another dimension of the African diaspora?"; Paul E. Lovejoy, *Jihad in West Africa During the Age of Revolution* (Athens: Ohio University Press, 2016), 89, 157–158, 187; Edward E. Curtis IV, *The Call of Bilal: Islam in the African Diaspora* (Chapel Hill: The University of North Carolina Press, 2014), chapter 2; and Ehud R. Toledano "African Slaves on Ottoman Eastern Mediterranean: A Case of Cultural 'Creolization'?" in Eyüb Özel, Suha Ünsal, and Kudret Emirogli (eds.), *The Mediterranean World: The Idea, the Past and the Present* (Istanbul: Iletism Yayinlari, 2006), 107–124. See also Professor Chouki El Hamel's online project, "De-Constructing the Maghrib: A StoryMap: Demonstrating the Maghrib's Africanity. The Origins Debate on Race and Slavery in Morocco." https://storymaps.arcgis.com/stories/a227b874713745b0b86ca63ac515d597 (Accessed: July 119, 2023).

far reaching implications in other under-studied geographical areas, including North Africa and the Middle East, which remained to be fully considered.[8] By making a complete critical edition of *Hatk al-Sitr ʿammā ʿalayhi sūdān Tūnis min al-kufr* ("Piercing the Veil: Being an Account of the Infidel Religion of the Blacks of Tunis"), this book, *The Blacks of Tunis in al-Timbuktāwī's Hatk al-Sitr*, is an effort to shed light on the under-studied dimensions of the West African jihad movements during the Age of Revolutions on the Maghribi frontiers of *Dār al-Islam*.

1 Bori in the Maghrib in Historical Context

Unlike the indigenous African-based religions such as Voodoo, Condomblé, Obeah and their variants that spread across the Americas in the western hemisphere through the transatlantic slave trade, the case of the *Sūdān Tūnis*' (Blacks of Tunis) deviant religious expressions that fueled al-Timbuktāwī's wrath is far more complex. Like Gnawa, Zar, and similar Sūdānic African religious practices, understanding the Bori presence in North Africa is best contextualized against the backdrop of the of the *longue durée* interrelated historical developments in the western and central Sūdān that intersected with the rise Islam in the western Arabian Peninsula.[9] Within less than a century following the death of the Prophet of Islam, Muḥammad ibn ʿAbdallāh (d. 42/663), his successors, known as the caliphs, continued his message, spreading Islam in the Arabian Peninsula and Maghrib (North Africa, or the western land of Islam) through military conquest. From the eleventh century CE, the nascent expanding monotheistic religion was spread peacefully through trade and proselytization into what the early Muslim geographers and historians dubbed the Land of the Blacks (*bilād al-sūdān*). Grasping the process of Islamization, particularly the rise of the late eighteenth- and nineteenth-century Islamic reformation

8 Lovejoy, *Jihad in West Africa During the Age of Revolution*, 158.

9 For a discussion of indigenous African Religions in the context of the Islamic world, see, John O. Hunwick, "The Religious Practices of Black Slaves in the Mediterranean Islamic World," in Paul Lovejoy (ed.), *Slavery on the Frontiers of Islam* (Princeton, NJ: Markus Wiener, 2004), 149–172; Curtis, *The Call of Bilal*; Chouki El Hamel, "Constructing a Diasporic Identity: Tracing the Origins of the Gnawa Spiritual Group in Morocco," *Journal of African History* 49, no. 2 (2008): 241–260; Richard C. Jankowsky, *Stambeli*; Ehud R. Toledano, "African Slaves on Ottoman Eastern Mediterranean"; Ismael Montana, "African Religions in the Maghreb and the Middle East," in *Oxford Encyclopedia of Slavery, the Slave Trade, and Diaspora in African History*. Published online: 24 February 2022. https://doi.org/10.1093/acrefore/9780190277734.013.1166.

and jihad movements, and the intersection of slavery, race and enslavement in these movements is paramount to understanding al-Timbuktāwī's dogmatic approach and harsh condemnation of the practitioners of the Bori cult in Tunisia.

Since the early 1960s, historians and scholars of African religion from various disciplines preoccupied with the complexity of what some have termed "African Islam"[10] in the Sūdānic African space have elucidated numerous theoretical frameworks or approaches to advance our understanding of the history, roots, and the process of Islamization across time and space. Synthesizing some of these theoretical and interpretative approaches propounded by pioneering scholars such as John Spencer Trimingham, Mervyn Hiskett, Nehemia Levtzion, and many others,[11] David Robinson, in his book *Muslim Societies in African History*, has succinctly highlighted one such approach in the form of a process of "*islamization* and *africanization*."[12] I find this to be pertinent to this study if we are to critically comprehend al-Timbuktāwī's main issues against the indigenous African religious practices that he condemned during his sojourn in the Maghrib.

Here, the tripartite analytical approach exemplified in Robinson's elucidation of the "*islamization* and *africanization*" framework in Sūdānic Africa is a useful lens to uncover the underlying historical factors that shaped and informed al-Timbuktāwī 's condemnation of the Bori in the Maghribi frontiers of *Dār al-Islam*. Even more, this framework helps to situate his dogmatic and extreme theological viewpoints advocating for the re-enslavement and the murder of his fellow Sūdānic citizens associated with Bori within the context of the *longue durée* process of Sūdānic Africa's interaction with Islam.[13] According to this framework, during the early stage of its expansion Islam was characterized by its association with foreign merchants involved in trans-Saharan com-

10 See Marloes Janson, "Islam in Sub-Saharan Africa," in Martin Shanguhyia and Toyin Falola (eds.), *Palgrave Handbook of African Colonial and Postcolonial History* (New York: Palgrave Macmillan New, 2018), 951–977.

11 See John Spencer Trimingham, *Islam in West Africa*, Oxford: Oxford University Press, 1959; Mervyn Hiskett, *The Development of Islam in West Africa*, London: Longman, 1982; Peter B. Clarke, West *Africa and Islam: A Study of Religious Development from the 8th to the 20th Century*, London: Edward Arnold, 1982; David Robinson, *Muslim Societies in African History: New Approaches to African History* Cambridge: Cambridge University Press, 2004; Nehemiah Levtzion, *Islam in West Africa: Religion, Society and Politics to 1800*, Brookfield, VT: Variorum, 1994; Nehemiah Levtzion and Randall L. Pouwels, eds., *The History of Islam in Africa*, Athens, OH: Ohio University Press, 2000.

12 Robinson, *Muslim Societies in African History*.

13 Ibid., 27.

merce.[14] These merchants, made up predominantly of indigenous Berber communities in the Maghrib, were themselves novices in the nascent expanding religion. Unlike in the Maghrib, where Islam expanded through military conquest and was met with local resistance, the early Muslim community from the Maghrib who spread Islam in the *bilād al-Sūdān* during this stage were mostly concerned with revitalizing their preexisting commercial interactions peacefully with Sūdānic Africa. Drawing on the dichotomy of countryside versus urban Islam propounded by Levtzion and other scholars, Robinson described this phase of the process as a "quarantine Islam."[15] Perhaps being protective of their religious and cultural traditions, the Sūdānic African rulers may have consciously housed these foreign merchants in separate quarters to prevent them from intermingling with the local populace. We know from al-Bakrī and the early historical accounts dating back to this period that other than engage in their trade, very little if any attempt at all was made by these merchants to spread Islam beyond the confines of their quarantine zone, either to the rulers or the local population.[16] From the account of the Kano Chronicle, it is also possible to surmise that by the end of the fourteenth century CE, under the purview of the ruling elites and kings (*Sarki*s in Hausa), Bori held sway in the social and governing structure of the city-states of Hausaland. According to the chronicle, Sarkin Kajaji (792–812/1390–1410), who was the son of the first Sultan of Kano, for instance, and reigned during its warfare against Zaria, attributed his victory to a Bori oracle, thus attesting to the place of Bori within Hausa society.[17] M.G. Smith and the authors of several historical ethnographic studies in central Sūdān have underscored that before it was reduced to a spirit possession cult in the wake of the Islamic renewal and reform movement discussed below, Bori was considered an indigenous religion associated with the kingship and political structure of Hausa states and society.[18]

14 Ibid., 28.

15 Ibid., 28; David Robinson, *Chiefs and Clerics: Abdul Bokar Kan and Futa Toro, 1853–1891*, Oxford: Clarendon Press, 1973. See also Nehemia Levtzion, "Merchants vs. Scholars and Clerics: Differential and Complementary Roles," in Nehemia Levtzion and Humphrey J. Fisher (eds.), *Rural and Urban Islam in West Africa* (Boulder, CO: L. Rienner Publishers, 1987), 38–42.

16 J.F.P. Hopkins and Nehemia Levtzion, ed. and trans., *Corpus of Early Arabic Sources for West African History* (Cambridge: Cambridge University Press, 1981), 97–81. See also, *El-Bekri, Description de l'Afrique septentrionale*, ed. and trans. William Mac Guklin de Slane, Tangiers: Adolphe Jourdan, 1859 & 1913.

17 Murray Last, "Historical Metaphor in the Kano Chronicle," *History in Africa 7*, (1980): 161–179.

18 See, for instance, M.G. Smith, *Government in Kano, 1350–1950*, Boulder, CO: Westview Press, 1997; Nicolas Guy, *Dynamique sociale et appréhension du monde au sein d'une société*

During the second phase of Robinson's process of "*islamization* and *africanization*" intensifying mostly around the thirteenth century onward and through the conversion of local rulers and their immediate circles, Islam spread beyond the merchants' quarantine zones into the palaces and courts of the Sūdānic African rulers and into the spheres of the local populace.[19] This development, however, was mostly confined to the urban centers where local merchants such as the Dyula had become active participants in the southern termini of the thriving trans-regional commerce. Increasingly, many of the local Dyula merchants, also working closely with the local rulers, had embraced some of the socio-economic values associated with trans-Saharan commerce. Hence, in such centers as Timbuktu, Djenné, and Gao in western Sūdān, and Bornu, Kano, Katsina, and Alkalawa in central Sūdān, many of the Sūdānic rulers began to sponsor the building of mosques while supporting Sufi brotherhoods (*tariqas*) whose marabouts and holy men had been credited for the peaceful consolidation of Islam across the *bilād al-Sūdān*.[20] Inevitably, the perception that the material benefits brought about Islam would strengthen the Sūdānic kingdoms in western and central Sūdān played an even higher role in facilitating its consolidation in the Sūdānic space. During this phase, not only did the local Sūdānic rulers increasingly convert to the expanding Islamic religion, they also employed Muslim clerics in their courts to serve as political counsellors or scribes for political ends. Many of these rulers even made Islam the official religion, as did Mansa Musa of the Kingdom of Mali prior to performing his sensational pilgrimage to Mecca in 724/1324. Upon his return from pilgrimage, Mansa Musa recruited architects, scholars, and judges (*quḍāt*) to spur the development of his kingdom, thus laying the foundation for Timbuktu and Djenné to become prominent centers of Islamic learning in the western Sūdān, where al-Timbuktāwī—and, long before him, Aḥmad Bābā al-Timbuktī—both received their education.[21] Exactly twenty-six years after Mansa Musa's pilgrimage, Ibn Battuta, who visited Timbuktu shortly after the great ruler's death,

hausa, Paris: Institut d'ethnologie, 1975; J. Paden, *Religion and Political Culture in Kano*, Berkeley: University of California Press, 1973.

19 Robinson, *Muslim Societies in African History*, 28; Levtzion and Pouwels, *The History of Islam in Africa*.

20 See John Hunwick, "Songhay, Borno and the Hausa States, 1450–1600," in J.F. Ade Ajayi and Michael Crowder (eds.), *History of West Africa*, vol. 1, 3rd ed. (Cambridge: Cambridge University Press, 1985), 323–372. See also Lamin Sanneh, *The Crown and the Turban: Muslims and West African Pluralism*, Boulder, CO: Westview Press, 1997.

21 See Ousmane Oumar Kane, ed. *Islamic Scholarship in Africa: New Directions and Global Contexts*, Woodbridge: James Currey, 2021.

painted a glowing picture of its daily life, depicting the level and progress of Islamization in Mali while also reminding his readers how its king and ruling elites approvingly and scrupulously observed their indigenous religious beliefs in his court.[22] In the extant literature, this phase in the process of "*islamization* and *africanization*" has been described as "court Islam."

The third phases of "*islamization* and *africanization*," occurring around the end of the eighteenth century, witnessed an intense level of Islamization in the central Sūdān region, particularly in the Hausaland.[23] From the 1500s until the late 1780s, successive rulers across the central Sūdān emulated the examples set by Mansa Musa in the Malian Empire and others such as Sultan Muhammad Rumfa (867–904/1463–1499) of Kano, who invited Muḥammed b. ʿAbd al-Karīm al-Maghīlī (d. 909/1503–1504 or 911/1505), a prominent Berber Islamic scholar, to serve as his political advisor and even commissioned him to compose a treatise on the arts of governance according to the Sharia.[24] As the growth and expansion of trans-Saharan commerce injected a much-needed economic boost to the economy of the Hausa city-states, its rulers, attracted by the prospects for the development of their states, increasingly surrounded themselves by learned Muslim scholars and clerics as advisors and scribes in their courts, as had other leaders in the western Sūdān before them. During this period, Hausa political and aristocratic titles such as *Sarki* (king) were transformed into Islamic equivalents such as *emīr*, *Sultān*., etc. And despite openly adopting Islam as the religion of their polities, most of the local Hausa populace remained predominantly attached to their indigenous religious belief system of Bori. It must be emphasized that while Bori reflected the indigenous religious belief system, its leaders and authorities too followed suited by emulating the prevailing trend of admixture of African culture with Islam by infusing Muslim names or titles into Bori practices.[25] A main feature of this phase is that the increased pattern of Islamization did not result in a complete break with Bori as a non-Islamic religious practice. Many of the rulers who took on Islamic titles and surrounded themselves with Muslim clerics while still realizing the overall significance of Bori to their society reduced it, instead, to a cult status

22 Said Hamdun and Noel King, *Ibn Battutta in Black Africa, 1600–1960*, Princeton, NJ: Markus Wiener Publishers, 2011.

23 Robinson, *Muslim Societies in African History*, 28.

24 See Usman dan Fodio, *Bayān wujūb al-hijra ʿalā l-ʿibād*, trans. F.H. El-Masri (Khartoum: Khartoum University Press & Oxford University Press, 1978), 29; John Hunwick, *Sharia in Songhay: The Replies of al-Maghili to the Questions of Askia al-Hajj Muhammad*, Oxford: Oxford University Press, 1985.

25 Robinson, *Muslim Societies in African History*, 148.

by declaring its adherents as "*maguzawa*" or "Magians."[26] Robinson, explaining the rationale behind this trend notes that: "In Hausaland before Uthman's reform Muslims worked in a different way. They institutionalized the status of *dhimmis*, 'protected community,' for non-Muslim groups who adhered to Bori traditions." These Bori adherents, Robinson continues, even though "not literate [in the scripture] in any language, [...] by analogy with the 'people of the Book' they were drawn under the umbrella of Islam and given protection from war and enslavement."[27]

It is worth stressing that the recognition of Bori as a religious minority within the expanding Islamic space in the central Sūdān was more than a sheer act of religious syncretism. It was rooted in the culture of religious accommodation and tolerance accorded to religious minorities (*dhimmis*) belonging to the People of Book (*Ahl al-Kitāb*) such as Jews, Christians, Zoroastrians, and Magians living under the sovereignty of the early Muslim rulers. To illustrate this culture of religious accommodation and tolerance, for example, when the second Rāshidūn caliph, ʿUmar Ibn al-Khaṭṭāb, was stabbed by a non-Muslim named Abū Luʾluʾ, a Zoroastrian and a fire worshipper, he still admonished his companions to respect the rights of non-Muslims when on his death-bed and said: "Admonish whosoever becomes caliph after me concerning the fair treatment of the non-Muslims. He must fulfil his pledge of protection towards them and should fight for their rights."[28] It is clear from the above acknowledgment of the Bori practitioners as a religious minority that such consideration was rooted in theological precedent vis-a-vis the People of the Book.

It must be stressed that not all the Muslim rulers of the central Sūdān, however, demoted the Bori practioners to a religious minority status. Out of recognition for its therapeutic and communal value and importance to the welfare of his subjects, the Sultan of Gobir, for instance, accorded the Bori authorities equal recognition in his court alongside the Muslim clerics.[29]

With the increased pattern of Islamization and the growth of religious establishments outside the local court system, actions like the one exhibited by the Sultan of Gobir created tension between Islamic reform-minded *ʿulamāʾ* and the rulers of Hausaland. Such tensions during the late eighteenth century

---

26 Ibid., 141.

27 Ibid., 202. See also Murray Last, "History as Religion: De-constructing the Magian "Muguzawa" of Nigerian Hausaland," in *L'invention religieuse en Afrique: Histoire et religion en Afrique noire* (Paris: Karthala, 1993), 45–57.

28 Abū ʿAbdallah Muḥammad bin Ismāʿil al-Bukhārī, *ʾAl-Jāmiʿ al-Saḥīḥ: Saḥīḥ al-Bukhārī*, vol. 9 (Cairo, n.d.), 209.

29 Robinson, *Muslim Societies in African History*, 142.

marked a momentous shift, introducing a renewal and reformation of Islam according to the strict and fundamental teaching of the Islamic faith. This shift had a major implication in changing the status of Bori's adherents as full-fledged followers of Hausa indigenous religion or "*maguzawa*" from a marginalized religious minority into infidels who could be enslaved, on the pretext that worshipping *iskoki* or Bori spirits was tantamount to idol veneration, which Islam strictly prohibits. Such criticism, which resulted in a never-before-seen structural and cultural change, was spearheaded by the rise of the charismatic Fulfulde cleric, Uthman Dan Fodio (d. 1232/1817). Born in Gobir in 1167/1754, and descended from the Torodbe clans of the Fulfulde, his family had migrated to Hausaland from the early 1400s from the Futa Toro area, where an earlier Islamic reformation movement and a less militant form of jihad under the leadership of Nasir al-Din (d. 1084/1674) took place in during the last quarter of the seventeenth century.[30] [See Map 1.] A few years after his involvement with the affairs of the Gobir palace, and following the footsteps of Jibrīl b. ʿUmar, his former teacher, who had initiated him into the Qādiriyya Sufi order and warned the Hausa kings of a need for reform, Dan Fodio renounced his support of the Sultān of Gobir and begun to direct criticism against the learned scholars associated with his court as "vile scholars" (*ʿulamāʾ al-sūʾ*), and the sultān and his counterparts throughout Hausaland as corrupt.[31] He then embarked on a holy war (*jihad*) against the Sultān of Gobir for disregarding what he condemned as socio-economic corruption, and for the state's mingling Islam with heretical and pagan practices.[32] Within a few years after openly denouncing the prevailing socio-economic and religious environment in the region, he proclaimed that he had a vision from God (Allah) arming him with a "sword of truth" to carry out his holy war to purify Hausaland, riddled as it was with religious innovations, corrupt political leadership, and ʿulamāʾ *al-sūʾ*.[33] As will

30 Usman dan Fodio, *Bayān wujūb al-hijra ʿalā lʿibād*, 1; Mervyn Hiskett, "An Islamic Tradition of Reform in the Western Sūdān from the Sixteenth to the Eighteenth Century," *Bulletin of the School of Oriental and African Studies* 25, nos. 1/3 (1962): 577–596; B.G. Martin, "Unbelief in the Western Sūdān: Uthman Dan Fodio's Ta'lim al-Ikhwan," *Middle Eastern Studies* 4, no. 1 (1967): 82; David Robinson, "Revolutions in the Western Sudan," in Nehemia Levtzion and R. Pouwels (eds.), *The History of Islam in Africa* (Athens, OH: Ohio University Press, 2000), 131–151.

31 Usman dan Fodio, *Bayān wujūb al-hijra ʿalā lʿibād*, 7.

32 See Usman dan Fodio, *Bayān wujūb al-hijra ʿalā lʿibād*, 3; Mervyn Hiskett, "Kitāb Al-Farq: A Work on the Habe Kingdoms Attributed to ʾUṯhmān Dan Fodio," *Bulletin of the School of Oriental and African Studies* 23, no. 3 (1960): 558–579; Robinson, *Muslim Societies in African History*, 144.

33 Hiskett, *Sword of Truth*, 61–62; Usman dan Fodio, *Bayān wujūb al-hijra ʿalā lʿibād*, 4.

be detailed in Chapter 1, Dan Fodio's holy war and jihad movement attracted eager followers who replicated his message, teachings, militant and revolutionary changes, especially in the Niger Bend.[34]

One outcome of these late eighteenth-century developments was that Bori—which until the outburst of Dan Fodio's militant jihad movements had been encouraged by the Hausa ruling elites—was now invariably condemned by the jihadi leadership as a polytheistic religious practice (*shirk*), and its adherents charged as infidels (*kuffār*).[35] Thus, in laying down the theological and philosophical foundation, precepts, or principles to govern the newly established Sokoto or the Hamdallahi caliphates, the leadership of these radical jihad movements was unanimous in considering the practitioners of indigenous African religious practices such as Bori as infidels. As the foundation of these Islamic caliphates took hold during the post-jihad era, it was not uncommon to justify their enslavement, as well as that of adherents of similar indigenous African religious practices, on the grounds that they were pure nonbelievers (*kuffār bi-l-aṣālat*).[36]

Here it must be emphasized that al-Timbuktāwī 's viewpoints concerning intolerance of the Bori practice in the Maghrib was directly related to the teachings of the Caliphate of Hamdallahi in the Niger Bend established by Shaykh Aḥmadu Lobbo (d. 1260/1845), which was an offshoot of Dan Fodio's jihad. An important dimension of the teaching of these two jihad movements was the similarity of their goals to comparable Islamic reformation movements calling for the return of Islam to its fundamental roots, including the Wahhābis whose founder, Muḥammad Ibn ʿAbd al-Wahhāb, issued a proclamation admonishing the rulers of the Maghrib against all forms of religious innovations (*bidʿa*). Unsurprisingly, the heightened polemical debate over the Wahhābi Proclamation, or *al-Jadal al-Wahhābiyya*, occurring on the eve of al-

---

34 For more on the jihad movements in western and central Sūdān, see Louis Brenner "Muslim Thought in Eighteenth Century West Africa: The Case of Shaikh Uthmain b. Fudi" in Nehemiah Levtzion and John O. Voll (eds.), *Eighteenth Century Renewal and Reform Movements in Islam* (Syracuse, NY: Syracuse University Press, 1987), 39–68; Murray Last, "Reform in West Africa: the Jihad Movements of the Nineteenth Century," in J.F. Ade Ajayi and Michael Crowder (eds.), *History of West Africa*, Vol. II (Harlow: Longman Group Ltd., 1987), 1–47; Nehemiah Levtzion and John O. Voll, "Introduction" in Nehemiah Levtzion and John O. Voll (eds.), *Eighteenth Century Renewal and Reform Movements in Islam*, eds. (Syracuse, NY: Syracuse University Press, 1987), 3–20.

35 Usman dan Fodio, *Bayān wujūb al-hijra ʿalā lʿibād, 8.*

36 See Murray Last and Muhammad A. Al-Hajj, "Attempt at Defining a Muslim in 19th Century Hausaland and Bornu," *Journal of the Historical Society of Nigeria*, 3, no. 2 (1965), 231–240.

Timbuktāwī 's sojourn in the Maghrib, was strikingly consistent with the intellectual debate and religious environment that accompanied the rise of the Islamic jihad movements in western and central Sūdān. Yet while capitalizing on the controversy over the Wahhābi Proclamation to banish Bori as a deviant religious practice in the Maghrib, al-Timbuktāwī also joined Tunisian religious establishments in criticizing Wahhābi views on the issue of veneration of the saints (*tawassul*). He proved that, like Dan Fodio and Aḥmadu Lobbo, he too was a Sufi and that his worldviews, while identical to those of the Wahhābis on the issues of religious innovations (*bid'a*), were rather shaped by the context of "*islamization and africanization*" in the *bilād al-Sūdān*.

Contemporary and modern scholars have debated the consequences of the jihad movements in western and central Sūdān, particularly on slavery and enslaving practices, with scholars such as Abdulahi Mahdi citing the Sokoto Caliphate jihad as a key factor in the expansion of the volume of the trans-Saharan slave trade during the nineteenth century.[37] In the past as well as in recent years, several historians have also examined the repercussions of the jihad movements in the trans-Atlantic context in the Americas. Numerous studies on the jihad led by Dan Fodio, for instance, has resulted in fruitful contributions about its effects on slave resistance, the volume of the Atlantic slave trade, and the diffusion of Islamic literature across the Atlantic world.[38] While Allan Austin, Michael Gomez, Sylviane Diouf and many other scholars have elucidated on the varied forms of spiritual struggles of enslaved Muslims in the Americas,[39] other historians such as Paul Lovejoy, João José Reis, Manual Bar-

37 Abdullahi Mahadi, "The Aftermath of the Jihad in the Central Sudan as a Major Factor in the Volume of the Trans-Saharan Slave Trade in the Nineteenth Century," in Elizabeth Savage (ed.), *The Human Commodity: Perspectives on the Trans-Saharan Trade* (London: Frank Cass, 1992), 111–128. See also Lovejoy, *Jihad in West Africa During the Age of Revolution*, 156–158.

38 See Paul E. Lovejoy, "The Central Sudan and the Atlantic Slave Trade," in Robert W. Harms et al. (eds.), *Paths Towards the Past: African Historical Essays in Honor of Jan Vansina*, Atlanta: African Studies Association Press, 1994; João José Reis, *Slave Revolt in Brazil: The Muslim Uprising of 1835 in Bahia*, trans. Arthur Brakel, Baltimore: Johns Hopkins University, 1993.

39 Paul E. Lovejoy, *Jihad in West Africa During the Age of Revolution*; Reis, *Slave Revolt in Brazil*; Manuel Barcia, "An Islamic Atlantic Revolution: Dan Fodio's Jihad and Slave Rebellion in Bahia and Cuba, 1804–1844," *Journal of African Diaspora*, Archeology, *and Heritage* 2, no. 1 (2013): 6–19; Toby Green, *A Fistful of Shells: West Africa from the Rise of the Slave Trade to the Age of Revolution*, Chicago: University of Chicago Press, 2019. See also Allan D. Austin, *African Muslims in Antebellum America: Transatlantic Stories and Spiritual Struggles*, New York: Garland Publishers, 1997; Philip D. Curtin, ed. *Africa Remembered*,

cia, and Toby Green have recently expanded our understanding of how Dan Fodio's Islamic jihad movement—as well as those of the nineteenth century—intersected with revolutionary developments associated with the Age of Revolutions, which until very recently had been discounted.[40]

Within western and central Sūdān and across the Sahara to the Maghrib and the Middle East, both contemporary and recent scholarship has also yielded a series of critical interrogations of the repercussions of the jihad movements on the intersection of slavery, religion, race, and Blackness. As will be in shown in this study, exactly two hundred years prior to al-Timbuktāwī 's condemnation of the Blacks of Tunis to enslavement on account of their religious deviance, Aḥmad Bābā (d. 1036/1627), who was taken as a captive to Marrakesh following the Moroccan invasion of the Songhay Empire in 1591, laid the foundation a rich intellectual discourse questioning the association of the *bilād al-Sūdān* with notions of *kufr* and enslavement. While staying in Morocco between 1593 and 1608, following his capture, and confronted with an abhorrent association of his Sūdānic homeland with disbelief and enslavement, he wrote his famous treatise "The ladder of ascent towards grasping the law concerning transported Blacks" (*Miʿrāj al-Suʿud ila nayl hukm majlūb al-Sūd*) as a rebuttal of the conflation of the *bilād al-Sūdān* with slavery.[41] Generations of scholars in the *bilād*

Madison, WI: University of Wisconsin Press, 1967; Sylviane A. Diouf, "African Muslims in Bondage," in Joanne M. Braxton and Maria I. Diedrich (eds.), *Monuments of the Black Atlantic: Slavery and Memory* (Piscataway, NJ: Rutgers University, 2004), 77–90.; Sylviane A. Diouf. "Devils or Sorcerers, Muslims or Studs: Manding in the Americas," in Paul E. Lovejoy and David V. Trotman (eds.), *Trans-Atlantic Dimension of Ethnicity in the African Diaspora* (New York: Continuum, 2003), 139–157; Maureen Warner-Lewis "Religious Constancy and Compromise Among Nineteenth Century Caribbean-Based African Muslims," in Behnaz A. Mirzai, Ismael M. Montana and Paul E. Lovejoy (eds.), *Slavery, Islam and Diaspora*, (Trenton, NJ: Africa World Press, 2009), 237–268; Ivor W. Wilks, "Salih Bilali of Massina" in Philip D. Curtin (ed.), *Africa Remembered* (Madison, WI: University of Wisconsin Press, 1967), 145–151; Mbaye Lo and Carl W. Ernst, *I Cannot Write My Name: Islam, Arabic, and Slavery in Omar ibn Said's America*, Chapel Hill: The University of North Carolina Press, 2023; Dobronravin, Nikolay, "Literacy among Muslims in Nineteenth Century Trinidad and Brazil," in Behnaz Mirzai Asl, Ismael M. Montana and Paul E. Lovejoy (eds.), *Slavery, Islam and Diaspora* (Trenton NJ: Africa World Press, 2009), 217–236.

40 Lovejoy, *Jihad in West Africa During the Age of Revolution*, 1–7; Paul E. Lovejoy, "Muslim Freedmen in the Atlantic World: Images of Manumission and Self-Redemption," in Paul E. Lovejoy (ed.), *Slavery on the Frontiers of Islam* (Princeton, NJ: Markus Wiener Publishers, 2004), 233–262; Paul E. Lovejoy "Slavery, the Bilad al-Sudan, and the Frontiers of the African Diaspora," in Paul E. Lovejoy (ed.), *Slavery on the Frontiers of Islam* (Princeton, NJ: Markus Wiener Publishers, 2004), 1–30.

41 See Aḥmad Bābā, *Miʿrāj al-Suʿūd: Aḥmad Bābā's Replies on Slavery*, ed. John Hunwick and Fatima Harrak, Rabat: Institute of African Studies, 2000. On the discourse on enslavement

al-sūdān, including leadership of the jihad of Dan Fodio, taking their cues from Aḥmad Bābā and confronted with the aberrant form of enslavement of the denizens in the Sokoto Caliphate also elaborated on the relationships between the jihad, unbelief, slavery and enslavement.[42]

Scholars and historians such as John Hunwick, Chouki El Hamel,[43] and more recently Bruce Hall and Bashir Salau, among others, have shown that issues of race and unbelief fueled the enslaving practices within the broader process of Islamization discussed above. While Hunwick and El Hamel have led the way in interrogating the conflation of race, unbelief, and slavery within the key canonical compendia,[44] Bruce Hall critiques race in the Niger Bend as a matter of both social and cultural construction and representation, rooted in the idea of Arab or Islamic notions of lineage and genealogical attachment, but which nevertheless had deleterious consequences on the racialization of slavery. As Hall has rightly shown through this prism of how race was viewed in Northwest Africa, enslavement was racialized by those claiming Arab ancestry—sometimes despite their physiological features of Blackness—to justify the enslavement of those with non-Arab ancestry or descent.[45] Salau, on the other hand, drawing on the writing of Muhammad Bello, insists that in the Sokoto Caliphate, religious grounds determined the aberrant enslavement practices

in central Sūdān, see Ahmad M. Kani, *Diyāʿ al-siyāsāt wa-fatāwī-l-nawāzil mimmā huwa fī furūʿ al-dīn min al-masāʾil*, Cairo, 1988. Jennifer Loftkranzt, "Intellectual Discourse in the Sokoto Caliphate: The Triumvirate's Opinions on the Issues of Ransoming, ca. 1810," *Journal of African Historical Studies*, 45, no. 3 (2012), 385–401; Paul Naylor, *From Rebels to Rulers: Writing Legitimacy in the Early Sokoto State*, London: James Currey, 2021 (especially chapter 4.) Chris Gratien, "Race, Slavery, and Islamic Law in the Early Modern Atlantic: Ahmad Baba al-Tinbukti's treatise on enslavement," *The Journal of North African Studies* 18, no. 3, (May 2013) 454–468; Timothy Cleaveland, "Aḥmad Bābā al-Timbukti and his Islamic Critique of Racial Slavery in the Maghrib," *The Journal of North African Studies* 20, no. 1 (2015): 42–64.

42 See Paul Lovejoy, "The Context of Enslavement in West Africa," in Jane Landers and Barry Robinson (eds.), *Slaves, Subjects, and Subversives: Blacks in Colonial Latin America* (Albuquerque: University of New Mexico Press, 2006), 9–38.

43 John O. Hunwick, "Islamic Law and Polemics Over Race and Slavery North and West Africa (16th–19th Century)," in Shaun E. Marmon (ed.), *Slavery in the Islamic Middle East* (Princeton, NJ: Markus Wiener Publishers, 1999), 43–68; John O. Hunwick, "Aḥmad Bābā on Slavery," *Sudanic Africa* 11 (2000): 131–139.

44 Chouki El Hamel, *Black Morocco: A History of Slavery, Race, and Islam*, Cambridge: Cambridge University Press, 2013.

45 See Bruce S. Hall, *A History of Race in Muslim West Africa, 1600–1960* (New York: Cambridge University Press, 2011), 53; Bruce Hall, "The Question of 'Race' in the Pre-Colonial Southern Sahara," *Journal of North African Studies* 10, 3–4 (2005): 339–367. See also Mahmood Mamdani, "Introduction: Trans-African Slaveries: Thinking Historically," *Comparative Studies of South Asia, Africa and the Middle East* 38, 2 (2018): 185–210.

more than race.[46] While this growing scholarship on the racialization of slavery in the Islamic context has informed the framework of the current study, my goal in presenting a translation and critical edition of al-Timbuktāwī 's *Hatk akl-Sitr* is to highlight the reverberations of the jihad movements in the Maghribi frontiers of *Dār al-Islam*.

2 Who Was al-Timbuktāwī?

The little we know about al-Timbuktāwī comes from the biographical sketches deduced from the prefaces of his two short treatises: *Hatk al-Sitr*, which he dedicated to the Tunisian ruler Ḥammūda Pāsha, and *Shikāyat al-Dīn al-Mohammadī*, addressed to the Moroccan religious authorities. Aḥmad b. al-Qāḍī b. Abī Bakr b. Yūsuf b. Ibrahīm al-Timbuktāwī was born around 1152/1740 in present-day Mali into a prominent religious family of the Fulfulde, an ethnic group commonly associated with Islam in the western Sūdān. The exact place of his birth, however, remains uncertain.[47] *Hatk al-Sitr* and *Shikāyat al-Dīn* both indicate that he was born in "Dawjaqa," which most probably is a corruption of N'Dodjiga, an administrative district in the Mopti region of present-day Mali. [See Map 3.] In their introduction to the two texts, Mohamed El-Mansour and Fatima Harrak identified al-Timbuktāwī's place of birth with Diaguku in Futa Jallon, indicating that he might have migrated to Mali from there.[48] Based, however, on the location of N'Dodjika and its reputation as a major Islamic religious learning center dominated by the Fulfulde, it is most probably the birthplace of the author.

An important source of information about al-Timbuktāwī's life also comes from his self-identification as the son of a religious judge (*ibn al-qāḍī*), placed before the rest of his names, which indicates that he was from a distinguished religious class of the *ʿulamāʾ* of Timbuktu.[49] From the medieval through the modern period, the designation *al-qāḍī* (the judge) has been a privileged status attached to the titles of *ʿulamāʾ* who were distinguished as such and who occupied the upper echelons of Islamic societies. As Elias Saad has shown, in Timbuktu, for instance, most *ʿulamāʾ* distinguished by the title of *al-qāḍī*, based on the institution of judgeship (*qaḍāʾ*), belonged to a specific religious and social

46 Mohammed Bashir Salau, *Plantation Slavery in the Sokoto Caliphate: A Historical and Comparative Study* (Rochester: University of Rochester Press, 2018), 3. See also Naylor, *From Rebels to Rulers*, 130–135.

47 Montana, "Al-Timbuktāwī, Aḥmad b. al-Qāḍī," 148.

48 Harrak and El-Mansour, *A Fulani Jihadist in the Maghreb*, 13.

49 Montana, "Al-Timbuktāwī, Aḥmad b. al-Qāḍī," 148.

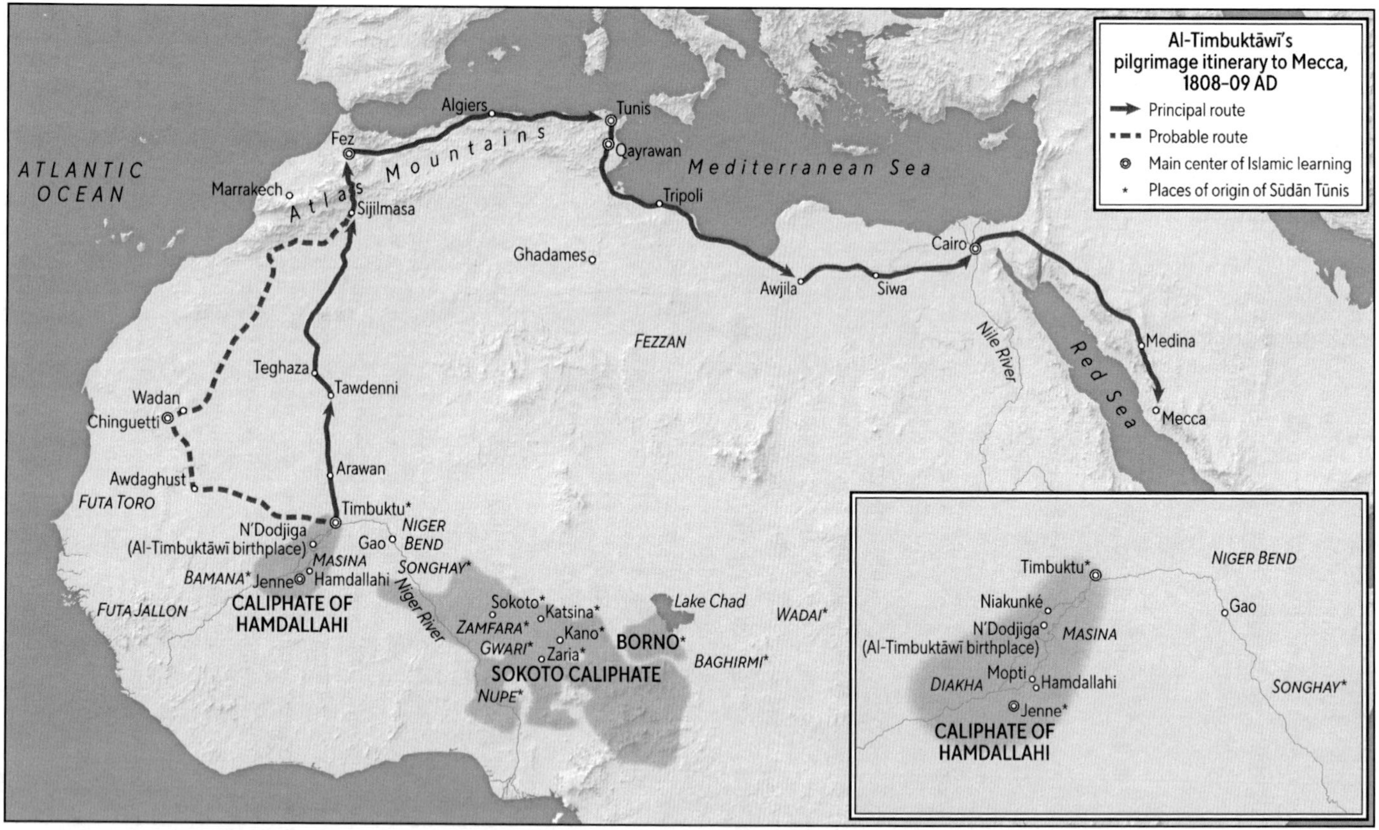

MAP 3 Al-Timbuktāwī's Itinerary to Hajj, 1808–1809

class.[50] According to al-Timbuktāwī, before joining the prestigious circle of the *ʿulamāʾ* in Timbuktu he obtained his early training in Qurʾānic and Islamic studies at Djenné, another important center of Islamic teaching and scholarship that ranks second to Timbuktu both in fame and intellectual output as a learning center.[51]

Notwithstanding his educational background and his religious and intellectual pedigree, which placed him among the distinguished class of religious scholars and jurists (*quḍāt*) in the Niger Bend, we are yet to locate al-Timbuktāwī's writings in the western or central Sūdān. The only possibility is put forward by ʿAlī Pereejo, who made reference to a certain al-Ḥajj Aḥmad b. Abī Bakr al-Fūtī in Djenné, strongly suggesting that he and al-Timbuktāwī may have been one and the same.[52] Given that while in the Maghrib al-Timbuktāwī wrote two treatises, *Hatk al-Sitr* and *Shikāyat al-Dīn*, within the span of a year, it is highly likely that he may have authored other works with similar depths in his homeland, even if these are yet to be discovered. Thus, since our efforts to fully locate any traces of al-Timbuktāwī in the western Sūdān with certainty have so far been unsuccessful, he is still considered among the little-known scholars of the region despite the intellectual prowess he exhibited, engaging in highly complicated and complex religious and juridical debates over matters of Islamic beliefs and theology at the intellectual centers of Tunis and Fez.

As will be detailed later in Chapter 1, apart from ʿAlī Pereejo's mention of al-Ḥajj Aḥmad b. Abī Bakr al-Fūtī as a revered Fulfulde scholar, and as the respected friend and possibly advisor to Aḥmad b. Muḥammad Būbu b. Abī Bakr b. Said (Aḥmadu Lobbo, d. 1260/1845),[53] who in 1818 founded the Māsina empire of Ḥamdallāhi, al-Timbuktāwī does not appear in the literature on the region;[54] neither Elias Saad, in his *Social History of Timbuktu*, nor the al-Furqan Foundation's comprehensive *Handlist of Manuscripts in the Center de Docu-*

50 See Elias Saad, *Social History of Timbuktu*, Cambridge: Cambridge University Press, 1983.

51 Al-Timbuktāwī, *Hatk al-Sitr*, p. 1, Folio A.

52 See Muḥammad b. ʿAlī Pereejo, *L'inspiration de l'éternel. Éloge de Shékou Amadou, fondateur de l'empire peul du Macina*, ed. and trans. Georges Bohas, Abderrahim Saguer, and Bernard Salvaing (Brinon-sur-Sauldre: Grandvaux, 2011), 71–73.

53 See ʿAlī Pereejo, *L'inspiration de l'éternel*, 71.

54 I thank Paul Naylor and Ali Diakite at the Hill Museum & Manuscript Library (HMML) who brought my attention to a letter collating the response of Aḥmadu Lobbo to al-Ḥāj Aḥmad ibn Abī Bakr al-Fūtī, believed to be the same esteemed Fulfulde scholar who ʿAlī Pereejo mentioned in the eulogy of Aḥmad Lobbo and described as a respected friend and possibly an advisor to Lobbo. This reference to al-Ḥāj Aḥmad ibn Abī Bakr al-Fūtī in this letter more than ever brings us closer to tracing al-Timbuktāwī's life with certainty in the western Sūdān. For this document see, Aḥmadu Lobbo to al-Ḥāj Aḥmad ibn Abī Bakr

mentation et de Recherches historiques Aḥmad Bābā in Timbuktu, for example, make any mention of him.[55]

Al-Timbuktāwī may have first left Timbuktu to go on pilgrimage, most probably at the end of 1807, and arrived in Tunis either in later that year or early 1808.[56] From the chronology of the events surrounding the Wahhābi controversy in Tunisia and Morocco, it is impossible, as Abdel Jelil Temimi indicates, that al-Timbuktāwī could have authored *Hatk al-Sitr* before the second decade of the nineteenth century. While Temimi dates the authorship of *Hatk al-Sitr* to 1227/1813,[57] other Tunisian historians, including Khalifa Chater and Rached Limam, have imprecisely dated it to between 1223/1809 and 1227/1813.[58] Perhaps the source of this disagreement can be attributed to Aḥmad Ibn Abī Diyaf, who reproduced the text of the Wahhābi proclamation and the response of the Tunisian *ʿulamāʾ* in his chronicle *Ithāf Ahl al-Zamān* without specifying the precise date of the proclamation.[59] The disagreement could also be attributed to the work of local Tunisians who were first to shed light on *Hatk al-Sitr* in the context of the Wahhābi controversy but did not provide an accurate date. Writing on Ḥammūda Pāsha's merits and his relationship with the *ʿulamāʾ*, Ibn ʾAbī Diyaf did not date the controversy precisely but did link it to Ḥammūda; as a result, copyists of the *Hatk al-Sitr* manuscript and later Tunisian historians have incorrectly dated it to 1227/1813 and not earlier. Yet the date of completion of *Shikāyat al-Dīn*—the second treatise al-Timbuktāwī wrote in Morocco, in which he referred Moroccan authorities to *Hatk al-Sitr*—was listed as Rajab 15, 1224/24 October 1809.[60] This undoubtedly proves that *Hatk al-Sitr* was written in 1222/1808, a few years before the death of Ḥammūda Pāsha, and not 1227/1813.

---

al-Fūtī, SAVAMA-DCI/Hill Museum & Manuscript Library, (SAV BMH 34003, p. 11), accessible online via https://w3id.org/vhmml/readingRoom/view/619930 accessed September, 22, 2023.

55 See Saad, *Social History of Timbuktu*; ʿAbd al-Muḥsin al-ʿAbbās (ed.), *Handlist of manuscripts in the Centre de Documentation et de Recherches Historiques Ahmed Baba, Timbuktu*, London: Al-Furqan Islamic Heritage Foundation, 1995.

56 Harrak and El-Mansour, *A Fulani Jihadist in the Maghreb*, 17.

57 Temimi, "Pour une histoire sociale de la minorité africaine noire en Tunisie."

58 Khalifa Chater, *Dépendance Et Mutations Précoloniales: La Régence De Tunis De 1815 À 1857* (Tunis: Publications de L'Université De Tunis, 1984), 147; Rached Limam, *Siyāsat Ḥammūda Bāsha fī Tunis* (Tunis: Manshūrāt al-Jamīʿa al-Tunisīyya, 1980).

59 Aḥmad Ibn ʾAbī Diyaf, *Itḥāf ahl al-Zamān bi Akhbār mulūk Tūnis wa ʿahdi al-Amān*, 7 vols, Tunis: al-Dār al-ʿArabiyya lil-Kitāb, 1999. See also Arnold Green, "A Tunisian Reply to a Wahhabi Proclamation: Texts and Contexts," in Arnold H. Green (ed.), *Arabic and Islamic Studies: In Memory of Mohamed al-Nowaihi* (Cairo: The American University of Cairo Press, 1985), 160.

60 Harrak and El-Mansour, *A Fulani Jihadist in the Maghreb*, 12. See especially footnote no. 2.

3 The Manuscript: *Hatk al-Sitr*

The manuscript that the current translation of *Hatk al-Sitr* is based upon is located in the Bibliothéque Nationale de Tunis under the title *Risālat Hatk al-Sitr ʿAmmā ʿalayhi Sūdān Tūnis min al-Kufr*, reference no. 21183. This copy of the manuscript is probably the most widely used of the three known copies of *Hatk al-Sitr* in the Bibliothéque Nationale de Tunis and is identical to another copy of the manuscript which is believed to be the mother copy. The presumed mother copy bears 18626 as its reference number and belonged originally to Ḥassan Ḥusnī's private library (under old reference No. 6796). This copy is marked as a gift donated to the Bibliothéque Nationale de Tunis by the family of Ḥassan Ḥusnī on September 22nd 1969. The presumed mother copy of the manuscript has a cover sheet with a summary of its contents and contains eleven folios or twenty-one pages of twenty-one lines per page, except for the first page which contains twenty lines and the last page containing twelve lines. According to this summary, the manuscript is probably the original copy of *Hatk al-Sitr* written by al-Timbuktāwī himself; yet Rached Limam, the first Tunisian historian to study and cite it at length, disputed this. According to Limam, this manuscript was copied by a certain Mohamed Miftah in September 1832, so it is not the original. Unfortunately, the name of the copyist and the date are not listed anywhere in this manuscript or in the volume of which it forms a part.

Besides manuscript no. 21183 and the above presumed mother copy of the manuscript originally from Ḥassan Ḥusnī's private library, one additional manuscripts of *Hatk al-Sitr* also exist with the same title and is located in the Bibliothéque Nationale de Tunis (reference no. 09563). This third manuscript no. 09563 is composed of seven folios with each folio containing twenty-five lines per page, except for the first page which contains twenty-three line and the last page containing twenty-six lines. This copy also contains a cover sheet describing its contents in four lines. As for manuscript 21183, it contains twelve folios, and has twenty-three pages in total with each folio containing twenty-two lines per page, except for the first page (nineteen lines) and the last (twenty lines). All three Tunisian manuscripts copies of *Hatk al-Sitr* are found in a bound volume of manuscripts at the Bibliothéque Nationale de Tunis, all measuring 23×27 cm.

A fourth manuscript of *Hatk al-Sitr* is in the King's Library in Rabat, Morocco; I am grateful to Professor Chouki El Hamel who kindly furnished me digital copy of this version of the manuscript. This manuscript (reference number 6832) contains twelve folios of twenty-two pages. Except for very minor differences in the stated date of the completion of the manuscript and a few annotations in the margins, it has the same structure as the three copies at the Bibliothéque Nationale de Tunis and is also written in a clear Maghribi script.[61]

When I first developed an interest in *Hatk al-Sitr* as the subject matter of my Masters thesis at York University in 1999, I relied on manuscript number 21183, which was the only copy of the treatise available to me at the time. In the summer of 2019, however, on a research trip to the Bibliothéque Nationale de Tunis, I was able to finally consult the other two copies of *Hatk al-Sitr*. With the assistance of Dr. Rachida Smine, Head of the Manuscripts Department at the Bibliothéque Nationale de Tunis, I obtained original copies of all three manuscripts of *Hatk al-Sitr* in digital form. Like the copy of the manuscript from the King's Library in Rabat, all three copies are well-preserved, legible, and in excellent shape. I have now been able to collate and compare all four copies of *Hatk al-Sitr* in my possession. The three manuscripts from the Bibliothéque Nationale de Tunis are all written on a brownish paper, in black ink for the main text, and with red ink used to separate the prefaces of manuscripts 18626 and 09564. Also, the beginning of the main sections of all three manuscripts—such as the introduction, chapter headings, and the conclusion—are in red ink, making it easy to decipher the ends or beginnings of these sections within the text. Unless otherwise noted, all citations from the original manuscript of *Hatk al-Sitr* in this book are based on manuscript no. 21183.

Except for the length of their folios and the number of lines per page, manuscripts 18626 and 09564 are identical in content, the only difference being on the last page. While the cover page of manuscript 18626 contains a detailed summary of *Hatk al-Sitr* stating that it is probably the mother copy written by al-Timbuktāwī, the date of the completion of the manuscript is inserted on the upper right-hand margin of the last page as 1228/1813.[62] Perhaps the reason for this is that al-Timbuktāwī stated that the work was completed in عام جكرش (the year of Jakrash). From the handwriting, it is obvious that the date inserted is not part of the original text and is clearly the work of the cataloguer who wrote the detailed summary of the content of *Hatk al-Sitr* for this copy.[63] Meanwhile, manuscript 09564 listed the date 1223 between the words عام and جكرش, indicating that *Hatk al-Sitr* was indeed completed on Thursday 24 Rajab, 1228 /September 13, 1808.[64]

61 Aḥmad b. al-Qādī b. Yūsuf b. Ibrāhīm al-Fulānī al-Timbuktāwī, *Hatk al-Sitr ʿAmmā ʿAlayhi Sūdān Tūnis min al-Kufr*, Royal Library, Rabat: MS No. 6832, 1809.

62 Al-Timbuktāwī, *Ḥatk al-Sitr*, MS. No. 18626, p. 11, Folio A.

63 Al-Timbuktāwī, *Ḥatk al-Sitr*, MS. No. 21183, p. 22, Folio B.

64 Al-Timbuktāwī, *Ḥatk al-Sitr*, MS. No. 09564, p. 11, Folio B.

After collating manuscripts 18626 and 09564, it is clear that either the date 1228 (1813) was incorrectly inserted in the margins by the cataloguer or, as Rached Limam observed, manuscript 18626 was a copy and not the original. This leaves us with the possibility, as Fatima Harrak and Mohamed El Mansour noted, that manuscript 09564 might be the original copy.[65]

Manuscript 21183, on the other hand, is clearly a copy by an unknown scribe, who copied the manuscript on 29 Rajab 1301/1883, almost seven decades after the original copy was authored.[66] Except for some very minor observations, the content of this manuscript is the same as manuscripts 18626 and 09564, the only difference being that the copyist in two instances lists the complete Qurʾānic verses that al-Timbuktāwī cited in the text. In addition, there are three instances where it uses pronouns not found in manuscripts 18626 and 09564. All in all, however, none of these minor additions—neither the Qurʾānic verses nor grammatical syntax—have changed or tempered with the meaning of the text in any shape or form. The scribe also inserted four additional lines at the bottom of the text in the epilogue, the first being in praise of the Prophet Muḥammad and other three lines of poetry.[67]

All four copies of the manuscript seem to have been written in Maghribi script, with the possible exception of manuscript 21183, which is written in Sūdānic script and thus may have been closer to the one written by al-Timbuktāwī himself. The author's Arabic style, however, is replete with reiterations and a mixture of ungrammatical Sudanic ajami that is sometimes puzzling. Like the three copies of the manuscripts from the Bibliothéque Nationale de Tunis, the content of the copy of the manuscript from the King's Library in Rabat is indistinguishable from the Tunisian copies.

The content and structure of *Hatk al-Sitr* is divided consistently into three sections in all four copies of the manuscript. Section One comprises a prologue which, in turn, consists of a preamble and a long introduction. Section Two constitutes three titled chapters; Chapter 1 is titled "An Account Establishing the Polytheism (*Shirk*) of the Slaves" (*Ithbāt Shirk al-ʿAbīd*). Chapter 2 is titled "Names of Some of Their Deities" (*Dhikr Baʿd Asmāʾ Ālihatuhum*). The final chapter is titled "Describing Their Worship" (*Fī Dhikr Ṣifati ʿibādatuhum*). The third section of the treatise is the epilogue.

Although al-Timbuktāwī wrote *Hatk al-Sitr* in 1808 and *Shikāyat al-Dīn* the following year, his works were not known until *Hatk al-Sitr* was discovered

---

65 Harrak and El-Mansour, *A Fulani Jihadist in the Maghreb*, 9.

66 Al-Timbuktāwī, *Ḥatk al-Sitr*, MS. No. 21183, p. 23, Folio A.

67 Ibid., p. 23, Folio A.

and subsequently brought to the attention of professors Rached Limam and Abd al-Jalil Temimi, two leading Tunisian historians. Since the discovery of the manuscript, the treatise has appeared in a number of historical works by Tunisian writers, although it has not been studied critically. As part of his admirable attempts to bring the history of the Blacks of Tunis into mainstream history in Tunisia and the Arab world, Professor Temimi has also published the text of *Hatk al-Sitr* in a number of journals and in other edited works.

Like Harrak and El Mansour, who reproduced the text of *Hatk al-Sitr* alongside *Shikāyat al-Dīn al-Muḥammadī*, the late John Hunwick and Eve Troutt Powell also translated an excerpt in their source book, *The African Diaspora in the Mediterranean Lands of Islam*.[68] The most detailed of the existing reproductions of the text of *Hatk al-Sitr*, however, is that of Abd al-Jelil Temimi. First reproduced in an article, *"Min ajl kitābat ta'rīkh al-hayāt al-ijtimāʿiyyat lil-aqalliyāt al-ifrīqiyya bi-l-bilād al-tūnīsiyya: masādir wa-āfāq"* ("For a social history of the Black African minority in Tunisia"), published in 1987, Professor Temimi describes the importance of *Hatk al-Sitr* and its role in studying the neglected history of sub-Saharan or Sūdānic African minorities in the Arab world.[69] Through his examination of the treatise, Temimi observed that in spite of the fact that the Black population in Tunisia had been Muslims for centuries, *Hatk al-Sitr* nevertheless brought yet another secluded Sūdānic African community in the early nineteenth century to our attention. This community was specifically the Hausa Bori cult practitioners who were labeled by al-Timbuktāwī as "the infidel Blacks of Tunis" (*kuffār Sūdān Tūnis*).

Accordingly, while it is established that enslaved Sūdānic West Africans and their descendants readily converted to Islam and assimilated into local Islamic culture, *Hatk al-Sitr*, as we now know, demonstrates that notwithstanding their confession of the Islamic faith, this community was set apart from Tunisian society by their attachment to their ancestral beliefs and worship of the Bori cult. Professor Temimi's reproduction and publications of *Hatk al-Sitr* thus marked a starting point for approaching the history of neglected Black communities in Tunisia. Throughout the period the text was reproduced, between 1987 and early 1995, it gained the attention of several scholars, as noted earlier, but was not scrutinized, nor did it receive any detailed study when it reappeared in a series of journals and some edited editions. In 1985, the treatise, along with several other documents outlining Afro-Arab relations, appeared in

68 See John Hunwick and Eve Troutt Powell, *The African Diaspora in the Mediterranean lands of Islam* (NJ, Princeton: Markus Winer Publishers, 2002), 157–163.

69 Temimi, "Pour une histoire sociale de la minorité africaine noire en Tunisie," 49–56.

a volume edited by Yusuf Fadl Hassan. Subsequently, it reappeared again in Temimi's 1995 collection *"Dirīsāt fī-l-ta'rīkh al-'Arabī al-Ifrīqī"* (Studies in Arab-African Relations).[70]

Among other works written on the manuscript is Professor Khalifa Chater's short study of nineteenth-century Tunisian local sources, but the most important mention of *Hatk al-Sitr* since Temimi's work on the subject appears in Rached Limam's monograph *Siyāsat Ḥammūda Bāsha fī Tūnis* (Ḥammūda Pāsha's Policy in Tunis) and his article, "Some Documents Concerning Slavery in Tunisia at the end of the 18th Century," Limam translated fragments of *Hatk al-Sitr* into English along with other archival sources dealing with the slave trade in Tunisia at the end of the eighteenth century.[71]

Moreover, in *Siyāsat Ḥammūda Pāsha fī Tūnis* Limam explained that the "negroes"—or rather Sūdānic West Africans—brought to Tunisia at the time of 'Alī Pāsha (d. 1066/1756) were initially recruited as palace guards (*bawwāba*), much like the slave soldiers (*'abīd al-bukhārī*) of the Sultan of Morocco. Following the death of 'Alī Pāsha, many of the Sūdānic West African community began to cluster into communal groups and started to practice their own religious beliefs and other social customs. In was in this context that Aḥmad al-Timbuktāwī, having arrived in Tunis on his way to pilgrimage, witnessed these practices and was shocked and horrified by them. After his return from *ḥajj*, he felt the need to write this treatise for Ḥammūda Pāsha to unveil what he perceived as the cult's threats to Tunisian society, particularly to women.

The text of *Hatk al-Sitr* contains a number of Hausa words and a great deal of repetition, and Professor Temimi's works on the treatise, without doubt, left more work to be done on the manuscript. After collating the extant texts published by Professor Temimi with the present manuscript, it was found that more extensive and serious corrections still needed to be made to the text. I have attempted to eradicate most of the previous uncorrected mistakes that were left unnoticed by Professor Temimi, and have also tried to rectify mistakes in the manuscript by using the following method: square brackets [ ] have been used in the text in order to clarify what the author refers to, and ordinary brackets ( ) have been used to identify terms which might otherwise be obscure or to give the meaning of a word or phrase which may be unclear. Also, since Hausa

70 Ibid., 49–56.

71 See Chater, *Dépendance Et Mutations Précoloniales*, 147; Khalifa Chater, "La traite au XIXe siècle d'après des sources tunisiennes," in André Martel (ed.), *Les arms et la Toge* (Montpellier: Centre d'Histoire et d'etudes de Defense nationale de Montpellier, 1997), 681–691; Limam, *Siyāsat Ḥammūda Bāsha fī Tūnis*, 16–19. Rached Limam, "Some Documents Concerning Slavery in Tunisia at the End of the 18th Century," *RHM* 8 (11) (1981): 351–354.

was not al-Timbuktāwī's mother tongue, his spelling of the Hausa words was sometimes incorrect. I have chosen to ignore these unusual spellings and transliterate them accordingly as written in Hausa. *Sarkin Gida* is therefore used instead of *Sharikin Gida*, *Dandufu* instead of *Dundufu*, and Zamfara instead of Jamfara, etc. It also appears that manuscript 21183, upon which the current translation is based, was not originally paginated; the present pagination was presumably added by the cataloguer, who also wrote a short introduction to the manuscript. The manuscript is numbered serially in an organized form.

4 Structure of the Book

The importance of this book lies not only in presenting a critical edition of *Hatk al-Sitr* with an English translation of the text, but also in the accompanying detailed chapters aimed at shedding light on the historical and intellectual environments that informed al-Timbuktāwī's ideas and his authorship of this important treatise. As well as presenting *Hatk al-Sitr's* detailed documentation of the Hausa Bori cult in nineteenth-century Tunisia, its ritual structure, deities, annual *ziyārāt* ceremonies, and musical instruments, the book examines the demographic and other defining characteristics of the enslaved Sūdānic Africans whom al-Timbuktāwī labelled *Sūdāni Tūnis*. It is hoped the book will significantly contribute to the literature on enslaved sub-Saharan Africans' religious practices beyond Tunisia and the Maghrib, and that it will also be of interest to scholars of slavery and African Diaspora studies in general. Another merit in presenting this critical edition and translation of *Hatk al-Sitr* lies in its contribution to our understanding of the repercussions that the late eighteenth- and nineteenth-century jihad movements of western and central Sūdān had in the Maghrib. While the effects of these jihad movements have attracted a sustained attention over the past several decades, their repercussions in the Maghrib are yet to receive their fair share of attention.

The book is divided into two parts. Part 1 begins with an introduction, placing *Hatk al-Sitr* within the broader historical context of the Islamization processes of the *bilād al-Sūdān*, in addition to shedding some light on the life of al-Timbuktāwī and discussing the technical specification of *Hatk al-Sitr*. Following the introduction, Chapter 1 focuses on the religious and intellectual milieu that informs al-Timbuktāwī's authorship of *Hatk al-Sitr*. Here, I discuss his encounter with the Wahhābi Controversy in Tunis. To understand al-Timbuktāwī's doctrinal outlook, especially on issues of *shirk*, *takfīr*, *tawassul* and slavery, this chapter examines the effects that the late eighteenth- and nineteenth-century Islamic jihad and reform movements in western and central Sūdān had on his ideas. Chapter 2 and 3 highlight the demographic profile and the religious and social organization of the enslaved Sūdānic West Africans whom al-Timbuktāwī labelled *Sūdān Tūnis* and condemned to *kufr* and re-enslavement. Part 1 concludes with an epilogue and an overview of the broader implications of *Hatk al-Sitr* in advancing our understanding of the intersection of slavery, Islam, and diaspora communities. Part 2 presents the English translation of *Hatk al-Sitr* and the original text in Arabic.

CHAPTER 1

Religious and Intellectual Milieu

> O learned scholars (*ʿulamāʾ*)! It is unlawful for you to remain silent about this sedition (*fitna*) after knowing the truth, for it is mentioned in the hadith—and you know better than I—"When sedition occurs and the scholar remains silent, the curse of Allah will be upon him."[1]
>
> AL-TIMBUKTĀWĪ

∵

In Tunis, where al-Timbuktāwī wrote the most important of the two treatises he authored while in the Maghrib, change was in the air during his visit. A heated religious polemic triggered by a Wahhābi proclamation denouncing Sufism as religious innovation (*bidʿa*) appeared, at a time when the presence of western and central Sūdānic communities was increasing as a result of augmented trans-Saharan slave trade.[2] Hailing from western Sūdān, and concerned as he was with the pristine practice of Islam, like the Wahhābis, he joined the polemical debate and expressed his radical outlook on the overarching questions of

1 *Musnad Ibn Ḥanbal*, 2:457.

2 On the caravan slave trade to the Regency of Tunis, see Abdullahi Mahadi, "The Aftermath of the Jihad in the Central Sudan as a Major Factor in the Volume of the Trans-Saharan Slave Trade in the Nineteenth Century," in Elizabeth Savage (ed.), *The Human Commodity: Perspectives on the Trans-Saharan Trade* (London: Frank Cass, 1992), 111–128; Jamil M. Abun-Nasr, "The Tunisian State in the Eighteenth Century," *Revue de l'Occident Musulman et de la Méditerranée* 33 (1982): 33–66; Ralph A. Austen, and Dennis. D. Cordell, "Trade, Transportation, and Expanding Economic Networks: Saharan Caravan Commerce in the Era of European expansion, 1500–1900," in Alusine Jalloh and Toyin Falola (eds.), *Black Business and Economic Power* (Rochester: University of Rochester Press, 2002), 80–113; Adu Boahen, "The Caravan Trade in Nineteenth Century," *Journal of African History* 3, no. 2 (1962): 249–359; Michael Brett, "Ifriqiyya as a Market for Saharan Trade from the Tenth to the twelve Century AD," *Journal of African History* 10, no. 3 (1969): 347–364; Khalifa Chater, "Esclavage et Commerce transsaherien au XIXe siécle dans las Règences de Tunis et Tripoli," *Cahier de la Mediterranée* 65 (2002); Abdelhami Larguèche, *L'abolition de l'esclavage en Tunisie à travers les archives, 1841–1846, Collection Savoir*, Tunis: Alif: Société tunisienne d'étude du XVIIIème siècle, 1990.

© KONINKLIJKE BRILL NV, LEIDEN, 2024 | DOI:10.1163/9789004516175_003

association of other beings with God (*shirk*) and the intercession and veneration of saints (*tawassul wa tabarruk bi-l-awliyāʾ*) raised by the Wahhābi proclamation.[3]

Capitalizing on the polemical debate to articulate his views on the Wahhābi doctrine concerning matters of unbelief (*kufr*) and anathematization (*takfīr*), al-Timbuktāwī—a guest and resident scholar in the city—questioned the legitimacy of the Bori cult and the commitment to Islam of thousands of its western and central Sūdānic followers, who were still being brought into the Regency of Tunis as slaves. In dragging the Bori cult and its adherents into the center of this controversy, al-Timbuktāwī's aim was clear: to use the Islamic jihad leadership's condemnations of the cult in his western and central Sūdānic homeland as a window to contribute to the debate instigated by the Wahhābi proclamation, calling for the outright eradication of forms of religious practices that they condemned as *bidʿa*. While joining Tunisian *ʿulamāʾ* to refute the Wahhābi doctrine and believing that the people of Tunis had little knowledge of Bori, he thus seized the opportunity to eloquently describe the cult's practice, its ritual structure, deities, musical instruments, and influence on local Islamic culture, which he felt had gone unnoticed by the people of Tunis, particularly its religious authorities.

This chapter, placing *Ḥatk al-Sitr* in its religious and intellectual contexts, is divided into three sections. In the first section, I will discuss the context of the Wahhābi controversy and the Tunisian *ʿulamāʾ's* refutations of their doctrine as a backdrop to the authorship of this treatise. Next, I will discuss al-Timbuktāwī's viewpoints on the central issues raised in the Wahhābi proclamation and his application of its main question to the legitimacy of the Bori cult as it was practiced by the western and central Sūdānic community in the Regency. In the final section, drawing on the intellectual output of the jihad movements of Uthman Dan Fodio (1167–1232/1754–1817) in Hausaland and Shehu Aḥmadu Lobbo (1188–1259/1775–1844) in central Niger, I will illustrate the influences of these jihad movements—which sought, among other objectives, to change

3 On the rise and expansion of the Wahhabi movement, see Cole M. Bunzel, *Wahhābism: The History of a Militant Islamic Movement*, Princeton & Oxford, Princeton University Press 2023; Michael Cook, "On the Origins of Wahhabism," *Journal of the Royal Asiatic Society of Great Britain and Ireland* 2 (1992), 191–202; Anita L.P. Burdet, *The Expansion of Wahhabi Power in Arabia, 1798–1932: British Documentary Records*, Cambridge: Cambridge Archives Editions, 2013; Mohammed Ayoob and Hasan Kosebalaban, eds., *Religion and Politics in Saudi Arabia: Wahhabism and the State*, Boulder, CO: Lynne Rienner Publishers, 2009; Peter G. Mandaville, ed., *Wahhabism and the World: Understanding Saudi Arabia's Global Influence on Islam*, New York, NY: Oxford University Press, 2022; Simon Ross Valentine, *Force and fanaticism: Wahhabism in Saudi Arabia and Beyond*, London: Hurst & Company, 2015.

society through jihad or political reform—on al-Timbuktāwī's dogmatic outlook, which set his views apart from his Tunisian counterparts. By exploring these influences, particularly his intellectual links to the western and the central Sūdān, I argue that al-Timbuktāwī's application of the overarching questions surrounding the Wahhābi controversy by condemning the Bori cult and calling for the re-enslavement of its adepts provides a perspective that appears to reflect the sentiments and philosophy of the West African jihad movements on issues of anathematization (*takfīr*) and enslavement. His viewpoints should be considered as a previously unrecognized reverberation and resonance of these jihad movements in the Maghrib.

1 Encountering the Wahhābi Controversy

Over the last couple of decades, several historians and religious scholars have studied the role of the Muslim pilgrimage as an important conduit that linked the *bilād al-sūdān* with the wider Islamic world.[4] In the western and central Sūdānic lands of Muslim Africa, the pilgrimage tradition is believed to have taken off with the consolidation of Islam by the middle of the eleventh century; the journey enabled Muslims from the Sūdānic lands to fulfill their religious duty to complete the *hajj*, and also provided the opportunity for intellectual engagement with the established learning centers found along the pilgrimage routes, such as Fez, Chinguetti, Tlemcen, Qayrawan, Tunis, Cairo, and, of course, the holy cities of Mecca and Medina.[5] Al-Timbuktāwī, who spent a lengthy period in the prestigious learning centers of Tunis and Fez during his pilgrimage, must have traveled via the Chinguetti route, through modern-day Mauritania. [See Map 3] Highly educated in Islamic jurisprudence, al-Timbuktāwī was probably a disciple of Qādirī Sufism. Based on his credentials

4 On the pilgrimage tradition in West Africa, see Ousmane Oumar Kane, "The Transformation of the Pilgrimage Tradition in West Africa," in Ousmane Oumar Kane (ed.), *Islamic Scholarship in Africa: New Directions and Global Contexts* (Woodbridge: James Currey, 2021), 90–110; ʿUmar al-Naqar, *The Pilgrimage Tradition in West Africa: An Historical Study with Special Reference to the Nineteenth Century* Khartoum: Khartoum University Press, 1972; Ahmad Chanfi, *West African Ulama and Salafism in Mecca and Medina*, Leiden: Brill, 2015; J.S. Birk, *Across the Savanna to Mecca: The Overland Pilgrimage Route from West Africa to Mecca*, London: C. Hurst 1978; M.F.E. Peters, *The Hajj: The Muslim Pilgrimage to Mecca and the Holy Places*, Princeton: Princeton University Press, 1994.

5 See Fatima Harrak and Mohamed El-Mansour, *A Fulani Jihadist in the Maghreb: Admonition of Aḥmad Ibn Al-Qādī at-Timbuktī to the Rulers of Tunisia and Morocco* (Rabat: Institute of African Studies, 2000), 14–16.

and willingness to engage with the intellectual community in Tunis and Fez, it seems that his pilgrimage was, first and foremost, motivated by scholarly pursuits.[6] At the time he passed through Tunis and Fez, the intellectual scenes there were humming with polemical debate triggered by a Wahhābi proclamation sent to several quarters of the Muslim world, including the Maghribi states of Tunisia, Libya, and Morocco.[7] In Tunisia, the proclamation appeared in the country, probably immediately after the death of Muḥammad ʾIbn ʿAbd al-Wahhāb (1115/1703–1206/1792), the founder of the Wahhābi movement (*al-ḥaraka al-Wahhābīyya*).[8] A student of the Ḥanbalī school of law, prior to establishing himself as a notable scholar and an Islamic revivalist *par excellence*, ʾIbn ʿAbd al-Wahhāb traveled far across the Middle East and Asia in search of knowledge, studying under several *ʿulamāʾ* in Baghdad, Damascus, Kurdistan, and Isfahan, where he acquainted himself with the religious conditions of Muslims—a situation he lamented as deviation from the true path of Islam. To rectify this, ʾIbn ʿAbd al-Wahhāb wrote a considerable number of works in support of his teachings to return Muslims to a pristine version of Islam free from all forms of religious innovations. Among these was the aforementioned proclamation that was widely reproduced by his followers after his death and was sent to several parts of the Muslim world to win over other Muslims to his teachings and religious doctrine. At its core, the Wahhābi movement preached an austere form of Ḥanbalism by calling for strict adherence to the doctrine of the essential unity of God (*tawḥīd*), free from religious innovations (*bidʿa*) and *shirk* (the association of other beings with God). Among the innovative practices that the Wahhābis condemned as *bidʿa* and *shirk* include visitations (*ziyārāt*) to mosques or mausoleums housing the tombs of holy Muslim personalities, such as the Prophet, his Companions, members of his family, and saints. The Wahhābis also condemned sacrificial offerings at the tombs of the Prophet and saints. With this mission, the Wahhābis directed their early attacks on Shiʾism and Sufism—both of which were gaining ground at the time—by accusing those making visitations to mausoleums and the tombs of saints as

6 See especially the preface and introduction of *Ḥatk al-Sitr*. al-Timbuktāwī, *Hatk al-Sitr ʿAmmā ʿAlayhi Sūdān Tūnis min al-Kufr*, Tunis: MS No. 21183, Bibliotheque Nationale de Tunisie, 1813, 1–3.

7 Ismael M. Montana, "Al-Timbuktāwī, Aḥmad b. al-Qāḍī," in Kate Fleet et al. (eds.), *The Encyclopedia of Islam Three* (Leiden & Boston: Brill, 2022), 148–149; Harrak and El-Mansour, *A Fulani Jihadist in the Maghreb*, 17–19; and John Hunwick and Eve Troutt Powell, *The African Diaspora in the Mediterranean lands of Islam* (Princeton: Markus Wiener, 2002), 157.

8 See Arnold Green, "A Tunisian Reply to a Wahhabi Proclamation: Texts and Contexts," in Arnold H. Green (ed.), *Arabic and Islamic Studies: In Memory of Mohamed al-Nowaihi* (Cairo: The American University of Cairo Press, 1985), 160.

bidʿa and polytheism.[9] The proclamation warned that failure to refrain from these acts of *bidʿa* would not only render Muslims unbelievers (*kuffār*) but that those who did not comply with the Wahhābi doctrine would be subjected to the jihad of the sword.[10] With the support of Muḥammad Ibn Saʿūd (r. 1178–1217/1765–1803), the emir of Dirʿiyah—a small oasis town near Riyadh, in the Najd region—within a decade the movement transformed into a dynamic religious and political ideology aimed at establishing a state on the principles of pure adherence to Islam.

Prior to this alliance between Muḥammad Ibn ʿAbd al-Wahhāb and Muḥammad Ibn Sa'ūd, and the emergence of Wahhābism as a dynamic religious and political movement, both Najd and Ḥijāz had been ruled by the Ottoman Sultan, who appointed the Sharīfs of Mecca. Sharīfs appointed by the Sublime Porte manned the affairs of the Holy Sites in Mecca and Medina. Besides the appointments of Sharīfs, the Porte controlled the movements of people by deploying military units and employing paid tribesmen to provide security and protection, especially for pilgrim caravans traveling to the holy sites. Even though the Ottoman Empire did not control the entire Arabian Peninsula, with the above arrangements put in place they provided much-needed security and protection that reflected the Porte's presence and legitimacy in the Arabian Peninsula. The growing influence of Ibn ʿAbd al-Wahhāb and Ibn Sa'ūd's alliance resulted in a series of challenges to the Porte's legitimacy as the protector of the holy sites and pilgrims. After expanding from Najd to central and eastern Arabia and taking over al-Ḥasā and Qatīf by 1800, the Wahhābis, supported by forces from Ibn Sa'ūd, ventured out of the Arabian Peninsula, invading Iraq and Syria and plundering the Shīʿī holy city of Karbala. Resolved in their mission to uproot religious innovations (*bidʿa*) in all Muslim lands, they began by besieging the Holy Cities of Islam, capturing Medina in 1804; within two years Mecca fell, and the Sharīfs who had been guardians of the holy sites on behalf of the Ottoman Porte were expelled.

In the Maghrib, where the Wahhābi proclamation appeared during the last decade of the eighteenth century, the Wahhābis accused the political author-

9 On the Wahhābi movement and controversy in the Maghrib, see El-Ajīlī al-Tlīlī, "*Al-Wahhābiyya wa bilād al-Tūnisiyya zamman Ḥammūda Basha*," C.A.R, Université de Tunis, 1983; Green, "A Tunisian Reply to a Wahhabi Proclamation," 134–177; Abdul al-Razzaq Al-Ḥammāmī, "ʿUlamā' Tūnis wa-l-Daʿwat al-Wahhābīyya," *Ḥawliyyāt Jāmiʿat al-Tūnīssiyya*, 30 (1989), 49–78; Faraj ibn Ramaḍān, *Talāqqī al-Wahhābīyya fī Tūnis: maʿa wathā'iq al-murāsalāt al-mutabādala* (Tūnis: Dār Muḥammad ʿAlī lil-Nashr, 2013), 33; Jalloul Azzoubat, *Al-Qādī wa-l-Muftī Ismā'īl Tamīmī wa-l-radd ʿalā Dalālāt al-Wahhābīyya* (Tunis, 2016).

10 Green, "Tunisian Reply to a Wahhabi Proclamation," 166.

ities of condoning polytheism.[11] Here, as in the other areas of the Muslim world where the Wahhābis vehemently attempted to win over Muslims to their doctrine, the proclamation admonished political and religious authorities to denounce heretical practices that violated the scriptural and prophetic tradition or what they considered the pure form of Islam. According to the Wahhābis, the Sufi practices of seeking the intercession of saints (*tawassul*) and visitation (*ziyārāt*) to the tomb of the Prophet, which remained widespread, constituted acts of religious innovation (*bidʿa*) and the association of other beings with God (*shirk*), meriting severe punishment. But the proclamation did not stop there. It called on the political and religious authorities in the Maghrib to rid their lands of these polytheistic practices of heresy stemming from Sufism or face the consequence: jihad of the sword. Owing to the tone of the proclamation and the religious milieu characterized by the mass presence of Sufism and popular Islam in the Maghrib, it is not surprising that, even in cases where the Wahhābi proclamation was well received, it still evoked sharp refutations and denunciations, particularly among the *ʿulamāʾ* in religious centers in Tunis and Fez.[12]

Unlike in Morocco, where the response to the proclamation received official support on the orders of the Moroccan Sultān, Mawlāy Sulaymān (r. 1206–1237/1792–1822),[13] in Tunisia the proclamation prompted the sharpest refutation and rebuttal. The chief chronicler of the Husaynid Dynasty, Aḥmad Ibn Abī Diyaf (d. 1290/1874) who reported the events surrounding the appearance of the proclamation in Tunis, citing an unpublished refutation of it, dubbed it outright propaganda.[14] Ibn Abī Diyaf's account of the Wahhābi controversy in Tunis, even though he did not indicate the precise date the proclamation appeared in the country nor when its unpublished refutation was issued, suggests it was one of the most pressing issues during the reign of the Tunisian

---

11 Green, "Tunisian Reply to a Wahhabi Proclamation," 166, and Paul L. Heck, "An Early Response to Wahhabism from Morocco: The Politics of Intercession," *Studia Islamica*, 107, no. 2 (2012), 235–254.

12 On the Wahhābi controversy in Morocco, see Heck, "An Early Response to Wahhabism from Morocco," Harrak and El-Mansour, *A Fulani Jihadist in the Maghreb*; Ḥamādī al-Rudaysī and Asmāʾ Nuwayra, *Al-Radd ʿalā al-Wahhābīyya fī-l-qarn al-tāsiʿ ʿashar: nuṣūṣ al-Gharb al-Islāmī namūdhajan*, Beirut: Dār al-Ṭalīʿa lil-Ṭibāʿa wa-l-Nashr, 2008; and Mohamed al-Mansour, "Al-Harraka al-Wahhābiyya wa rudūd al-fiʿl al-Maghribiyya ʿinda Bidāyat al-Qarn al-Tāsiʿ Ashar," in *Al-Islām wa-l-Mujtamaʿ al-Maghribī fī al-Qarn al-Tāsiʿ ʿAshar* (Rabat, 1986), 175–191.

13 For response to the Wahhābi proclamation in Tunis, see Ibn Abī Diyaf, *Ithāf*, Vol. III, 75.

14 Ibn Abī Diyaf, *Ithāf*, Vol. III, 75, and Green, "Tunisian Reply to a Wahhabi Proclamation," 157.

ruler, Ḥammūda Pāsha (r. 1206–1229/1792–1814).[15] Based on the *ʿulamāʾ* of Fez's response to the proclamation, Rouisī and Nuwayrāt date its appearance in Tunis to 1803.[16] On the basis of events surrounding the first published refutation of the proclamation, dated around 1800, however, historian Arnold Green suggests that it may have appeared in Tunisia as early as 1795 or shortly after the death of Muḥammad Ibn ʿAbd al-Wahhāb.[17] Whatever the precise date of the arrival of the proclamation in Tunisia, we know that its appearance generated a heated and long-lasting religious controversy. Among the leading (scholars) *ʿulamāʾ* and members of the religious judiciary whose refutations to the proclamation Ibn Abī Diyaf published in his chronicle, *Itḥāf*, were Shaykh ʿUmar al-Maḥjūb (d. 1221/1807), who served as a Chief Muftī under Ḥammūda for the Maliki school, and Shaykh Ismāʿīl al-Tamīmī (d. 1245/1830), his student.[18]

A review of the Tunisian religious judiciary's response to the proclamation perhaps ought first to begin with an assessment of the importance Ḥammūda Pāsha accorded it. External concerns in terms of Tunis's relations with the Ottoman Porte and the contours of Ḥusaynid state socio-religious structure shaped Ḥammūda's attention and the importance he bestowed on it. As Green suggests, whereas the Moroccan Sultān Sulaymān (r. 1206–1237/1792–1822) appears to have been receptive and sympathetic to the Wahhābi doctrine, as a vassal state of the Ottoman Porte, political considerations concerning the Wahhābi threat and challenge to the legitimacy of the Ottoman Empire dominated Ḥammūda's response.[19] From the beginning, the Ḥusaynid dynasty, which came to power in 1705, aspired on varying levels for some kind of autonomy from the sovereignty of the Ottoman Sultan, but throughout the eighteenth century, until the French occupation in 1881, the Regency remained nominally attached to the Porte. As a vassal entity, Tunis had been concerned about the implications that the Wahhābis' sack of the Holy Cities posed to the sovereignty of the Ottoman Porte. This legitimate concern was the reason why Muḥammad ʿAlī (r. 1219–1264/1805–1848) led a series of military campaigns on behalf of the Porte against the Wahhābis in the Arabian Peninsula. In 1814, when news that Muḥammad ʿAlī's forces had regained control of the Holy Cities and defeated the Wahhābis reached Tunis, Ḥammūda ordered celebratory gunshots to mark the occasion.[20] As Green opines, the leading Tunisian *ʿulamāʾ* and judiciary

15 Ibn Abī Diyaf, *Ithāf*, Vol. III, 75.
16 El-Raouisī and Nuwayrāt, *Al-Radd ʿalā al-Wahhābīyya fī al-qarn al-tāsiʿat ʿashar*, 28.
17 Green, "Tunisian Reply to a Wahhabi Proclamation," 155–156.
18 Ibid., 157.
19 Ibid., 161.
20 Ibn Abī Diyaf, *Ithāf*, Vol. III, 75.

took this concern over the Wahhābi challenge to the integrity of the Ottoman Porte into consideration in their response to the Wahhābi proclamation.[21]

Equally crucial in heightening Ḥammūda's sense of urgency when he appealed to the religious judiciary to respond to the proclamation was the prevailing religious culture, characterized by what Leon Carl Brown termed as a spirit of accommodation between orthodoxy and mysticism in the Regency.[22] From the early eighteenth century, the political and religious landscape in Tunisia had been marked by accommodation and harmonious relations between the Ḥusaynid ruling class and the religious establishment, including the Sufi and the popular religious brotherhoods (*ṭarīqas*). As both Brown and Green have shown, many of the country's learned and leading *ʿulamāʾ* were members of the Sufi brotherhoods.[23] In 1803, Ḥammūda sent Ibrāhīm al-Riyāḥī as an emissary to Fez, where Moroccan *ʿulamāʾ* had also been debating the Wahhābi doctrine. While in Morocco, al-Riyāḥī joined the Tijaniyya brotherhood and later introduced it to the Regency before Aḥmad Bey (r. 1250–1271/1835–1855) embraced it himself. Meanwhile Ḥammūda himself was reportedly initiated into the Qādiriyya order by another leading Tunisian scholar (*ʿālim*) of the time, Shaykh ʿAlī b. ʿUmar al-Shāʿib, who had joined the *ṭarīqa* while on pilgrimage and was the first to introduce it to Tunis. According to Ibn Abī Diyaf, Ḥammūda built a shrine (*zāwiya*) in honor of ʿUmar al-Shāʿib in his native town of Menzel Bouzelfa. By the middle of the nineteenth century, both the Tijaniyya and Qādiriyya were flourishing in Tunis because of their support from the Ḥusaynid rulers, before their influence waned toward the latter part of the century.[24]

2 The Tunisian Response

As outlined above, the Wahhābi proclamation declared war on the Muslims they accused of religious innovations (*bidʿa*) and sought to ban them from visiting the tombs of the Prophet Muḥammad and his Companions in the

21 Green, "Tunisian Reply to a Wahhabi Proclamation," 161.

22 Carl L. Brown, *The Tunisia of Ahmad Bey, 1837–1855* (Princeton: Prince University Press, 1974), 174–175.

23 Carl L. Brown, "The Religious Establishment in Husaynid Tunisia," in Nikki R. Keddie (ed.), *Scholars, Saints, and Sufis: Muslim Religious Institutions in the Middle East since 1500* (Los Angeles and London: University of California Press, 1972), 80–81; Green, "Tunisian Reply to a Wahhabi Proclamation," 162.

24 See Arnold Green, "The Sufi Orders in 19th-Century Tunisia: Sources and Prospects," *Revue D'Histoire Maghrebine*, 13–14 (1979), 61–68.

heartland of the Middle East. In Tunisia, they accused Muslims of abandoning monotheism (*tawḥīd*) for polytheism (*shirk*), and for glorifying Sufi saints by visiting their tombs; they warned that "whoever does not respond to the[ir] summoning by means of proof and clear evidence, [they] shall summon him with the sword and the spear …"[25] Among the leading Tunisian *ʿulamāʾ* Ḥammūda Pāsha tasked to respond to the proclamation was ʿUmar b. al-Maḥjūb (d. 1221/1807), whose refutation of the proclamation is the only text Ibn Abī Diyaf reproduced in his *ʾItḥāf* alongside the complete text of the Wahhābi proclamation. It must be noted that ʿUmar b. al-Maḥjūb's refutation was preceded by an earlier rebuttal written around 1800 by Shaykh Ismāʿīl al-Tamīmī, his own student at Zaytūna.[26] While not in disagreement with al-Tamīmī's rebuttal of the Wahhābi doctrine, ʿUmar b. al-Maḥjūb's response went further to elucidate theological inconsistencies articulated in the Wahhābi argument on such issues as visitation (*ziyārāt*) to the tombs of the Prophet and saints (*awliyāʾ*), which they considered religious innovation.[27] Arming his response with evidence from the *ḥadīth* (sayings of the Prophet), ʿUmar b. al-Maḥjūb rejected the arguments of the Wahhābis and convincingly argued that seeking intercession with Allah through the blessing of the Prophet is a legitimate and permissible form of *tawassul*. As a case in point, he cited the action of ʿUmar ibn al-Khaṭṭāb, the second of the four Rāshidūn Caliphs and one of the closest Companions of the Prophet Muḥammad, as evidence. According to ʿUmar b. al-Maḥjūb, when praying for rain, the Caliph ʿUmar went to the tomb of the Prophet's uncle and invoked his name to pray and intercede for rain; if seeking the intercession of holy men was prohibited, ʿUmar would not have done this.

Basing his argument on this event and on other documented practices of the Prophet's companions, ʿUmar b. al-Maḥjūb further contended that when it came to the ban on erecting tombs and visiting them, the Prophet's prohibition of such practice was initially aimed at discouraging the continuation of pagan customs, and that it is established that the Prophet later encouraged the visitation of tombs in Islamic contexts and settings.[28] On the question of sacrificial animals and making votive offerings, ʿUmar b. al-Maḥjūb contended that banning this practice actually rested on the intention, not the act itself per se.

After rebutting these charges and allegations, ʿUmar b. al-Maḥjūb then concluded it was rather the Wahhābis who strayed from the straight path of Islam

25 Green, "Tunisian Reply to a Wahhabi Proclamation," 157.
26 Ibid., 159.
27 Ibid., 159.
28 Ibid., 159.

by their vicious attack on the Holy Cities of Mecca and Medina and declaring jihad on fellow Muslims who disagreed with their fanatical and extremist doctrine.[29]

3 Al-Timbuktāwī and the Wahhābi Controversy

When al-Timbuktāwī returned to Tunis from pilgrimage and began the authorship of his treatise, *Risālat Ḥatk al-Sitr ʿAmmā Alayhi Sūdāni Tunis min al-Kufr*, probably in the spring of 1808, the polemical debate instigated by the Wahhābi proclamation was at its peak. ʿUmar b. al-Maḥjūb, a prominent member of the Tunisian religious judiciary and the harshest critics of the Wahhābi doctrine, had just passed away. A year prior to his death, Ḥammūda Pāsha had deposed him from the position of Bash Mufti of the Maliki Mazhab after a disagreement, displeased with his attitude, although he continued to serve as the Chief Qāḍī of Tunis while also lecturing at the Zaytūna mosque until his death.[30] Since he authored the most damning refutation of the Wahhābi proclamation and their doctrine, his influence on the Wahhābi controversy no doubt served as a reference point for almost all the subsequent responses. Although ʾIbn ʿAbī Diyaf does not mention al-Timbuktāwī among the *ʿulamāʾ* who joined the debate in refuting the proclamation, based on the similarity of al-Timbuktāwī's views to those of ʿUmar b. al-Maḥjūb, one can clearly surmise that the former must have been thoroughly familiar with the content of the latter's refutation of the proclamation. Following ʿUmar b. al-Maḥjūb, al-Timbuktāwī outrightly rejected the Wahhābis' call for the excommunication of Muslims who sought intercession (*tawassul*) through the blessing of prophets and saints (*ʾawliyāʾ*). Citing the same scriptural evidence as ʿUmar b. al-Maḥjūb, al-Timbuktāwī concluded that turning to Almighty Allah through his prophets or saints was legally permissible, and that the Wahhābis' characterization of intercession as a religious innovation (*bidʿa*) had no legal grounds. Al-Timbuktāwī's elucidation of his opinion on this issue is worth quoting at length here:

> So what right do we have to excommunicate Muslims because of their turning to Allah [through the prophets and saints] (*tawassul*), when it is legally permissible, for saying such things as: "O Lord! Provide me with

29 Ibid., 159–160.
30 Ibid., 158.

> such and such by the honor of Muḥammad, blessings and peace of Allah be upon him, or the honor of one of his companions, or [a certain] angel or a saint"? The excommunication of people for this *tawassul* by the Wahhābis has no legal basis. And their assertion that *tawassul* is only lawful through someone who is alive not dead, and who is present not absent, requires legal proof. What seems obvious to me is that they have proceeded haphazardly in this matter, because they justify this prohibition by restricting *tawassul* to he who makes it an intermediary between himself and his Lord, and this happens in the case of someone who is alive and present. If they claim that *tawassul* is a kind of worshipping the dead and absent because some people worshipped their dead, then that is equally applicable to the living and present, for Pharaoh was worshipped during his lifetime.[31]

In a section devoted to "Refutation of the Wahhābis" in Chapter One of *Ḥatk al-Sitr*, after declaring that the Wahhābis' arguments were baseless, al-Timbuktāwī then introduced the Bori cult practiced by the recently enslaved western and central Sūdānic Africans into the debate. To al-Timbuktāwī, while seeking intercession through the blessing of the Prophet and *ʾawliyāʾ* after death or visiting their tombs did not amount to *shirk*, the practitioners of the Bori cult who sought intercession with God or the *ʾawliyāʾ* through idols, *jinn*, and musical instruments were indeed worthy of excommunication. According to al-Timbuktāwī, the actions of these slaves, immersed in their reprehensible "pagan" practices, were tantamount to the practices of the Arab polytheists whom the Prophet had combated.[32] Thus, while intercession with the Prophet and saints did not amount to an act of *shirk*, contrary to the Wahhābis' assertion, the "sedition of the slaves was pure polytheism."[33] This form of polytheism, which was widespread throughout North Africa and known among the people of Tunis, was plain *shirk*, not intercession with the Prophet of Allah's saints. Moreover, al-Timbuktāwī contended that "even if we suppose that these practices do not amount to polytheism, but mere immorality, it would be obligatory to prevent them because they entirely resemble the practice of unbelievers of the *bilād al-Sūdān*."[34]

As the title of his treatise—*Ḥatk al-Sitr ʿAmmā Alayhi Sūdān Tūnis min al-Kufr*, "Piercing the Veil: Being an Account of the Infidel Practice of the Blacks

31 Al-Timbuktāwī, *Ḥatk al-Sitr*, p. 11, Folio A.
32 Ibid., p. 10, Folio B.
33 Ibid., p. 9, Folio A.
34 Ibid., p. 17, Folio A.

of Tunis"—makes clear, al-Timbuktāwī's central goal was to unmask the true nature of the Bori as a polytheistic and infidel practice. According to him, this was the deviant religious cult practiced by the same Bori practitioners condemned as fire worshippers (*majuzawa* or *majūs*) in western and central Sūdān. Following this, he laid down a series of recommendations as a basis for the excommunication of the cult's practitioners and called for its outright ban as follows. That Ḥammūda Pāsha and Tunisian religious authorities should:

1. Prohibit the enslaved Sūdānic West Africans from intermarrying with Muslim women;[35]
2. Nullify any existing marriage between the enslaved Sūdānic West Africans and any Muslim and vice versa;[36]
3. Prohibit them from legal testimony or witness in religious matters;[37]
4. Prevent anyone to pray over their dead until they repent;[38]
5. Issue a fatwa to stipulate the manumission of any enslaved Sūdānic West African on refraining from the Bori cult. That is, no one should set any of them free if he/she knows the slave will join the Bori cult;[39]
6. As fire worshippers (*majus*), the enslaved Sūdānic West Africans are to be forced to embrace Islam by threat and whipping unconditionally;[40]
7. Prohibit people of Tunis from eating what they slaughtered for their gods for it is carcass;[41]
8. Relinquish and convert the principal communal lodge of the Bori practitioners (Dār Kofa) to a mosque, *madrasa*, or a hostel for soldiers;[42]
9. Destroy all the Bori pantheon and idols housed in their Bori compounds (*diyār*) and scattered around Tunis and throughout the regency;[43]
10. Ban their enslaved girls and women from private and public gathering other than weddings;[44]
11. Discipline and imprison any possessed enslaved girls/women until they repent, else they must be put to death;[45]

---

35 Ibid., p. 21, Folio A.
36 Ibid., p. 21, Folio A.
37 Ibid., p. 22, Folio B.
38 Ibid., p. 22, Folio B.
39 Ibid., p. 22, Folio B.
40 Ibid., p. 21, Folio A.
41 Ibid., p. 20, Folio B.
42 Ibid., p. 20, Folio B.
43 Ibid., p. 20, Folio B.
44 Ibid., p. 20, Folio B.
45 Ibid., p. 20, Folio B.

12. Forbid all the enslaved Sūdānic West Africans from going to the forest (*jilāz*) on the outskirts of Tunis, which they claim is inhabited by Bori spirits;[46]
13. Appoint a pious and knowledgeable person of the Holy Book and Sunna to monitor the actions of these enslaved Sūdānic West Africans;
14. Order the people of Tunis to shut their doors on these devils [slaves].

Because the principal adepts of the Bori cult were those he described as infidels and unbelievers from his own homeland, al-Timbuktāwī was utterly convinced that the people of Tunis had very little knowledge about the infidel beliefs and seditious practices (*fitna*) they were spreading in Tunisia. As such, he urged that doing away with this sedition was not only a religious duty binding and incumbent upon Ḥammūda Pāsha, but also a collective duty for everyone, especially the *ʿulamāʾ*, who should encourage Ḥammūda to "enjoin the good and forbid the wrong" by banning Bori because it is plainly polytheism. Here he wrote:

> It is impermissible for anyone to remain silent about this sedition (*fitna*) because it is not [merely] among those matters that fulfill the condition of commanding the good and forbidding the wrong (*al-amr bi-l-maʿrūf*), since this sedition is plain polytheism, and resisting polytheism is a [form of jihad], and jihad is a legal obligation even if it destroys one or one's wealth.[47]

Whether al-Timbuktāwī was privy to the culture of religious accommodation that prevailed throughout North Africa and made Tunis a subject of the Wahhābis' attack or not is a question that should not be difficult to establish. While the *ʿulamāʾ* of Tunis, like Fez, concerned themselves more with intellectual engagement, there is no doubt that al-Timbuktāwī's viewpoints reflected the attitudes of Islamic reformist leaders in his homeland of western and central Sūdānic milieu. In fact, the indigenous Sūdānic religious practices that the Sūdānic *shaykh* attacked had a long presence in the Regency and elsewhere in the Maghrib, perhaps dating back centuries. It is known to have commingled peacefully with the religious landscape throughout the Maghrib. Yet at the time of his stay in Tunis the presence of Bori practitioners, owing to the favorable economic conditions in Tunisia, markedly increased as a result of their displacement by jihad movements and political instability in western and central

46 Ibid., p. 20, Folio B.
47 Ibid., p. 4. Folio B.

Sūdān.[48] As a number of scholars have shown, following the burgeoning economic policies put in place by Ḥammūda Pāsha, trade after the last quarter of the eighteenth century between the Regency and western and central Sūdān was significantly revived.[49] For the first time since the Hilali invasion in the early eleventh century disrupted regular trade between Ifriqiyya and western and central Sūdān, the last quarter of the eighteenth century through the end of Ḥammūda Pāsha's rule witnessed a massive surge in the slave trade, representing the high point of the Tunisian portion of the trans-Saharan slave trade during the modern period. A few decades prior to Ḥammūda's revival of the trans-Saharan slave trade, his predecessor, ʿAlī Bey I, tapped into preexisting commercial and diplomatic ties with central Sūdān and imported male slaves to serve as his bodyguards. These bodyguards, described invariably as *bawwāba* (sing. *bawwāb*, meaning doorman in Arabic) or *kofāfi* (sing. *Kofa*, meaning door or doorman in Hausa) were drawn from the same geographical zone that supplied the bulk of the enslaved entering Tunis after the last quarter of the eighteenth century.[50] We now know that through the support of ʿAlī Bey to facilitate the settlement of the *bawwāba* or *kofāfi*, the Bori cult practice became localized in Tunis. By the turn of the nineteenth century, around the same time al-Timbuktāwī visited the city, the Bori practitioners, a result of the Ḥusaynid state's continued support, organized along the lines of the state-regulated religious brotherhoods. As will be detailed in Chapter 3, the state attached these enslaved Sūdānic West Africans to Sīdī Saʿad al-ʿAbīd, a scholar (*ʿālim*) and an ex-manumitted slave of Bornu origin who served as their spiritual patron. Through their affiliation with Sīdī Saʿad, they were recognized and controlled within the framework of the Husaynids' religio-political strategy of societal control of the local populace.[51] As Leon Carl Brown illustrated, this

48 Abdullahi Mahadi, "The Aftermath of the Jihad as a Factor in the Volume of the trans-Saharan Slave Trade in the Nineteenth Century," in Elizabeth Savage (ed.), *The Human Commodity: Perspectives on the trans-Saharan Trade* (London: Frank Cass, 1992), 111–128.

49 See Ismael M. Montana, *The Abolition of Slavery in Ottoman Tunisia*, Gainesville: University Press of Florida, 2013; Richard C. Jankowsky, *Stambeli: Music, Trance, and Alterity in Tunisia* (Chicago: University of Chicago Press, 2010), 43–45.

50 See Ismael M. Montana, "The Forgotten Sudanic Palace Guards of Ali Bey I: Their Genesis, Functions, and Legacy in Ottoman Tunisia," *Comparative Studies of South Asia, Africa and the Middle East* 38, no. 2 (2018): 296–309.

51 See Ismael M. Montana, "The Stambali of Husaynid Tunis: From Possession Cult to Ethno-Religious and National Culture," in Ehud R. Toledano (ed.), *African Communities in Asia and the Mediterranean: Identities Between Integration and Conflict* (Halle and New Jersey: Max Plank Institute and Africa World Press, 2011), 171–184.

Ḥusaynid religio-political strategy was based on the spirit of accommodation between orthodoxy and mysticism. Within this policy, as Brown writes:

> The pattern of accommodation between legalistic orthodoxy and illuminist mysticism in Ḥusaynid Tunisia was thorough and consistent both on the level of theology and in the specific institutional and personal relationships that characterized the daily life. Both ulama and the people accepted the idea of intercession between the individual believer and Allah, and it appears thus perfectly consistent that such persons-or-"saints"-should be granted a special veneration.[52]

When visiting Tunis in 1914, almost a century after al-Timbuktāwī's stay and condemnation of the Bori practitioners to death and re-enslavement, A.J.N. Tremearne, the British military officer and anthropologist who conducted a comparative study of the Bori cult in West and North Africa, could still witness the spirit of religious accommodation that Brown and other historians of Ḥusaynid Tunisia aptly describe as a key feature of the Tunisian state.[53] According to Tremearne, not only was the Bori cult—now known as Stambāli—integral to the popular religious landscape, but even some of the beys of Tunis embraced the cult and had private Bori temples dedicated to their service. All these led him to write in amazement that: "It is somewhat strange to find that whereas in Nigeria we [British colonial authorities] have forbidden the practice of the Bori rites in consideration of the Filani [*sic*] protests, here in North Africa (which is surely more Moḥammadan) the negroes are encouraged to be much more powerful that [*sic*] than the pure and undefiled True-Believers."[54]

4 Al-Timbuktāwī's Dogma in Context

To understand al-Timbuktāwī's harsh stance concerning the practice of the Bori in Tunis and the Maghrib, his arguments and doctrinal position ought to be contextualized in conjunction with the ideological currents that prevailed in his western and central Sūdānic homeland.[55] Less than a decade prior to his

52 Brown, *Tunisia of Ahmad Bey*, 174.

53 Ibid., 174.

54 Tremearne, *Ban of the Bori*, 23.

55 B.G. Martin, "Unbelief in the Western Sudan: 'Uthman Dan Fodio's *'Ta'līm Al-Ikhwān,'*" *Middle Eastern Studies* 4, no. 1 (1967): 50–97; Michael Gomez, *African Dominion: A New History of Empire in Early and Medieval West Africa*, Princeton: Princeton University Press, 2018.

pilgrimage, the region was witnessing the effects of Islamic reforms and revivalism that began in the two Futa regions in western Sūdān.[56] Beginning with Futa Jallon under Karamoko Alfa, in 1138/1726, and Futa Toro under Suleiman Baal and ʿAbd al-Qādir in the 1183/1770s, by the end of the eighteenth century these movements had spread westward to central Sūdān through the network of Torodbe *ʿulamāʾ*.[57] Uthman Dan Fodio (1167–1232/1754–1817), whose father was a Muslim cleric (*torodbe*), embarked on reforming Islam in Hausaland with the ultimate goal of purifying central Sūdān from the impure practice of Islam which he deemed to have been corrupted by the Hausa ruling class.[58]

As the Islamic reforms and revivalism took hold in central Sūdān, historians who have examined the effects of Uthman Dan Fodio's jihad in Hausaland singled out Central Niger as an area where the rapid success of the jihad and its intellectual output attracted the participation of armed volunteers and Muslim clerics from neighboring states, especially among the Fulfulde in the Niger Bend.[59] Many of these volunteers to the cause of jihad, particularly those from Central Niger, were enthused and inspired by the revolutionary literature that developed in tandem with the jihad in Hausaland and sought to replicate the process in the Niger Bend. As Christopher Brown and other historians have remarked, volunteering in the jihad in Hausaland and the prestige which Uthman Dan Fodio's reformist ideas enjoyed in the Bend had a profound effect in inspiring active reformist scholars to call for overthrow of the local and "pagan" authorities whom they perceived as standing in the way of Islamic reforms.[60]

Within this context, while there is no direct evidence to suggest al-Timbuktāwi set foot in Hausaland prior to his pilgrimage, it is impossible to rule out the effects of the Hausaland jihad on his religious and intellectual outlook as a Sufi, a reformist, and a scholar (*ʿālim*) intolerant of religious innovation (*bidʿa*). The similarity of his ideas to those of Dan Fodio would suggest

56 Paul E. Lovejoy, *Jihad in West African during the Age of Revolutions*, Athens, Ohio: Ohio University Press, 2016. See chapter seven especially.

57 On the origins of the jihad, see Lovejoy, *Jihad in West African during the Age of Revolutions*, particularly chapter three. See also Mauro Nobili, *Sultan, Caliph, and the Renewer of the Faith: Ahmad Lobbo, the Tarikh Al-Fattāsh and the Making of an Islamic State in West Africa* (Cambridge: Cambridge University Press, 2020), 13–25.

58 Lovejoy, *Jihad in West African during the Age of Revolutions*, 68–101; Paul Naylor, *From Rebels to Rulers: Writing Legitimacy in the Early Sokoto State*, London & Rochester: James Currey, 2021.

59 See Nobili, *Sultan, Caliph, and the Renewer of the Faith*, 128–133.

60 William A. Brown, "The Caliphate of Hamdullahi, ca. 1818–1864: A Study in African History and Tradition," Ph.D. dissertation, University of Wisconsin-Madison, 1969; 15; Nobili, *Sultan, Caliph, and the Renewer of the Faith*, 129–130; Naylor, *From Rebels to Rulers*, 61.

al-Timbuktāwī might well have been exposed to many of Dan Fodio's ideas on issues of *shirk*, *tawwaṣṣul*, and *takfīr*, all of which Dan Fodio wrote and elaborated on during the early phase of his jihad.[61] Only about four years prior to al-Timbuktāwī leaving on pilgrimage in 1807, Dan Fodio and the leadership of the jihad had been reorganizing the political map of Hausaland by reconceptualizing it as a territory of the *Dār al-Islām*.[62] As part of this process, many of the fundamental works Dan Fodio wrote during this period laid the religious, theological, intellectual, and philosophical foundations of the Sokoto Caliphate. Through these works, guidelines for social values and legal frameworks demarcating the religious identity of his followers—as opposed to the pre-jihad era, characterized as a state of darkness and ignorance—were established. In *Tamyīz al-Muslimīn min al-kāfirīn* (Distinguishing Muslims from the Infidels), one of his works written during the early phase of the jihad, Dan Fodio divided people in the new territory into the following eight categories and according to their degree of being a Muslim. F.H. El Masri's elaboration of Dan Fodio's division of the citizenry of the Sokoto Caliphate is worth reproducing for clarity as follows:

(1) the *ʿulamāʾ* whose belief is sound; they perform *ghusl* [major ablution] after *janāba* [a state of major ritual performance; they perform ablution [with water] before prayers and do not unduly perform *tayammum* [ablution with sand] except in case of necessity; they carry out the rest of the religious injunctions and do not show any sign of unbelief, such as venerating stones and trees and sacrificing animals at them or anointing them with *ʿajīn* [dough-libation?]; they do not deny anything in the *sharīʿa*. These are definitely Muslims.

(2) The *ṭalaba* [they do exactly as the *ʿulamāʾ*, and Dan Fodio repeats the same words as above]; these are definitely Muslims.

(3) Those who listen approvingly to what the *ʿulamāʾ* say and do exactly as the *ʿulamāʾ* and the *ṭalaba* do [Dan Fodio again repeats the same words]; these too, are definitely Muslims.

(4) The category of unbelievers who have never accepted Islam and their state is clearly unbelief.

(5) The category of those who mix acts of unbelief with acts of Islam. They have accepted Islam but failed to abandon such acts of unbelief as veneration of stones and trees by sacrificing animals at them and anointing them with 'dough'. These are also definitely unbelievers.

61 On the issue of *tawassul*, see Usman dan Fodio, *Bayān wujūb al-hijra ʿalā l-ʿibād*, trans. F.H. El-Masri, Khartoum: Khartoum University Press & Oxford University Press, 1978.

62 Ibid., 8–9.

(6) The sixth category, like the fifth, mix acts of unbelief with acts of Islam. They mock the religion of God and deny [some of] the injunction of the *sharīʿa*. These, too, are unbelievers.
(7) The category of innovators. These have accepted Islam and their belief is sound, but they intentionally perform *ṣalāt* without ablution. Nevertheless, no word of unbelief is heard from them, such as denial of the injunction of the *sharīʿa*, and no sign of veneration of stones or trees is observed from them. The scholars have advanced diverse rulings about this category [Dan Fodio quotes these ruling] but the accepted view is that they are disobedient Muslims (*ʿuṣāt*, sing. *ʿāsī*).
(8) The ignorant people who embraced Islam but have not understood it. They utter the Profession of Faith without believing in it because they do not care to know. These are unbelievers as far as their relations with God are concerned but as far as we are concerned, they are Muslims, except when they show acts of unbelief. In the past, when religious knowledge was widespread among people, scholars branded such people as unbelievers; but now that such knowledge has become scarce, they should be treated by us as Muslims, though they are unbelievers before God [Dan Fodio here quotes scholars, the majority among whom regard such persons as unbelievers.[63]

In commenting on this categorization of the citizenry of Hausaland according to their degree of Islamization, El Masri concluded that "the fifth and sixth categories are the syncretists, the former through weaving Islamic practices into their traditional cults and the latter by mocking at Islam or by denying some of its basic tenets."[64]

Besides the categorization of the citizenry of the new territory on the basis of the degree of their adherence to the true practice of Islam and the degree of conformity to religious observation, ethnic profile also played a role in Dan Fodio's division and categorization of the denizens of the nascent Sokoto caliphate. Accordingly, the main ethnic groups in Hausaland were the Hausa, the Tuareg, and the Fulfulde.[65] Non-Muslims among the Hausa were classified as *Maguzawa* based on the Arabic word *majus* (a magician or Zoroastrian), the same terms al-Timbuktāwī invoked as the basis for his fourteen-point recom-

63 Ibid., 8.
64 Ibid., 8.
65 See Naylor's excellent discussion of the Sokoto Caliphate's territorial policy and its implications on the enslavement of non-Muslim citizenry of the caliphate in chapter four of his book, *From Rebels to Rulers*, pp. 130–135.

mendations urging the ruler of Tunis to ban the Bori cult in Tunis.[66] Like Dan Fodio, Mohammad Bello, Dan Fodio's son, considered the non-Muslim Hausa group within the new Islamic territory in the caliphate to be true unbelievers born in the state of unbelief (*kuffār bi-l-ʾaṣṣāla*).[67] The historian Abdullahi Mahadi has argued that it was this categorization of the citizenry of the newly established Islamic caliphate that motivated the Jihad officials to use the ideals of the Jihad to enslave those they perceived as non-Muslim Hausa, particularly the Hausa masses, on the pretext that they were *kuffār bi-l-ʾaṣṣāla* and therefore legally enslaveable. El Masri also emphasized that the leadership of the jihad in the caliphate "used [this categorization of the citizenry of the nascent territory of Dār al-Islām] as an injunction of the sharia to charge the Hausa masses with unbelief" and thus subjected them to enslavement.[68]

While there is no known evidence linking al-Timbuktāwī directly to the jihad in Hausaland, the depth and intensity of the intellectual links between Hausaland and the Niger Bend, particularly the religious class of Timbuktu, heightened the possibility that, like several *ʿulamāʾ* from Timbuktu who were influenced by the Sokoto caliphate, he too might have been intellectually attuned to the revolutionary literature and was likely influenced by the religious doctrine, ideals, and philosophy of the jihad.

5 The Niger Bend Dimension

The dogmatic position exemplified in al-Timbuktāwī's scathing attack on the Bori practitioners in Tunis reflects not only the possible influence of Uthman and the revolutionary literature of the Sokoto caliphate on matters of *bidʿa*, *takfīr*, and *tawassul*, but it is also possible to trace his uncompromising stance on these matters to the extreme puritanical view of Islam in the central Niger Bend. As in central Sūdān, developments leading up to the jihad movement

---

66 Usman dan Fodio, *Bayān wujūb al-hijra*, 8. See also Al-Timbuktāwī, *Ḥatk al-Sitr*, p. 21, Folio A.

67 See Salahudeen Yusuf, *A History of Islam, Scholarship and Revivalism in Western Sudan, Being an Annotated Translation with Introduction of Infāqul-Maisūr fī Taʾrīkh Bilād al-Tukrūr of Sultan Muhammad Bello Bin Fodio* (Zaria: Tamaza, 2013), 300–301 and 309; Naylor, *From Rebels to Rulers*, 130–135; Paul E. Lovejoy, *Slavery, Commerce and Production in the Sokoto Caliphate of West Africa* (Lawrenceville, 2005), 14. See also Al-Timbuktāwī, *Ḥatk al-Sitr*, p. 12, Folio B.

68 Usman dan Fodio, *Bayān wujūb al-hijra*, 7–8. See Naylor's excellent maps delineating the non-Muslim regions subjected to enslavement based on Muhammad Bello's *Infāq al-Maysūr* (1812), in Naylor, *From Rebels to Rulers*, 133 and 135.

that Aḥmadu Lobbo (founder of the theocratic state in Masina) established in the Niger Bend were not dissimilar to the conditions that preceded Dan Fodio's Jihad in Hausaland.[69] In the centuries that followed the fall of Songhay in 1591 and the weakening of Mali, many of the clerics who received their religious training in the Bend, particularly in rural areas, grew intolerant of the increasing power of traditional rulers and their indifference to Islam.[70] Inspired by the jihad in Hausaland, the *ʿulamāʿ*, who had previously confined themselves to the prestige of learned circles, began to denounce the Fulfulde ruling elites and clans (*ardos*) of Djenné in Masina and the surrounding areas in the Inner Delta, in particular for their close attachment to magico-religious practices and superficial practice of Islam.[71] The denunciation of the Fulfulde ruling elites and *ardos* was followed by attacks on the Bambara, a non-Muslim group who controlled the Niger River. While the clerics criticized the Fulfulde for practicing a form of Islam that was far from pure, they admonished the Bambara as idolators.[72] By 1818, after some resistance, Lobbo successfully overturned the rule of the Fulfulde elites and *ardos*, overthrew the independent rule of the Bambara in Segu, and established a theocratic Muslim caliphate that governed the entire Inner Delta area, including the historically intellectual cities of Djenné and Timbuktu.[73]

In the aftermath of his successful overthrow of the Fulfulde elites and their *ardos* as well as Segu, Lobbo's principal goal, like those of the leadership of the Sokoto Caliphate in Hausaland, was to establish a pure brand and pan-Islamic identity over the territories inhabited by Fulfulde in the Inner Delta. He was enthusiastic about establishing the caliphate on a firm foundation grounded on strict and rigorous Islamic principles.[74] To achieve this goal, Lobbo, who

---

69 See Brown, "The Caliphate of Hamdullahi," 15; and Nobili, *Sultan, Caliph, and the Renewer of the Faith*, 127–153.

70 On the intellectual output of Uthman Dan Fodio's writings and ideas in the central and the western Sudan see Naylor, *From Rebels to Rulers*; Mauro Nobili, "Reinterpreting the Role of Muslims in the West African Middle Ages," *Journal of African History*, Vol. 61 (3) (2020): 327–340; and Charles C. Stewart, "Frontiers Dispute and Problems of Legitimation: Sokoto-Masina Relations 1817–1837," *Journal of African History*, 17, no. 4 (1976), 499.

71 Brown, "The Caliphate of Hamdullahi," 120; Paul E. Lovejoy, *Jihad in West Africa During the Age of Revolution* (Athens: Ohio University Press, 2016), 89; Nobili, *Sultan, Caliph, and the Renewer of the Faith*, 131–133.

72 Brown, "The Caliphate of Hamdullahi," 67–68, Nobili, *Sultan, Caliph, and the Renewer of the Faith*, 149–153. See also Bruce S. Hall, *A History of Race in Muslim West Africa, 1600–1960* (Cambridge: Cambridge University Press, 2011), 32.

73 Nobili, *Sultan, Caliph, and the Renewer of the Faith*, 128.

74 See Brown, "The Caliphate of Hamdullahi," 49–50, and Nobili, *Sultan, Caliph, and the Renewer of the Faith*, 127–133.

was not a first-rate cleric, relied on a top class of intellectual elites composed of forty clerics to head a Grand Council (*Dina*) which he established to provide moral and spiritual guidance to the state.[75] In addition to functioning as a privy council to the position of Commander of the Faithful (*Amīr al-Muʾminīn*) held by Lobbo himself, the Council among other matters set the standard for moral order, enforced strict adherence to the *sharīʿa*, and worked with the state judiciaries and moral police to impose strict observation of the *sharīʿa*, eliminate syncretic practices, and ban immoral conduct including dance, alcohol, and tobacco.[76]

Unlike his relation to the Hausaland jihad, al-Timbuktāwī's interaction with Masina can be established on a number of fronts. Firstly, if, as Brown implies, Lobbo relied on Fulfulde *ʿulamāʾ* first and foremost in building the intellectual foundations of the Masina state, then as a prominent Fulfulde *qāḍī* in Timbuktu—who, like Lobbo, had also studied in Djenné—it is possible that al-Timbuktāwī might have been a member of the Grand Council, comprising forty men of the learned class whose duty was to advise Lobbo on various state matters. After all, not only did he hail from a Fulde family background with high-standing intellectual pedigree within Djenné and Timbuktu's religious and intellectual establishments, but he was actually highly conscious of his identity as a pan-Fulde scholar.[77] In the preface of *Ḥatk al-Sitr*, he proudly identified himself as pan-Fulde (*al-fulāni ʿufuqan*),[78] clearly suggesting that he would likely have been central to the ideals of the Masina state to realize a "pan-Fulde brand" of Islam.[79] It is needless to mention that, as contemporaries, both al-Timbuktāwī and Lobbo studied in Masina, although by all accounts it seems that al-Timbuktāwī was far more educated in Islamic sciences as a scholar and thus could have been among those Lobbo could count on for counsel.

In fact, Muḥammad b. ʿAlī Pereejo's mention of a certain al-Ḥajj Aḥmad b. ʿAbī Bakr al-Fūtī in Djenné in his eulogy of Lobbo strengthens the probability that not only was al-Timbuktāwī a contemporary of Lobbo, but he was revered by him.[80] In mentioning Lobbo's virtues and his great deeds, ʿAlī Pereejo recounted a meeting between Lobbo and a notable scholar by the name al-Ḥajj Aḥmad b. ʿAbī Bakr al-Fūtī in Djenné over a meal, during which Lobbo comported himself carefully because he was in the presence of

75 Brown, "The Caliphate of Hamdullahi," 119.
76 Ibid., 50.
77 Ibid., 98.
78 Al-Timbuktāwī, *Ḥatk al-Sitr*, p. 1, Folio A.
79 Brown, "The Caliphate of Hamdullahi," 98.
80 ʿAlī Pereejo, *L'inspiration de l'éternal*, 71–73.

a notable scholar who commanded his respect. From the brief mention of al-Timbuktāwī in this eulogy, a number of conclusions can be inferred from the encounter: first, in using this encounter to stress Lobbo's virtues, al-Timbuktāwī is described as an esteemed and notable scholar, and as someone who might have been higher in stature than Lobbo in knowledge and perhaps age.[81] As such, the eulogist used their encounter to illustrate Lobbo's character, showing that he dealt with the noble class in his state with respect.

Second, in this eulogy the mention of al-Timbuktāwī's name is also prefixed with the honorific title *al-ḥajj*, given to male Muslims who have successfully performed the pilgrimage to Mecca. Clearly, this addition of *al-ḥajj* to his name establishes the social and religious identity that al-Timbuktāwī might automatically attain after his return from the pilgrimage. As a knowledgeable scholar with high standing within the strata of the Masina state, this must have only added to the prestige that only persons of his stature could attain. Consequently, al-Timbuktāwī may well have been among the top class of Fulde clerical elites whom Lobbo relied on to enforce the strict Islamic laws after the establishment of the state. As will be detailed in the next chapter, it was these strict religious, intellectual foundations nourished by the teachings of the Islamic jihad movements in western and central Sūdān that shaped and informed al-Timbuktāwī's appeal to the Tunisian religious and political authorities to ban the Sūdānic West African community from what he condemned as the highest form of infidel religious practices. The following chapter will examine the demographic, cultural, and religious characteristics that made this community the subject of al-Timbuktāwī's wrath.

81 Ibid., 71.

CHAPTER 2

Defining al-Timbuktāwī's Infidel Blacks of Tunis (*Sūdān Tūnis*)

> Realize—may Allah guide us all—that it is not our intention to judge all slaves (*ʿabīd*). Rather, we only disfavor those whose deeds are indicative of unbelief (*kufr*), or whose speech implies as such, or who have appointed a leader, be they a man or woman, in their pantheon, or who assist in continuing this sedition (*fitna*) after it being established [as wrong] because he is content with such unbelief—for being content with unbelief is itself unbelief.[1]
>
> AL-TIMBUKTĀWĪ

Drawing on al-Timbuktāwī's efforts to single out the portion of the Black population of Tunis (*Wusfān*) he label *Sūdān Tūnis* and his eloquent and evocative portrayal and description of their syncretic religious practices, this chapter seeks to address the following questions: Who were al-Timbuktāwī's *Sūdān Tūnis* really? What were the attributes and the distinguishing characteristics that made them the subject of his religious excommunication and condemnation as infidels (*kuffār*), and how did they differ historically or structurally from the broader Tunisian Black population (*Wusfān*) from whom the author consciously strived to distinguish them? Were Tunisian political and religious authorities, as al-Timbuktāwī alleged, ignorant or indifferent to the *Sūdān Tūnis*' thriving deviant religious practices at the time of his sojourn in Tunis? In other words, were the syncretic and deviant religious practices of *Sūdān Tūnis* in any sense part and parcel of the religious landscape that prompted the Wahhābi movement to issue its proclamation admonishing Ḥammūda Pāsha to rid his land from all forms of religious innovation (*bidʿa*) or face the consequence of jihad of the sword?

1 Aḥmad b. al-Qādī b. Yūsuf b. Ibrāhīm al-Fulānī al-Timbuktāwī, *Hatk al-Sitr ʿAmmā ʿAlayhi Sūdān Tūnis min al-Kufr*, Tunis: MS No. 21183, Bibliotheque Nationale de Tunisie, 1813.

© KONINKLIJKE BRILL NV, LEIDEN, 2024 | DOI:10.1163/9789004516175_004

As he declared in the above vignette in the introduction to *Hatk al-Sitr*, al-Timbuktāwī's central goal was to justify the excommunication of a distinct enslaved Black community of Tunis, who were at the heart of what he condemned as infidel forms of worship or pure acts of idolatry and polytheism (*shirk*). This category of Blacks was the principal subject of his wrath for spreading their degenerate religious manners among the people of Tunis, particularly "Muslim women," and "weak-minded men."[2] In condemning *Sūdān Tūnis* in the harshest terms, al-Timbuktāwī lamented that the primary reason behind the silence and indifference of Tunisian religious authorities towards their sedition (*fitna*) was that it was perpetrated neither by the Jews nor the Christians of the land, but rather by adherents of the Hausa Bori spirit possession cult. The same group the leadership of the Islamic Jihad movements in western and central Sūdān invariably condemned as idolators (*mushrikīn*) and fire worshippers (*maguzawa*; *bamaguge* in Hausa) from the Arabic word *majus* (a magian, or Zoroastrian).[3] In central Sūdān, for instance, Fulfulde *ʿulamāʾ* and the leadership of the Sokoto caliphate's jihad and its successor movements, particularly in al-Timbuktāwī's own homeland in the Niger Bend, used injunctions of the *sharīʿa* (Islamic law) to justify the enslavement of the masses associated with indigenous religious beliefs and practices, especially the Bori cult. To demonstrate the characteristics of the Bori cult's practitioners to Tunisian religious and political authorities, al-Timbuktāwī strove to single them out from the larger Black population in the Regency, labelling them *Sūdān Tūnis*. And since the Black population (*Wusfān*) themselves were heterogeneous, comprising free Blacks (the *Ahrār*) and free Blacks of slave descent (*Shwāshīn*), all of whom he may have encountered during his sojourn in Tunis and travels elsewhere in the Maghrib, the *shaykh* was careful not to conflate *Sūdān Tūnis* with these other Black groups who may have shared some of their physical or religious characteristics but were never the subject of his wrath. Hence the need to consciously distinguish *Sūdān Tūnis* with qualifiers that not only highlighted their geographical places of origin, but also aspects of the religious practices that made them the subject of his condemnation for mingling Islam with their superstitious Bori rites.

2 Al-Timbuktāwī, *Hatk al-Sitr*, p. 11, Folio B.

3 The term *majus*, originally applied to Zoroastrians, may have been derived from the Old Persian *magush* in reference to the priestly class of Zoroastrians. Perhaps certain elements of the old Persian religion, which involved fire in worship, resembled Bori rituals and therefore prompted jihad leaders in central Sūdān to apply the term to the Hausa Bori cult practitioners. See Joseph Greenberg, *Influence of Islam on Sudanese Religion* (Seattle: University of Washington Press, 1966), 13. See also Usman Dan Fodio, *Bayān wujūb al-hijra ʿalā lʿibād*, trans. F.H. El-Masri, Khartoum: Khartoum University Press & Oxford University Press, 1978.

As he makes apparent in the above vignette to this chapter, not all slaves (*ʿabīd*) were exclusively part of the category of Blacks he labeled *Sūdān Tūnis*. Those he designated as such were, by and large, a recent category of enslaved Sūdānic West Africans brought into the Regency predominantly during the Husaynid era (1705–1957). Among the attributes of this category of the "Blacks of Tunis" at the time of the author's stay is that they had both strong and continuing ties with the *bilād al-Sūdān* (the land of the Blacks). Taking his cue from the attitudes of the Islamic jihad leadership in western and central Sūdān towards the Bori practitioners, al-Timbuktāwī thus castigated them as infidels from his own native land "*min al-kuffār baladnā al-Sūdāniyya*,"[4] even though most of them were enslaved from territories where Islam was well-established and predominated, such as Hausaland in central Sūdān.

The process of al-Timbuktāwī's attempt to differentiate those he castigated as *Sūdān Tūnis* in relation to the broader Black population of the city (*Wusfān*), charging them with unbelief (*kufr*), needs to be examined against the backdrop of the *shaykh*'s own clerical and ideological viewpoints discussed in the previous chapter as well as external factors that played a role in the politics and dialectics of this differentiation. On the one hand, is his differentiation of *Sūdān Tūnis* from other Black groups within the spectrum of the general usage of the word *ʿabīd*—literally meaning slaves, but vaguely implying both the enslaved and also freed slaves of Sūdānic descent and their descendants. Because the term *ʿabīd* in its generic sense was already a major determinant and index of legal and social identification of the entire Black population of the Regency, al-Timbuktāwī thus did not consider it sufficient to differentiate those he labeled *Sūdān Tūnis* from other portions of the *Wusfān* population, particularly the much older category of freed slaves and their descendants, the majority of whose presence in the Regency far predated that of the *Sūdān Tūnis* class and could be traced back to the Muradid period in the region.

In addition to the terminological definitions established around the various groups of *ʿabīd*, external elements in the dialectical process of al-Timbuktāwī's branding of this more recent category of the Sūdānic community as infidels (*kuffār*) also point to their place of origin as perhaps their most significant marker. Geographically, the regions of Africa lying south of the Greater Sahara were termed *bilād al-Sūdān*. At the time of al-Timbuktāwī's stay in the Maghrib and his authorship of *Hatk al-Sitr*, the term derived from the Arabic word *al-Sūdān* (literally meaning "Blacks") had been coined by medieval Arab and historical geographers and their counterparts in Africa south of the Greater

4 Al-Timbuktāwī, *Hatk al-Sitr*, p. 2, Folio B.

Sahara[5] to refer to the population inhabiting the geographical sphere of the *bilād al-Sūdān*.[6] But while this term came to historically signify the area populated by Blacks, its meaning was also shaped by the Hamitic myth that imbued the *bilād al-Sūdān* with notions of a curse, unbelief, idolatry, inferiority, and ultimately as being a bastion or reservoir of enslavement, especially in relation to the heartland of the Islamic Middle East.[7] Proponents of this myth, who ascribe it to the Old Testament, hold the view that Black Africans, believed to have been descendants of Ham, had been cursed in punishment for Ham observing his father's nakedness as he bathed, and that his father's curse made him and his descendants the slaves of his brothers Shem and Japheth and their descendants comprising Arabs, Europeans, and central Asians.[8] As stated in the introduction, in the sixteenth century, when Aḥmad Bābā issued a fatwa responding to a North African merchant disturbed by the indiscriminate enslavement of Blacks, he sharply refuted the generalization associating the *bilād al-Sūdān* with unbelief (*kufr*) and disputing that it was a bastion of slavery and enslavement.[9] Despite Aḥmad Bābā's fatwa debunking this mis-

5 Both Abdul al-Raḥman as-Saʿdī and Maḥmud Kaʿtī utilized the term in their historical works and were followed by Sultan Mohammad Bello in his book, *Infāq al-Maysū fī ta'rīkh bilād al-Takrūr*, ed. Bahajia Shadhili, Rabat: Publications of the Institute of African Studies, 1996.

6 See Abū ʿUbayd Allah b. ʿAbd al-ʿAzīz al-Bakrī, *Kitāb al-masālik wa-l-mamālik*, ed. William Mac Guklin de Slane with Arabic title *Kitāb al-mughrib fī dhikr bilād Ifrīqiya wa-l-Maghrib* (Algiers, 1911), 77–87; Abū ʿAbdallāh Muḥammad b. Muḥammad al-Sharīf al-Idrīsī, *Nuzhat al-mustāq fī ikhtirāq al-āfāq*, ed. and Fr. trans. by R. Dozy and M.J. De Goeje, *Description de l'Afrique et de l'Espangne par Edrisi* (Leiden: Brill, 1866), 106–109. Both sources are cited from Nehemiah Levtzion and J.F.P. Hopkins, eds., *Corpus of Early Arabic Sources for West African History* (Princeton, 2000).

7 See Chouki El Hamel, *Black Morocco: A History of Slavery, Race, and Islam* (Cambridge: Cambridge University Press, 2013), 62–86. See also Terence Walz and Kenneth M. Cuno, *Race and Slavery in the Islamic Middle East: Histories of Trans-Saharan Africans in Nineteenth-Century Egypt, Sudan, and the Ottoman Mediterranean* (Cairo & New York: The American University in Cairo Press, 2010), 8; Terence Walz, "Sudanese, Habasha, Takarna, and Barabira: Trans-Saharan Africans in Cairo as Shown in the 1848 Census," in Terence Walz and Kenneth M. Cuno (eds.), *Race and Slavery in the Islamic Middle East: Histories of Trans-Saharan Africans in Nineteenth-Century Egypt, Sudan, and the Ottoman Mediterranean* (Cairo & New York: The American University in Cairo Press, 2010), 52–53.

8 John Hunwick, *West Africa, Islam, and the Arab World* (Princeton: Markus Wiener Publishers, 2006), 79. See also Bruce S. Hall, *A History of Race in Muslim West Africa, 1600–1960* (Cambridge: Cambridge University Press, 2011), 40, 45–47; Jonathan A.C. Brown, *Slavery and Islam* (London: One World Academic, 2019), 120–121.

9 Hunwick, *West Africa, Islam, and the Arab World*, cf. chapter eight on Arab views of Black Africans and slavery; John Alembillah Azumah, *The Legacy of Arab-Islam in Africa: A Quest for Inter-Religious Dialogue* (Oxford: One World, 2001), 125.

conception, successive Islamic states in western and the central Sūdān, taking their cue from the historical construct of the *bilād al-Sūdān* as a zone of enslavement, used Islamic religious injunctions and waged jihad against innocent masses, whom they derided as enslaveable infidels.[10] A case in point is Askiya Mohammad I (846–944/1443–1538), who in 1498 resorted to jihad as a pretext for enslaving thousands of innocent people from the Mosi perceived to dwell outside the frontiers of *Dār al-Islām*.[11] By the late nineteenth century, the Islamic Jihad movements had broadened the scope of this indiscriminate and aberrant enslaving practice under the pretext of Islamization. As John Alembillah Azumah succinctly notes, "while most the jihad leaders of West Africa condemned the enslavement of fellow Muslims, their activities led to substantial raiding of non-Muslim communities."[12]

Indeed, despite the flourishing debate in western and central Sūdān contesting anathematization (*takfīr*) and illegal enslavement, the jihad and religious leadership—including the likes of al-Timbuktāwī—could not escape the racial connotations associating the *bilād al-Sūdān* with notions of unbelief (*kufr*) and enslavement. Henceforth, to stress the unique identity of the Bori cult's adherents, al-Timbuktāwī employed the term *Sūdān Tūnis* not only to categorize but also to distinguish them as infidel others. His singling out this portion of the Blacks of Tunis for his condemnation partly explains—particularly from the standpoint of the prevailing intolerance of the jihadi establishments in western and central Sūdān—his advocacy for their re-enslavement, because they were according to him "*kuffār bi-l-ʾaṣl*"[13] (idolators by descent) for remaining in their original state of unbelief, and thus could only expect enslavement.

Before any consideration of the distinguishing characteristics of this group of the Blacks of Tunis (*Wusfān*) who were subject to al-Timbuktāwī's wrath and of how this group's deviant religious practices can be fitted within the context of the Husaynid socio-religious framework, a reflection on al-Timbuktāwī's construct of the term *Sūdān Tūnis* is necessary to unpack the meaning of this concept and to situate the community in their specific and broader historical contexts.

10 Aḥmad Bābā, *Miʿrāj al-Suʿūd*, in *Miʿrāj al-Suʿūd: Aḥmad Bābā's Replies on Slavery*, ed. John Hunwick and Fatima Harrak (Rabat: Institute of African Studies, 2000), 11–12. See also Brown, *Slavery and Islam*, 119.

11 Azumah, *The Legacy of Arab-Islam in Africa*, 147; Brown, *Slavery and Islam*, 105 and 107.

12 Azumah, *The Legacy of Arab-Islam in Africa*, 147.

13 Al-Timbuktāwī, *Hatk al-Sitr*, p. 12, Folio B. See also Usman dan Fodio, *Bayān wujūb al-hijra*, 8.

1 *Sūdān Tūnis* Defined

Prior to al-Timbuktāwī's coining the term *Sūdān Tūnis* to designate and categorize the enslaved Sūdānic West Africans he encountered in Tunisia, neither the local Tunisian nor the early European sources that are replete with fragmentary references and information about the origins of the enslaved Blacks in the Regency used this term. The *Majba* Census records were assembled during the early 1860s and contain the most detailed demographic information classifying Black groups into five main categories including: (1) *ʿabīd* (slaves); (2) *Shwāshīn* (older category of freed slaves or free Blacks of enslaved descent); (3) *al-muwalladūn* (mixed race of Sūdānic descent); (4) *al-muwalladun al-ʿajām* (mixed race of Sūdānic descent who were non-native speakers of Arabic); and (5) foreign-born slaves. The term *Sūdān Tūnis* was not used.[14] As stated above, the etymology of the term as al-Timbuktāwī used it is derived from the Arabic word, *al-Sūdān* (singular, *ʾaswad*, which means black). Historically, the term had been used since medieval times to describe people of swarthy or dark skin whose place of origin lay nearest to North Africa, the Islamic Middle East, and Europe as *al-Sūdān* (literally meaning Black people). The *al-Sūdān* or "the Black race" were separated from the Mediterranean and the Caucasian races and the main centers of Arab civilization by great stretches of the Saharan dessert.[15] As al-Timbuktāwī sought to differentiate the adherents of the Bori cult from the larger Tunisian Black population (*Wusfān*), his use of the term *Sūdān* in the first place was clearly invoked from a quasi-racial and ethnographic lens. Undoubtedly, his frame of reference might also have been shaped and informed by the varied meanings of the term as used in the Arab classical or medieval geographical and historical works depicting the region south of the Sahara as *bilād al-Sūdān* and its inhabitants as *al-Sūdān*.[16]

Also, as a member of the religious establishment and scholars associated with the Islamic Jihad movements in his western Sūdānic homeland in the Niger Bend, al-Timbuktāwī's use of the term *al-Sūdān* in relation to the larger Black Tunisian population (*Wusfān*) was not entirely separate from his perception of the *bilād al-Sūdān* as a land of heathens. At the time he wrote his

14 On the Majba Census classification of Black groups in Tunis, see Ismael M. Montana, "European Capitalism and the Effects of Commercialization on Agriculture," *Labor History*, 58 (2) (2017), 202.

15 Bruce S. Hall, *A History of Race in Muslim West Africa, 1600–1960* (Cambridge: Cambridge University Press, 2011), 27.

16 On the concepts of *al-Sūdān* and *bilād al-Sūdān*, see Hunwick, *West Africa, Islam, and the Arab World*, 10; Hall, *A History of Race in Muslim West Africa*, 2, 4. See also Jonathan Brown, *Islam & Blackness* (London: Oneworld Academic, 2022), 8.

treatise, he employed the term to specifically categorize the Masu-Bori (adepts of the Hausa spirit possession cult) as "different others" and to stress their unique identity that resulted largely from their syncretic religious deviancies and Sūdānic geographical places of origin. Thus, the term *Sūdān Tūnis*, meaning Blacks of Tunis, was coined by al-Timbuktāwī to specifically designate the Bori adepts and not every *ʿabīd* or *Wusfān* group, as he clarified himself in the introduction of the treatise. In the broader historical sense, he was writing of a distinct class of enslaved and freed slaves or their immediate descendants. The majority of this group were born in the western and central Sūdān. This category of Blacks of Tunis was distinct from *Shwāshīn*, a much older pre-existing category of freed slaves and their descendants. As will be detailed below, the *Shwāshīn*, although many of them had legally been freed and become part of the free-born population, were nonetheless generally referred to as "slaves" (*ʿabīd*).[17]

2 *Sūdān Tūnis* in Historical Context

From the time of the Aghlabids down to the Husaynid periods, diplomatic exchanges that occurred intermittently between the rulers of these dynasties and the *bilād al-Sūdān* can be said to have accounted for the gradual increased presence of enslaved Sūdānic West Africans from central Sūdān in the Regency. Starting with the Aghlabids (184–296/800–909), the Fatimids (296–566/909–1171), the Zirids (361–543/972–1148), and the Muradids (1022–1114/1613–1702) successive rulers of Ifriqiyya and their Husaynid successors all employed enslaved Africans, obtained from western and central Sūdān, for various social, economic and political ends as domestic servants, concubines, eunuchs, agricultural laborers, and slave soldiers.[18] Yet because of the sporadic nature of the caravan slave trade during these periods and due to the paucity of contemporary sources, we have very little evidence to suggest the existence of cohesive enslaved Sūdānic West Africans communal households or organizational structure along the lines of ethno-religious affiliation that became prevalent after the middle of the eighteenth century CE. This lack of evidence on the social,

17 See Geneviève Bédoucha, "Un noir destin: travail, status, rapport dépendence dans une oasis du sud-tunisiene," in Michel Cartier (ed.), *Le Travail et ses représentations: text rassemblés*, Paris: Édition des archives contemporaire, 1984.

18 Abdeljelil Temimi, "Les affinites culturelles la Tunisie, la Libye, le centre et l'ouest de l'afrique a l'epoque moderne," in Abdeljelil Temimi (ed.), *Etudes d'Histoire Arabo-Africaine*, Zaghouan, 1994.

religious and organizational structure of the enslaved Sūdānic Africans during this period led historian of the Ifriqiyya period Michael Brett to rightly surmise that enslaved Sūdānic Africans imported into the Regency before the middle of the eighteenth century may have been absorbed into the local tribal system through the clientele system of dependency or *walā'*.[19]

In contrast to the Ifriqiyya's time period, which was characterized by the intermittent and sporadic import of enslaved Sūdān West Africans into the Regency, the momentous economic and political transformations that occurred after the beginning of the Husaynid Dynasty coupled with the rise of the late eighteenth- and nineteenth-century Islamic jihad movements in western and central Sūdān created conditions that sustained the import of enslaved Sūdānic West Africans from the *bilād al-Sūdān* to a greater degree than in previous periods. As will be detailed in this section, the enslaved Sūdānic West Africans imported into the Regency after the turn of the eighteenth century can be considered to represent the nucleus elements of those Blacks of Tunis (*Wusfān*) whom al-Timbuktāwī labelled *Sūdān Tūnis*. By the late eighteenth century, as trade relations between the Regency and the *bilād al-Sūdān* increasingly flourished, Tunisia became one of the main termini of the central trans-Saharan trade route in the Maghrib. Throughout this period, thriving Mediterranean and regional commerce resulted in the Regency becoming a major inter-regional center for long-distance trade, with commercial activities between the Regency and the *bilād al-Sūdān*, the Middle East, and the western Mediterranean thriving, to the extent that some historians have dubbed Tunis the breadbasket of the western Mediterranean. The result of this development on the expansion and acceleration of the caravan slave trade with western and central Sūdān was transformational. Compared to the earlier period, when both the volume of the slave trade was meagre due to the irregular operations of the trade, in the period after the mid-eighteenth century not only did the volume of the enslaved increased but the circumstances of their enslavement also differed markedly, owing to the political conditions in the *bilād*

19 Michael Brett, "Ifriqiyya as a Market for Saharan Trade from the Tenth to the twelve Century AD," *Journal of African History* 10, no. 3 (1969), 347–364; Michael Brett, "Population, Culture and Race in Egypt, the Sahara and North Africa" (unpublished paper presented at the Workshop on the Long-Distance Trade in Slaves Across the Sahara and the Black Sea in the 19th Century, Bellagio: Italy, 10–16 December 1988: 1–7), B.G. Martin, "Kanem, Bornu, and the Fezzan: Notes on the Political History of a Trade Route," *Journal of African History* 10, no. 1, (1969): 15–27. See also Marta Scaglioni's excellent study of the process of integration of freed slaves into the dominant tribal lineage, *Becoming the Abid: Lives and Social Origins in Southern Tunisia* (Milano: Ledizioni, 2020), 58–59 and 85.

al-Sūdān.[20] As a number of historians have shown, the eruption of the jihad movements from the second half of the eighteenth century and their consolidation by the early nineteenth century fueled slave export across the Sahara to North African and Middle East Eastern destinations of the slave trade.[21]

Several sources, including diplomatic correspondence and travelers' accounts from the late eighteenth century, shed light on the process of the growth of the Sūdānic West African community in Husaynid Tunisia during this period in quantitative terms. One such account came from Robert Trail, the British Consul in the Regency of Tunis.[22] In 1788, Trail was tasked by the British Foreign Office to procure information about the trade in slaves carried out in the dominions of the Bey of Tunis and to state the numbers of slaves brought to the city, as well as distinguishing those who were natives of Asia from those who were natives of Africa. Responding to the British government almost a year later, in 1789, Trail—whose account relied on intelligence about the scope and the extent of the trade he gathered directly from Ghadames merchants trading with the *bilād al-Sūdān*—revealed that slaves brought by these merchants came principally from the heart of Hausaland in central Sūdān, a hotbed of the Bori cult.[23]

Less than two decades following Trail's report, Louis Frank, Ḥammūda Pāsha's private physician, who was in Tunis at the time of al-Timbuktāwī's stay

---

20 Adu Boahen, "The Caravan Trade in Nineteenth Century," *Journal of African History* 3 no. 2, (1962); Brett, "Ifriqiyya as a Market for Saharan Trade"; Ismael Montana, "The Trans-Saharan Slave Trade of Ottoman Tunisia, 1574 to 1782," *The Maghreb Review* 33, no. 2, (2008): 132–150; Commandant Rebillet, *Relations commerciales de la Tunisie avec le Sahara et le Soudan*, Nancy: Imprimerie Berger-Levrault, 1895; and C.W. Newbury, "North Africa and Western Sudan Trade in the Nineteenth Century: A Reevaluation," *Journal of African History* 8 no. 2, (1966): 233–246.

21 Paul E. Lovejoy, *Jihad in West Africa During the Age of Revolution* (Athens: Ohio University Press, 2016), 157. See also Abdullahi Mahadi, "The Aftermath of the Jihad in the Central Sudan as a Major Factor in the Volume of the Trans-Saharan Slave Trade in the Nineteenth Century," in Elizabeth Savage (ed.), *The Human Commodity: Perspectives on the Trans-Saharan Trade* (London: Frank Cass, 1992), 111–128; Ralph Austen, "The Trans-Saharan Slave Trade: A Tentative Census," in Henry Gemery and J.S. Hogendorn (eds.), *The Uncommon Market: Essays in the Economic History of the Atlantic Slave Trade* (New York: Academic Press, 1979), 23–76; and H.C. Danmole, "Islam, Slavery and Society in Nineteenth Century Illorin, Nigeria," *Journal of the Pakistan Historical Society, [Pakistan]* 42, no. 4 (1994): 341–353.

22 Robin Hallett, *The Penetration of Africa: European Exploration in North and West Africa to 1815*, New York: Praeger, 1965; Robin Hallett, ed., *Records of the African association, 1788–1831*, London: T. Nelson, 1964.

23 Hallet, *The Penetration of Africa*, 207.

there from 1806–1810, also provided some useful information about the geographical origins of enslaved Sūdānic West Africans in Husaynid Tunisia. Frank's account, *Description de cette régence*, documented aspects of the caravan trade between the Regency and the *bilād al-Sūdān*, noting the number of regular and annual slave caravans and slave merchants, and documenting the treatment of slaves; he reported that Bornu and Fezzan were the most important source areas of the enslaved entering Tunis.[24] Unlike in Cairo, where Frank lived and worked prior to serving as Ḥammūda Pāsha's physician, he noticed that the number of the enslaved population in the Regency during this time was considerably higher than in Egypt, and he attributed their higher number to the lack of disease.[25] Indeed, unlike in the Regency, in Egypt disease and epidemics killed the enslaved easily, particularly during the same period. But what really accounted for the increased presence of enslaved Sūdānic West Africans in the regency, according to Frank, was Ḥammūda Pāsha's trans-Saharan trade policy, which he praised and described as the first phase of the Husaynid rulers' attempts to expand Tunis commercial trade with the *bilād al-Sūdān*. Historians have also attributed Ḥammūda Pāsha a's successful commercial policy to a number of factors, including the measures he took against the intervention of the Algerian Turkish military general (*deyets*) after the ousting of ʿAlī Bey I (r. 1147–1169/1735–1756) and their confiscation of much of the Regency's treasury, particularly its gold reserve. Ḥammūda's resolve to replenish the depleted gold reserve and to modernize the Regency resulted in his successful trans-Saharan policy aimed at obtaining gold from the *bilād al-Sūdān* to mint and revive his monetary policy. To achieve this goal, he provided trade incentives to Ghadames merchants by granting them special trade permits (*teskeres*) to operate the caravan slave trade.[26]

Ḥammūda's trans-Saharan trade policy coincided with the peak of jihad warfare in central Sūdān, which led to thousands being annually enslaved by the jihad leadership. This no doubt resulted in an increased influx of Hausa Bori practitioners in the Regency of Tunis. In his book, *Siyāsat Ḥammūda Bāsha fī Tunis* (Ḥammūda Pāsha's Policy in Tunis), Rached Limam argued that this increased influx of enslaved Sūdānic West Africans from the *bilād al-Sūdān* during the reign of Ḥammūda Pāsha marked the starting point of the presence of

24 Louis Frank, *Tunis. Descrition de cette régence*, in J.J. Marcel (ed.), *L'Univers pittoresque: Histoire et description de tous les people* (Paris, 1850).

25 Frank, *Tunis*, 116.

26 Ismael M. Montana, *The Abolition of Slavery in Ottoman Tunisia* (Gainesville: University Press of Florida, 2013), 36–37.

Bori adherents in the Regency.[27] Elsewhere, Limam explains the religious and cultural implications of the presence of Sūdānic West Africans and states:

> With the passing of years, the number of Negroes [*sic*] in Tunisia from Black Africa increased, especially during the second half of the eighteenth century. Their presence resulted in various manifestations on the part of the Negroes [*sic*], coming from the fact that most of these [slaves] were atheists or pagans, although some of them had become converted to Islam, their new religion had remained superficial. As a result, this minority gathered into groups and communities in order to practice their religious rite, beliefs and previous traditions.[28]

Other brief yet illuminating accounts that shed light into origins of the enslaved Sūdānic West Africans come from a number of European travelers and residents in the regency. A case in point is an account that James Richardson—founder of the British and Foreign Anti-Slavery movement based in Malta, who led tireless abolitionist campaigns in Tunis and Morocco—gave on the volume of enslaved West Africans on the eve of the abolition of slavery in 1845. Richardson collected this information during his stays in the Regency to promote the abolitionist campaign. Of the nearly two and a half million people he estimated to be the Regency's population, he listed 200,000 as "negroes," half of whom he said were free.[29] Two thirds of those he counted as "negroes" resided in Tunis. As a result of his travels to Ghat and Fezzan to determine the source of enslaved Black Africans entering the Regency, Richardson wrote that they came principally from central and western Sūdān. Describing the caravan trade that existed in the southern part of the Regency during the same period, the French consul in Sousse, De Rayaud E. Pellissier (d. 1858) also reported that the slaves who were brought there were numerous, and that while many of them came from Bornu, a considerable number were brought from the Niger Basin.[30] Similarly, Amos Perry, who served as the United States Consul General in Tunis

27 Limam, *Siyāsāt Ḥammūda Bāsha fī Tūnis* (Tunis: Manshūrāt al-Jamīʿa al-Tunisīyya, 1980), 302–304.

28 Rached Limam, "Some Documents Concerning Slavery in Tunisia at the End of the 18th Century," *RHM* 8, no. 11 (1981), 351.

29 James Richardson, *An Account of the Regency of Tunis*, London [Unpublished] See also, F.O. 100/29., 1845.

30 Henri Jean François Edmond Pellissier de Reynaud, *Description de la Régence de Tunis*, Exploration scientifique de l'Algérie pendant les années 1840, 1841, 1842. *Sciences historiques et géographiques*, 16, (Paris, 1853).

in the early 1860s and wrote to General Hussein in 1863 inquiring about the impact the abolition of slavery had in Tunisia, also delved into the origins of the enslaved Sūdānic West Africans. Perry was not particularly knowledgeable about the geography of the *bilād al-Sūdān*, so his description of the places of origin of the enslaved, unlike the aforementioned accounts, was imprecise. His report, colored by accounts of the Atlantic slave trade, remarked that most of the enslaved Sūdānic West Africans in the Regency originated from the frontiers of the "Soudan" and from the tropical region called "Nigritia." Unlike Frank, who had written extensively about the Blacks in Egypt and Tunis, and Pellissier, who had been member of the French Exploration Scentifique de l'Algerie from 1840–1842 before serving as French consul in Sousse, Amos was more interested in the effects of the abolition of slavery in the Regency and less about the source areas of the enslaved. However, broad though his description of the source areas of enslaved Sūdānic West Africans in the Regency might have been, he too traced their origins to *bilād al-Sūdān*.[31]

Until the late nineteenth century, the distinct characteristics of enslaved Sūdānic West Africans continued to render them the subject of interest of several fascinating eyewitness accounts. Amongst such interesting accounts from this period was that of Henry Charles Robinson.[32] In 1891, when John Alfred Robinson—one of the first few Cambridge scholars on the Hausa language—died, the executive committee of the Church of Christ appointed Henry Charles Robinson to complete the late scholar's mission, commissioning him to travel to West Africa to study Hausa. However, due to climate conditions and security considerations in parts of Hausaland, it was advised that Robinson shorten his stay by making a preliminary study of both Hausa and Arabic in either Tripoli or Tunis until conditions improved. In Tripoli, where Robinson spent his first days, he observed a community of some six to seven hundred native Hausa speakers out of a population of three thousand. He reported that the majority of those Hausa speakers were not slaves. Robinson expounded on the origin of the community and stated:

> The greater part of these have come from across the desert as slaves or servants, and, though most of them can speak two or more languages, they are quite uneducated and illiterates. There are however a certain num-

31 Perry Amos, *Carthage and Tunis: Past and Present* (Providence: Providence Press Company, 1869), 217.

32 Charles Henry Robinson, *Hausaland Or Fifteen hundred Miles Through the Central Soudan*, London: S. Low, Marston and company, 1896.

> ber of educated natives of the Hausa "Malam" from a word meaning to teach, who are to be found en route as pilgrims to or from Mecca. It is no uncommon occurrence for many as thousand pilgrims from the interior to embark at Tripoli in a single day.[33]

While in Tunis, Robinson reported that there were about a thousand natives of Sūdānic West African groups in Tebessa, in the southern part of the Regency alone. According to him, majority of these Sūdānic West Africans spoke "Bournese" and not Hausa. Robinson added that those who spoke "Bournese," obviously referring to Kanuri, outnumbered those who spoke Hausa, but that they were all subject to a "Negro king" who was himself a former slave dealer and had been appointed chief over all the enslaved Sūdānic West Africans. According to Robinson, all the Sūdānic West Africans paid tribute to this "Negro" chief.[34]

Additional valuable information on the Sūdānic West Africans' presence in the Regency from this period comes from the writings of the local Tunisian historian and traveler, Muḥammad b. ʿUthmān al-Ḥachāʾishī.[35] Besides al-Timbuktāwī's writing, al-Ḥachāʾishī's account perhaps provides the most penetrating insights into the geographical and ethnic origins of the enslaved Blacks drawn into the Regency under the Husaynids. His account of his journey through the Sahara, *Voyage au pays des Senoussie à traverse la Tripolitaine et les pays Toureg*, contains detailed information about the slave trade and his observation on the religious and communal lives of the Sūdānic West Africans whose presence in the Regency, like Frank, he credited to Ḥammūda Pāsha for his revival of the trans-Saharan commerce. Much like al-Timbuktāwī, al-Ḥachāʾishī paid attention to the places of origin and ethnic backgrounds of the Sūdānic West Africans. He observed that they were brought from several places from the western Sūdān, particularly from Bornu, Wadai, Kano, Timbuktu, Sokoto, Kawar and Ghat.[36] Like al-Timbuktāwī al-Ḥachāʾishī described the social and religious organization of the enslaved Sūdānic West Africans at length. It should be mentioned, however, that although al-Ḥachāʾishī's account

33 Robinson, *Hausaland*, 22–23.

34 Robinson, *Hausaland*, 23.

35 Muḥammad b. ʿUthmān al-Ḥachāʾishī, *Al-Rihla al-Saḥrāwiyya ʿabra arāḍī Tarābulus wa-bilād al-Tawāriq*, Fr. trans. Muḥammad Lasram, *Voyage au pays des Senoussia à travers la Tripolitaine et les pays Touareg*, Librairie maritime et coloniale: Tunis, 1903.

36 See, Al-Ḥachāʾishī, *al-Riḥla al-Sahrāwiyya*; Muḥammad b. ʿUthmān al-Ḥachāʾishī. *Al-ʿAdāt wa al-taqālīd al-Tūnīsiyya: al-hadiya wa-l-fawāʾid al-ʿilmiya fī-l-ʿadāt al-Tūnīsiyya* (Tunis, 1994), 300–302.

derived primarily from his own journey to the Sahara, in his description of the Bori compounds (*diyār*) he includes lodges that were named after Bori priestesses and differ somewhat from those al-Timbuktāwī reported on. Unlike the ethnically-centered structure of the Bori compounds al-Timbuktāwī described, the compounds al-Ḥachā'ishī wrote about were associated with powerful Bori priestesses whose names also reflected their ethnicities or regional places of origin. It is possible that during his time the Bori compounds may have been more associated with the powerful Bori priestesses; or perhaps, like al-Timbuktāwī, he was simply fascinated by the dominance of these women and thus ascribed the compounds to them owning to their immense power and influence over the *Sūdān Tūnis* community.[37]

Well into the early nineteenth century, firsthand anthropological and sociological accounts continued to provide insights into the geographical and ethnic background of the Sūdānic West Africans community. One of the most important of this category of accounts is Major A.J.N. Tremearne's *Ban of the Bori: Demons and Demon-Dancing in West and North Africa*. Besides al-Timbuktāwī, Robinson, and al-Ḥachā'ishī, Tremearne was the first anthropologist who undertook a detailed study of the Hausa diasporic communities and colonies in North Africa.[38] Tremearne's study of the Hausa communities in North Africa was not limited to the Regency, as he also studied the Hausa in Tripoli and Algeria. From his comparative study of Bori adherents in these North African regencies, it is clear that the largest Hausa communities were found in Tunis, where they also predominated culturally.

M.G. Zawadowski's short study, "Le Role des Nègres parmi la population Tunisienne," is another remarkably informative sociological work about the religious practices of the enslaved Sūdānic West Africans. Describing the ways in which their religious ceremonies were acculturated into Sufism in Tunis, Zawadoski provided insights into the origins of those who were involved in this acculturation process. He noted that in the regency of Tunis there were two distinct groups of Blacks: the first was the Wargliyya, a term applied to Blacks from the Oases.[39] According to Zawadoski, the Wargliyya were those possessing the moral traits of Berbers but with some Black physical characteristics. The Wargliyya were different from a second category of Sūdānic Africans whom Zawadowski classified as *Wusfān*. Although Zawadowski did not men-

37 Al-Ḥachā'ishī, *al-ʿAdāt wa-l-taqālīd al-Tūnīsiyya*, 300.

38 See A.J.N. Tremearne, *The Ban of the Bori; demons and demon-dancing in West and North Africa* (London: Heath, Cranton & Ouseley Ltd, 1914).

39 See G. Zawadowski, "Le rôle des negres parmi la population tunisienne," *En Terre d'Islam*, no. 2eme semestre (1942): 146–152.

tion the specific ethnicities and places of origin of those he classified as *Wusfān*, he did, as Frank and Tremearne before him, provide some useful information highlighting their religious and social organizational characteristics that distinguished them from the Wargliyya.[40]

3 Bori as a Mechanism for Identifying *Sūdān Tūnis*

Both al-Timbuktāwī and Tremearne showed that the religious lives of the Sūdānic West Africans revolved around a considerable number of Bori pantheons and temples.[41] As in central Sūdān, in the Regency the structure within the cult was modeled in accordance with the hierarchical structure of surrounding society. In al-Timbuktāwī's account, for instance, one gets a picture of a complex hierarchy of Bori spirits and deities as well as the organizational structure of the cult's adepts.[42] According to al-Timbuktāwī, the most important or the Holiest of Holiest of the Bori deities was *Sarkin Gida*, also known in local terms as Sovereign of the Jinn and the Desert (*Sultān al-Jinn wa al-Ṣaḥrā*).[43] Another deity, *Sarkin Gwari*, was considered next to *Sarkin Gida* in ranking, and was regarded as the local "governor" of Tunis (*qāʾid*). Even though *Sarkin Gwari* was considered inferior to *Sarkin Gida*, he was accorded the status of being the patron of the town.[44]

Attached to each of the Bori temples was a Bori priestess, referred to in local Tunisian parlance as *ʿarīfa* (pl. *ʿarāʿif*) and occasionally in Hausa as *sarauniya* (queen). Tremearne also mentions the term *chika* as another title used by Bori adepts to refer to the priestess.[45] According to Tremearne, both mean 'wise.' However, *ʿarīfa* refers to a woman in charge of other women, and may have been connected with her role as a diviner, whereas *chika* implies a magician and is connected to singing, particularly in religious rites.[46] Conversely, Tunisian ethno-musicologist Mohammed Aziza, noting a phonetic resemblance between *ʿarīfa* and "orisha,"[47] which also came from southwest Nigeria,

40 Zawadowski, "Le rôle des negres parmi la population tunisienne," 149–151.
41 Al-Timbuktāwī, *Hatk al-Sitr*, p. 5, Folio A.
42 Tremearne, *The Ban of the Bori.*
43 Al-Timbuktawi, *Hatk al-Sitr*, p. 5. Folio A.
44 Ibid., p. 6, Folio B.
45 A.J.N. Tremearne, "Bori Beliefs and Ceremonies," *Journal of the Royal Anthropological Institute* 45 (1915).
46 Tremearne, "Bori Beliefs and Ceremonies."
47 For more on orisha, see Alex Cuco, *African Narratives of Orishas, Spirits and Other Deit-*

suggests that the former may have been derived from the latter.[48] Aziza further posits that the term orisha was corrupted and, as a result, became *ʿarīfa*.[49] This view, however intriguing, is highly unlikely, since most scholars of indigenous African religion treat Bori and the Ifa religion, in which orisha play a key part, as separate and distinct religious practices. While both Bori and Ifa can be traced to northern and southwestern Nigeria, they differed in their ritual and organizational structure. Like Zar, the Bori cult diffused from its northern Nigerian context across the Sahara and the Islamic Middle East, whereas the Ifa religion, like Voodoo, took hold in the Americas in the context of the trans-Atlantic slave trade.[50]

The *ʿarīfa* herself was usually an elderly freed former slave, who was selected to maintain the liturgical rites of the Bori temple. It was her duty to perform the ritual liturgy in the temples, and she was considered by the Sūdānic West African communities as a spiritual being to be worshipped. She commanded respect from the community and was never called by her given name, but was rather referred to as the "old lady" (*ʿajūz*).[51] In performing their liturgical duties, the priestesses were believed to be supernatural mediums of the Bori spirits and were consequently not allowed to marry anyone, except Bori jinn.[52] Their liturgical duties involved the ritual healing of cult members and their clients, organizing Bori ceremonies, and the maintenance of the Bori temples. Socially, the priestesses also served as protectors of the community, especially for enslaved and freed females. They also inducted newly arrived enslaved Sūdānic West Africans from the *bilād al-Sūdān* into the temple.[53] They enjoyed enormous influence among the Bori community and settled disputes among its female adherents. Each *ʿarīfa* had assistants ranked hierarchically from the deputy priestess (*kasheka*) to the lower-level lieutenants and spokeswomen (*magajiyas*). Similar to the hierarchy of the Bori pantheon, the *kasheka* was considered to be the deputy, ranking next to the chief priestess.

---

ies, Denver, CO: Outskirts Press, 2020; and Tracey E. Hucks, *Yoruba traditions and African American religious nationalism*, Albuquerque: University of New Mexico Press, 2012.

48 See Mohamed Aziza, *Formes traditionnelles du spectacle*, Tunis: Sociéte tunisienne de diffussion, 1975.

49 Ibid.

50 Ismael M. Montana, "African Religion in the Maghreb and the Middle East," in *Oxford Encyclopedia of Slavery, the Slave Trade, and Diaspora in African History*, published online, 24 February 2022. https://doi.org/10.1093/acrefore/9780190277734.013.1166.

51 Al-Timbuktāwī, *Hatk al-Sitr*, p. 6, Folio B.

52 Ibid., p. 19, Folio A.

53 Ibid., p. 19, Folio A.

Bori houses were considered sacred. In fact, no one except the Bori priestesses were allowed to enter them without being in a complete state of ritual purification (*wuḍūʾ*). In addition, in each temple there was a mattamore—an underground storage bin or granary, used for storing musical instruments, flags, and other items associated with the Bori rituals.

An important dimension of these rituals was music.[54] The ceremonies involved the creation of an atmosphere that induced a state of trance, and for this purpose music was indispensable. The use of stringed instruments to invoke the special musical rhythm of the Bori spirits was essential to the worship circle. Al-Timbuktāwī described some of these Bori musical instruments used to invoke the Bori spirits, for example the *gumbri* and *dan dafu*.[55] The *Sūdān Tūnis* believed the *gumbri*, which was strung with beads, cowrie shells, coins, and cloth, to be sacred and to have been handed down by God to Bilāl Ibn Abī Rabāḥ, the Companion of the Prophet Muḥammad and the first muezzin to give the Muslim call to prayer (*adhān*).[56] Due to their sacred status, apart from the priestesses and the male musicians no one was allowed to touch these instruments, unless they were in a state of complete ritual purification that included the sprinkling and rubbing of blood from ritual sacrifices onto the instruments.

Two other important aspects of Bori worship at the temples were the sacrificial slaughters for the mattamore at the beginning of every year and demonstrations of pious devotion every Friday, which included ritual slaughter. The sacrifice was typically of a hen or goat of a certain kind or color and other practices involving spirit possession and ritual dance:

> If they offer a sacrifice to the mattamore, they eat as much of the meat as they can, then they bury the rest of it in the mattamore, but without breaking any of the bones. No one may enter that place with them unless he is in a state of ritual purity—despite which, you never see any of them bowing or prostrating except for two reasons: to pick something up from the floor or prostrating to an idol.[57] In addition, they light fires in those mattamores for the entire night, undoubtedly for some form of sorcery. Do you not see them practice mortification of the flesh, piercing their abdomens and foreheads with knives when worshipping the jinn, and

54 See Al-Sadiq al-Rizqi, *Al-Aghānī al-Tūnīsiyya* (Tunis, 1989).
55 Al-Timbuktāwī, *Hatk al-Sitr*, p. 6, Folio B.
56 Ibid., p. 6, Folio B.
57 i.e., They never bow to God as part of their worship.

> maintaining that the blade doesn't enter their stomachs? I swear by my life, were they to put a knife in my hand I would plunge it into their stomachs until it came out of their backs. This is a form of sorcery that extends beyond their unbelief.[58]

Al-Timbuktāwī noted that sacrifice was intended to result in therapeutic healing for the cult members and their Muslim clients:

> Another aspect of their worship is that when they are worshipping their idols they take a hen, either red, black, or white, according to the idol, and bring coriander seeds and other grains, burn incense around it and cleanse and then feed those grains to the hen. If it eats the grains they ululate and place their hands in a begging position behind them, prostrating to their gods, and believe that they have accepted their offering and are pleased with it. If, however, the hen does not eat the grains, they take it ill and believe that their gods have rejected their offering and are wroth with them. Then they humble themselves before them and say: "O our masters, why is it that you are angry with us? Why is it that you do not accept our offering?" If the hen then eats, they do as was described above. After this they slaughter it without invoking Allah's name; sometimes they slaughter it by cutting the nape of the neck. At the time of slaughtering they drink its blood.[59] If the hen refuses to eat altogether they bring another one and claim that their gods were not satisfied with that [first] offering.
>
> If a sick person or one in need comes seeking health or the fulfilment of a need, they tell him to bring a hen of such and such type, then they do with it as was described above and rub the person over with the blood if he is sick. The sick or needy then prostrates to their gods. If the one in charge of the ceremony is a slave woman who is possessed by the jinn, the servant prostrates to the jinn, who is in her head. Then they say to him: "Your requests are granted" and they order him to offer a sacrifice to their gods every year on the same day. And every year they take from him what he has [of financial means], who may well grow poor as a result.[60]

Al-Timbuktāwī observed that drinking the blood of sacrificial slaughters was a major aspect of Bori rituals:

58 Al-Timbuktāwī, "Hatk al-Sitr," p. 5, Folio A, and p. 6. Folio B.

59 See Tremearne, *The Ban of the Bori*, 72, 199, and 261.

60 Al-Timbuktāwī, *Hatk al-Sitr*, p. 14, Folio B.

> Another aspect of their worship involves drinking the blood [of the sacrificial animal] when making offerings to their gods, believing that it is, in fact, the jinn who drink that blood. Even if there was nothing more to their sedition than this, it would be enough to have it done away with, in view of the unlawfulness of consuming flowing blood from a sacrificial animal. For Allah, Most High, says: "He has only forbidden you dead animals, blood, the flesh of swine, and that which has been dedicated to other than Allah."[61]

As a result of the above practices and their belief in the power of Bori spirits, al-Timbuktāwī charged the *Sūdān Tūnis* with blasphemy, even though these practices formed part of the culture of religious pluralism which the Husaynids encouraged.[62]

4 *Sūdān Tūnis* and the Husaynid Dynasty

Ascertaining the beylical authorities' efforts to integrate the Sūdānic West African community into the religio-political system necessitates a distinction between them and other related groups of the Black population of servile origins such as the *Shwāshīn* (free Blacks of slave descent). Social discourse has often lumped these related yet distinct categories of servile classes together as a homogenous group. As Viviana Pâcques and a number of scholars have pointed out, several key differences, apart from the longevity of the *Shwāshīn*'s presence in the Regency, exist between these groups. One is their patterns of social organizational structure. Whereas the *Shwāshīn* were tied to the indigenous tribal structure through kinship, real or fictional, the Sūdānic West Africans who were brought to the region during the eighteenth and nineteenth

61 Ibid., p. 15, Folio A.

62 On the Husaynid beys' liberal approach to religious pluralism, see Lucette Valensi, "The Problem of Unbelief in Braudel's Mediterranean," in Gabriel Piterberg et al. (eds.), *Braudel Revisited: The Mediterranean World 1600–1800*, (Toronto: University of Toronto Press, 2010), 17–34; Lucette Valensi, "Is Religion Always Relevant? The Case of Tunisia (First Half of the 19th century)," in Lothar Gall and Dietmar Willoweit (eds.), *Judaism, Christianity, and Islam in the Course of History: Exchange and Conflicts* (Berlin & Boston: De Gruyter Oldenbourg, 2011), 415–424; Sophie Ferchiou, "Stambali, La fête des 'autres gens': Présentation d'un film ethnologue," in Sophie Ferchiou (ed.), *L'Islam pluriel au Maghrib*, Paris: CNRS Éditions, 1996; and Carl L. Brown, "The Religious Establishment in Husaynid Tunisia," in Nikki R. Keddie (ed.), *Scholars, Saints, and Sufis: Muslim Religious Institutions in the Middle East since 1500*, Los Angeles and London: University of California Press, 1972.

centuries, mainly as slaves, were rather loosely integrated into the indigenous social organizational structure.[63] As Carl Brown has rightly indicated, unlike the *Shwāshīn*, the *ʿabīd* or recently imported class of enslaved Sūdānic Africans did not assimilate into *walā* ʾ (clientage) dependency relationships with the local Tunisian lineage system.[64] That is, they lived outside the kinship structure that bound the *Shwāshīn* to local Tunisian culture. Moreover, the *Shwāshīn*, being freed slaves who had long been assimilated into the indigenous tribal structure, functioned as sharecroppers, an occupation that typified and characterized their distribution throughout the southern parts of Tunisia. While many Sūdānic West Africans shared the same occupation in oasis agriculture, the vast majority of them were employed in domestic settings.

Within the ritual structure of what Viviana Pâcques called "Bilalian tradition," a marked distinction also exists between Sūdānic West Africans and other Black populations of servile origins.[65] Both Keiko Takaki and Muhammad Al-Juwayli concluded that while Sūdānic West Africans' religious and ritual practices revolved around the Hausa Bori cult, the vast majority of the *Shwāshīn*, based mostly in southern Tunisia, did not identify with the Bori. Even though Sīdī Saʿad al-ʿAbīd is generally considered a patron of the Black population of servile origin, the vast majority of *Shwāshīn* did not adhere to the Bori cult and were attached to different Sufi saints, such as Sīdī al-Mansūr, whose followers were prevalent in southern Tunisia.[66]

Without a doubt, the Bori cult practice, which al-Timbuktāwī condemned as religious innovation (*shirk*), calling for the re-enslavement of its practitioners, clearly illustrates its acculturation into the religious pluralism the Husaynids encouraged. To be sure, the nexus of this acculturation process can be traced as far back as the special measures ʿAlī Bey I took to facilitate the settlements of the military regiments he recruited from central Sūdān. When ʿAlī Bey I (r. 1835–1856) commissioned and imported Sūdānic military regiments from central Sūdān for use as his bodyguards, the Bey allowed them to establish what al-Sabaʿī described as clubhouses (*nawādī*).[67] As will be detailed in the next

63 Bédoucha, "Un noir destin," 82–85.

64 Brown, "Color in Northern Africa," 8.

65 Viviana Pâques, *L'arbre cosmique dans la pensée populaire et dans la vie quotidienne du nord-ouest Africain* (Paris: Institut d'Ethnologie, 1964), 7–12.

66 Mohamed Hedi, Al-Juwayli *Mujtama ʿātun li l-dhākira, mujtama ʿātun lil-nisyān* [*Societies to be remembered; Societies to be forgotten*]. *A Monograph on the Black Minority in Southern Tunisia*, (Tunis: Ceres, 1994), 84.

67 Limam, Limam, *Siyāsat Ḥammūda Bāsha fī Tūnis*, 241; Keiko Takaki, *The Stambali: A Black Ritual Group of Tunisia: The Slave Trade Background and Present Situation* (Tokyo: Monbusho Kagaku Kenkyuhi, 1992), 161–163.

chapter, the clubhouses functioned as religious and social spaces for these regiments. Dār Kofa, for instance, the biggest of these clubhouses, provided a space for the regiments and their kinsmen to practice their ancestral religion, which al-Sabaʿī reported they conducted only among themselves.[68] Based on the religious culture of the region where these regiments originated, this ancestral religion was none other than the Bori cult. By the late nineteenth century, while Dār Kofa continued to function as a social and religious space, its physical character had evolved to becoming a major temple for housing the greatest of the deities associated with Bori. Because of this transformation, at the time of his stay in Tunis al-Timbuktāwī equated Dār Kofa with the *Kaʿba al-Musharraf* (the holiest place of Islam, in Mecca), as the Sūdānic community from every corner of the beylic gathered there during the annual visitation (*ziyārāt*) season which started in Shaʿabān and lasted for three months.[69]

Information about the origins of Dār Beylik—another clubhouse—also attest to the acculturation process that facilitated the inclusion of the Sūdānic West Africans in the Husaynids' societal integration project. Dār Beylik was the second of the clubhouses ʿAlī Bey I allowed the *Bawwāba* regiment to establish. At the turn of the twentieth century, unlike al-Timbuktāwī, who was shocked to see the Bori cult thriving in Tunis, Tremearne was fascinated by its acceptance and accommodation by the beylical authorities. In comparing the treatment of the Bori cult in Northern Nigeria and Tunisia, Tremearne remarked that "whereas in Nigeria we [British Colonial authorities] have forbidden the Bori rites in consideration of the Filani [*sic*] protests, here in North Africa, (which is surely more Mohammedan) the negroes are encouraged to continue them."[70] Tremearne went on to reveal that "in fact, in Tunis, one of the cousins of the Beys has a private temple, and in Tripoli several members of the Karamanli encouraged the rites."[71]

The acceptance and accommodation of the Bori by prominent members of the beylical authorities was more than sheer tolerance. Fascinating as it appeared to Tremearne, it was premised on the Husaynids' religio-political scheme of societal integration, with a clear objective to command the loyalty of the indigenous populace. Evidently, from the start of their implementation of this policy, Sīdī Saʿad al-Istanbūlī, an ex-slave and popular Sufi saint, was among

68 Al-Sabaʿī, "Private Papers." Cf. Limam. *La Politique de Hammouda Pacha*, 241, footnote no. 2. On the Diyar, see also Richard C. Jankowsky, *Stambeli: Music, Trance, and Alterity in Tunisia* (Chicago: The University of Chicago Press, 2010), 34 and 55–59.

69 Montana, "Al-Timbuktāwī on Bori Ceremonies of Tunis," 180.

70 Tremearne, *The Ban of the Bori*, 23.

71 Ibid.

the religious establishments to which Ḥusayn Ibn ʿAlī provided fiscal support in order to integrate his followers to the state's centralization policy.[72]

The little available information about the early life of Sīdī Saʿad reveals that he was of Bornu origin. He settled in Tunis following his manumission by his former master in Istanbul. Al-Wazīr al-Sarrāj, a contemporary historian of the early Ḥusaynid dynasty, attested to the sainthood of Sīdī Saʿad and depicted him as one of the pious learned men who was inducted into sainthood during the reign of the founder of the dynasty.[73] The oral tradition of his enslaved Sūdānic African followers also remembers him as a former slave of Bornu origin known as a pious *ʿālim* (scholar) who rose to sainthood after distinguishing himself amongst forty unknown Sufi disciples (*al-arbaʿīn al-Dhakkārāt*) of his time.[74]

Sīdī Saʿad's mausoleum (*zāwiya*), located in Morneg, about six kilometers north of Tunis, also illustrates the Husyanids' deliberate efforts to integrate the Sūdānic West Africans into Tunisian society. According to al-Ḥachā'ishī, this edifice was built by Husayn Ibn ʿAlī, founder of the dynasty. In its origin, the *zāwiya* was part of a grand structure containing more than forty rooms.[75] Throughout the eighteenth and nineteenth centuries, many of these rooms were reserved for the beylical authorities and indigenous dignitaries partaking in the annual visitation (*ziyārāt*) organized at the site. Hundreds of Bori practitioners who came from outside Tunis for the visitation were accommodated and fed during their stay, which lasted up to two weeks.[76] In terms of its administration, similar to the support allocated to the religious institutions, during Sīdī Saʿad's lifetime the beylical authorities apportioned him a special endowment budget and a regular monthly stipend of up to ten piastres.[77] Sustenance and support of the *zāwiya* from the beylical authorities continued well beyond the death of Sīdī Saʿad in the eighteenth century. In the early 1960s, when the Neo-Dustur Party rose to power after Tunisian independence in 1957, Habib

72 See Mohammed al-Wazīr al-Sarrāj, *Al-Ḥulal al Sundusiyya fī l-Akhbār al-Tūnīsiyya* (Tunis, 1970–1973), vol. 2, part 2, folio 135; Chérif Mohamed-Hédi, "Hommes De Religion Et Pouvoir Dans La Tunisie De L'epoque Moderne," *Annales Economies Sociétés Civilizations*, 35, no. 3–4 (1980): 584.

73 al-Sarrāj, *Al-Ḥulal al Sundusiyya*, vol. 2, part 2, folio 135; Ferchiou, "Stambali, La fête des 'autres gens,'" 211; Montana, "The Stambali of Husaynid Tunis," 178–179; Jankowsky, *Stambeli: Music, Trance, and Alterity in Tunisia*, 60.

74 El-Cheikh Hammadi el-Bidali; Abdel Hamid and Abdelmajid, interview by the author. Sidi Abdel Salem, (Tunis), August 23, 2000.

75 Al-Ḥachā'ishī, *Al-ʿādāt wa al-taqālīd al-Tūnisiyya*, 212–213.

76 Ibid., 212–213.

77 Chérif, "Hommes de religion," 590.

Bourguiba—president of the country from 1957 to 1987—shut down the *zāwiya* along with several others in a vigorous campaign to eradicate popular Islam and Maraboutism, aspiring to build a modern secular state.[78] Up until this period, the *zāwiya* was supervised, under French colonial rule, by a state-appointed official over the Sūdānic West African community called the Bash Agha.

The Bash Agha held a distinct judicial and administrative position that the Husaynids had created in order to oversee matters pertaining exclusively to the enslaved and freed slave communities of sub-Saharan African descent. The holder of this title, also known in Arabic as the "governor over the dark skinned" (*al-hākim fī-l-kishrat al-sawdā'*), had deputies under his jurisdiction known as slave officials (*qā'id al-ʿabīd*).[79] According to Louis Frank, who served as Ḥammūda Pāsha's private physician and stayed in Tunis from 1802 to 1806, persons appointed to this position were usually drawn from the black eunuchs who had served in the beylical courts. However, the most important characteristic of a Bash Agha, according to Frank, was that he must be fluent in the languages of the Sūdānic community whom he served as a judge and a governor, because not all of them spoke Arabic.[80] Among his duties was to oversee matters involving the community he represented at the beylic court. With regard to the supervision of the *zāwiya* of Sīdī Saʿad, the Bash Aghas issued permits allowing the membership of Bori ethno-communal houses to take turns in organizing a procession (*kharja*) to the *zāwiya* during the annual visitation season.[81]

Within the broader contours of Tunisian society, the extent of the Bash Aghas' administrative and juridical authority involved settling disputes between the enslaved Sūdānic Africans and their Tunisian masters. Frank stated that the office of the Bash Agha was a site of refuge for enslaved West Africans fleeing abusive masters. Once a slave escaped to this office, the owner had to pay a fine of up to five piastres before he could redeem the slave.[82] As a case illustrating this office's authority, in 1844 a female slave who fled her master's house alleging ill treatment sought refuge at the Austrian consulate. The Austrian consul, Bavarra, wishing to use the runaway slave case to exact political and economic concessions from the beylical authorities, did not bother to refer the matter to them, as custom and courtesy required, but insisted on intervening between the slave and her master. Furious at the consul for violating established rules concerning runaway slaves, the Bey instructed him to

78 Ferchiou, "The Possession Cults of Tunisia," 214.

79 Frank, *Tunis*, 119.

80 Ibid., 119.

81 Al-Ḥachā'ishī, *Al-ʿādāt wa al-taqālīd al-Tūnisiyya*, 303.

82 Frank, *Tunis*, 119.

direct her to the office of the Bash Agha and described it as the main site for settling disputes between slaves and their masters.[83] Correspondence between the office of the Bash Agha and the Office of the Prime Minister (*wizārat al-kubrā*) also revealed that the Bash Agha's role within the beylical administration was extensive.[84] Other records, such as census data collected during the 1850s and 1860s, attest that under the supervision of the Bash Agha, slave officials (*qā'id al-ʿabīd*) were dispatched to collect taxes from agricultural proprietors who employed enslaved labor.

As mentioned above, the economic developments taking place in the Regency as a result of Ḥammūda Pāsha's deliberate trans-Saharan commerce policy had done more than augment the presence of the Sūdānic West Africans. As the number of enslaved West Africans increased, the Hausa Bori, which had been the basis for the clubhouses, expanded considerably. Apart from Dār Kofa and Dār Beylik, established at the time of the *Bawwāba*, during his stay in Tunis al-Timbuktāwī recorded up to ten houses, each reflecting ethnicity and the regional origins of its primary inhabitants from western and central Sūdān.[85] By the late 1860s, al-Ḥachā'ishī reported additional Bori houses, making the total fourteen. As was the case in all the destinations of the caravan slave trade, particularly in the Maghrib and the Ottoman Empire, the Sūdānic West Africans invoked Hausa and Kanuri aristocratic titles such as the female patron of the household (*inna*) and deputy of the king (*galadima*) to govern their internal matters. Despite this internal structure of governance, communal life was strictly regulated by the beylical authorities through the office of the Bash Agha. The role of the Bori priestess within the hierarchical structure of the Bori compounds has been mentioned above. In matters involving the community and wider Tunisian society, each Bori compound, in addition to being headed by a Bori priestess (*ʿarīfa*), had a superintendent called the *galadima*. Each *galadima* served as a representative of the ethnic membership of his appointed Bori compound, especially in interpersonal relations in the residential area where his compound was located. Among his duties, a *galadima* was to supervise the membership of the Bori compound and represent their concerns and interests before the Bash Agha.[86] Compared to the Bori priestess, who

83 Ahmad Bey to the Austrian consul, 24 Shawwal 1258/29 September 1842, Document 10 and 11, Dossier 421, Carton 230, Séries Historiques, Archives du Government Tunisienne.

84 Lettres des Caid de Sahel, Correspondences des Caids, Dossier 425-Carton 36, Archives du Government Tunisienne.

85 Al-Ḥachā'ishī, *Al-ʿādāt wa al-taqālīd al-Tunisiyya*, 300–301.

86 Lettres des Caid de Sahel, Correspondences des Caids, Dossier 425-Carton 36, Archives du Government Tunisienne. See also Montana, "Bori Colonies," 162–164.

was revered among the community and could settle internal disputes among the female membership within Bori communal compounds, the *galadima* was only responsible for reporting disputes or issues within the community to the office of the Bash Agha.

5 *Sūdān Tūnis* and Questions of Legal Status: *ʿAbīd* and *Maʿātīq*

Understanding the distinguishing characteristics of the West and Central Sūdānic Africans labelled *Sūdān Tūnis* by al-Timbuktāwī can hardly be appreciated without giving further attention to their juridical and legal status in the Regency. As shown above, the contemporary accounts examined in this chapter depict them, by and large, as slaves (*ʿabīd*) brought from the *bilād al-Sūdān*, mainly during eighteenth and the nineteenth centuries, although at the time of al-Timbuktāwī's stay, many of this category of Blacks of Tunis (*Wusfān*) had been manumitted and were thus, legally speaking, freed slaves (*maʿātīq*). Socially speaking, however, they were classified as slaves (*ʿabīd*) and lumped together with those who were legally enslaved. Carl L. Brown, for instance, commenting on this generalization and blurring together these distinct legal categories, noted that: "Just as the word *khādim* in Arabic came to mean "Negro" [*sic*] or more particularly a "Negro" [*sic*] woman, so is the term *ʿabd*, (pl. *ʿabīd*)."[87] Indeed, in Tunisia, as in most parts of the Arab and Muslim world, although the term *ʿabd* in essence means a slave, it has no etymological link to skin color but has commonly been used to refer Black people (*al-Sūdān*). Seen from this perspective and eager to consciously distinguish those he labeled *Sūdān Tūnis* from the pre-existing older generation of *ʿabīd* in the Regency, al-Timbuktāwī may well have been aware of this generalization. Throughout *Hatk al-Sitr*, he diligently applies the term *ʿabīd* to Bori practitioners, largely to emphasize the connection between their legal status and geographical origins from the *bilad al-Sūdān*. Thus, to al-Timbuktāwī, the Sūdānic West Africans were conceptually and legally speaking *ʿabīd* (slaves), with *riqq* (the conditions of being a slave) being their original status. His most interesting illustration of the status of this category of the *Wusfān* as *ʿabīd* in the legal sense stems from his use of several modalities to emphasize what he considered their reprehensible manners towards the people of Tunis. In particular, when admonishing the Tunisian religious authorities about this class of *ʿabīd*, he constantly referred to them as "those slaves" (*hāʾulāʾ al-ʿabīd*) and to

87 Carl L. Brown, "Color in Northern Africa," *Daedalus* 96 (1967), 467.

their religious deviance as the polytheism of slaves (*shirk al-ʿabīd*), the idolatry of slaves (*kufr al-ʿabīd*), and so forth.[88] According to al-Timbuktāwī, the legal status of the Sūdānic West Africans as slaves (*ʿabīd*) was far from theoretical.[89] It had legal implications, and one such implication is miscegenation, that is to forbid them from intermarriage with free Muslim women (*manʿ al-ʿabīd min nikāḥ al-Muslimāt*).[90]

Similarly, al-Ḥachā'ishī, writing over three decades after the abolition of slavery in Tunisia, portrayed the Sūdānic West Africans as being slaves (*ʿabīd*). However, this was more in line with the socio-economic conception of the term than the juridical and legal notion that al-Timbuktāwī had employed. The accounts of Frank and Tremearne also portrayed the Sūdānic West Africans as a distinct group of recent slaves. In particular, Tremearne classified them exclusively as recent former slaves "taken into slavery some thirty to fifty years ago, [who] although no longer slaves … have no status."[91]

6 *Maʿātīq*

It is discernable from al-Timbuktāwī's theological ordinances and advocacy for the re-enslavement of the Sūdānic West Africans that not all of those classified as *ʿabīd*, technically speaking, were actually enslaved, according to the legal conception of the term, making re-enslavement possible. From the early eighteenth century to the early nineteenth century, a considerable number of the enslaved Black Africans brought to the Regency under the Husaynids had, in many respects, already been liberated. Accordingly, such liberated slaves became freed slaves (*maʿātīq*, sing. *ʿatīq*) and were, consequently, entitled to a clientelistic tie (*walā'*), usually established between a freed slave and the master who freed them, whereby the freed slave became integrated into the family of the former master. Thus, once a liberated slave (*ʿatīq*) obtained freedom, they could not be re-enslaved provided their manumission (*ʿitq*) was uncontested. Moreover, the *ʿatīq*'s entitlement to clientelistic ties (*walā'*) granted them rights and privileges: not only could a freed slave inherit from their former master, for example, but they could also marry a free person. In *Hatk al-Sitr*, however, al-Timbuktāwī dialectically advocated for the re-enslavement

88 Al-Timbuktāwī, *Hatk al-Sitr*, p. 3, Folio A; p. 17, Folio A; p. 4, Folio, B.
89 Ibid., p. 21, Folio A; p. 3, Folio A; p. 5, Folio A.
90 Ibid., p. 22, Folio A.
91 Tremearne, The *Ban of the Bori*, 25–29.

of manumitted slaves (*maʿātīq*).[92] This unusual dialectical ordinance from the Timbuktu cleric and *shaykh*, as well as the theological implication of branding some Sūdānic West Africans enslaveable infidels, was based on a number of factors. Culturally and demographically, the new group of *maʿātīq* constituted part of the group of Sūdāniv West Africans which had already been branded by the *shaykh* as infidels (*kuffār*). Thus, though the pre-existing class of Blacks of Tunis (*Wuṣfān*) in the Regency were *maʿātīq* and not *ʿabīd*, technically speaking, al-Timbuktāwī did not differentiate between them and those Sūdānic West Africans who were legally slaves. Rather al-Timbuktāwī deemed both categories to be idolaters by descent (*kuffār bi-l-ʾaṣl*) and fire-worshippers (*majus*), largely because of their association with the Bori cult, which had already made them subject to religious condemnation in the *bilād al-Sūdān*. Ultimately, he invoked the more familiar correlation of the doctrine of anathematization (*takfīr*) with the enslavement of the *bilād al-Sūdān*, advocating that the Sūdānic West Africans must be kept enslaved because their manumission might lure them into the Bori cult. He consequently called upon the religious authorities to keep every manumitted slave (*ʿatīq*) in slavery: "It is also incumbent upon every mufti to issue a fatwa ordering that no one should set a slave or a slave free knowing that that slave will join them [masu-Bori] in this *fitna* (dissension)."[93] Aware that such a harsh clerical stance would not gain the support of the Tunisian *ʿulamā*ʾ, the expected criticism of his advocacy of re-enslavement was forestalled by al-Timbuktāwī: "And if someone says to me, 'On what grounds do you term them [the Blacks of Tunis] 'slaves' when they are emancipated, and an emancipated person is free?' Then my reply to him is, 'Because they have returned to the source of slavery, which is unbelief.'"[94]

Given the historical, demographic and cultural characteristics of the manumitted slaves (*maʿātīq*), it is clear that they were, indeed, part of the Sūdānic West African category brought into the Regency during the Husaynid era. Throughout the Husaynid era, slaves were frequently manumitted en masse; indeed, by the early 1800s, it can be estimated that up to a thousand slaves were likely to have been manumitted per annum. A few years prior to al-Timbuktāwī's sojourn in the Regency, Louis Frank, for instance, was intrigued by the large size of the freed slave population. Compared to Egypt, where Frank had lived before coming to serve Ḥammūda Pāsha, and which had a large share of the caravan trade, the Regency of Tunis, despite having a smaller share of the

92 Al-Timbuktāwī, *Hatk al-Sitr*, p. 22, Folio B.
93 Ibid., p. 22, Folio B.
94 Ibid., p. 12, Folio B.

trade, had a substantial number of freed slaves. Frank attributed this to several factors. In addition to religious imperatives, customary practices precipitated mass emancipation. Indeed, evidence of Husaynid practices demonstrate that it was customary in the beylic to routinely liberate large numbers of slaves, especially following the death of a member of the ruling family or the accession of one of the Bey's family to power. As an illustration to this practice, Frank observed that generally, "When a wife of the Bey is about to die, all the people of the same rank hasten to purchase some or many slaves, whom they immediately grant freedom to."[95] The number of these slaves, according to Frank, sometimes amounted to almost two hundred. Other European travelers attest to the custom of mass manumission in the Regency. For instance, Sesilasso, another European traveler, reported that following the death of Hussein Bey in 1835, six hundred Black women and two hundred male slaves were set free by his successor.[96] Likewise, upon his accession to the throne and before his final blow to slavery in the Regency, Ahmed Bey himself ordered the manumission of a large number of slaves.

Furthermore, mass emancipation was common among both wealthy and poor segments of the population. Frank cited the example of a wealthy man who manumitted ten of his slaves and took care their settlements. Frank reported that "after he fell off from his horse and was almost killed at the spot, the [rich man] made a vow that if he recovered, he would grant freedom to ten of his slaves. When he recovered, he not only fulfilled his promise, but he also assisted the slaves in their settlements."[97] Such practices explain, in part, the existence of the large body of manumitted slaves (*ma'ātīq*) in the Regency. Although legally freed, socially and demographically these slaves remained part of the Sūdānic West African category of *'abīd*.

7 Conclusion

Differentiating al-Timbuktāwī's *Sūdān Tūnis* amidst the heterogeneous Black population (*Wusfān*) of the Regency of Tunis during the eighteenth and nineteenth centuries requires not only a firm grasp of them as a meaningful category, but also insight into the socio-historical and religious contexts that

95 Frank, *Tunis*, 119.

96 Raymond Burgard, "Sesilasso en Tunisie: Voyage du prince de lacker-Muska en 1935," *Revue Tunisienne* 10, no. 2, (1932): 217–243.

97 Frank, *Tunis*, 119.

made them a distinct community. Notwithstanding al-Timbuktāwī's dogma, his efforts at distinguishing these Sūdānic West Africans as slaves (*ʿabīd*), portrayed as infidels and idolaters (*kuffār*) who originated from his own native land, *bilād al-Sūdān*, raises certain dialectics of identification that have significant implications on slavery, religious practice, and the ethnographic characteristics of Black groups in the Maghrib. As Stuart Hall states, the "ensemble of identity-position" is constituted "out of specific histories and cultural repertoires of enunciation."[98] That is to say, the Sūdānic West African community designated *Sūdān Tūnis* were not labeled as such without the acknowledgment of this dialectics of an identification process that can be explained in socio-historical terms. On the one hand, their identification as a distinct community within the larger Black (*Wusfān*) population—including both slaves and former slaves, as well as those integrated into household structures and local-born Blacks—represents an important aspect of their isolation as recently enslaved Blacks from the *bilād al-Sūdān*. This demarcation is of great importance in that it underscores the historical and structural contexts underlying differences between the diverse categories of the Black population in nineteenth century-Tunisia. Thus, unlike the historical contexts and social organizational patterns of the pre-existing *ʿabīd* groups, those of the practitioners of the Bori cult were products of the Husaynid era.

Having been brought as recent slaves from the *bilād al-Sūdān*, the religious, social and communal lives of the Sūdānic West Africans, unlike those of the older and ancient generation of freed slaves in the Regency, were invariably patterned on religious and cultural elements derived from their western and central Sūdānic homelands. In addition, the socio-religious culture of the Husaynids that sought to integrate these new arrivals ultimately allowed for the process of acculturation that transformed Bori to Stambali. This process, as shown above, was facilitated by the early Husaynids' ordination of the ex-slave, Sīdī Saʿad, who served as the saint and spiritual patron of the "detribalized" Sūdānic West Africans. Whereas the Sūdānic West Africans were principally Bori practitioners and by and large followers of the Black slave saint, Sīdī Saʿad, most *Shwāshīn* did not form part of the Bori cult and Stambali ritual circles. Likewise, the *Shwāshīn* were far more integrated into Tunisian society, and compared to the Sūdānic West Africans, were more clan-like. Unlike the Sūdān West Africans, who lived apart in Bori colonies headed by *galadimas*, the *Shwāshīn* were headed by their *shaykh*s and their social organizational pat-

98 See *Stuart Hall, Representation: Cultural Representation and Signifying Practices*, London Thousand Oaks, California: Sage in Association with the Open University, 1997, 234.

terns were modeled after the local segmentary structure, with their households firmly established upon local principalities (*ʿurūsh*).

Not surprisingly, when al-Timbuktāwī encountered the Bori practice in Tunis, he identified Sūdānic West Africans as the sole practitioners of the cult.[99] Yet, unaware of the pluralistic religious culture promoted by the Husaynids, al-Timbuktāwī was quick to condemn the Bori practice as religious innovation (*shirk*) and charge its practitioners with unbelief (*kufr*).

---

99 Montana, "Al-Timbuktawi on Bori Ceremonies of Tunis," 177.

CHAPTER 3

Sūdān Tūnis and Their Imprint on Urban Space

> At the head of the pantheon is Sarkin Gida. This deity is housed in Dār Kofa, where they [the slaves] all assemble every *Shaʿbān*, just as Muslims assemble at the Kaʿba during the holy month of the pilgrimage.
>
> AL-TIMBUKTĀWĪ

∵

One of the defining characteristics of the category of the Black Tunisian population that al-Timbuktāwī dubbed *Sūdān Tūnis* was their affiliation with a series of Bori communal compounds modelled along the Hausa concept of *gidade* (sing. *gida*) which correspond to the local Tunisian concept of *diyār* (sing. *dār*), both meaning households or compounds. One such communal compound was what al-Timbuktāwī knew as Dār Kofa, which was known as *gidan jamāʿat* in Tremearme's time a century later. As outlined in the above vignette, this household, Dār Kofa, housed *Sūdān Tūnis's* principal religious deities and according to al-Timbuktāwī attracted droves of the Bori adherents as pilgrims to Tunis annually. From the late eighteenth through the twentieth centuries, this communal compound was pivotal in defining the social and religious lives and characteristics of the *Sūdān Tūnis* community. This final chapter places Dār Kofa and its auxiliary units that developed during the peak of the caravan slave trade in their specific context of the Husaynids' centralization scheme and the societal control of the populous of the beylic. When and why Dār Kofa and its auxiliary compounds came into being not only reveals valuable information about the spatial contours and transformation of these compounds over the course of the era of the slave trade and its abolition, but also the mechanism of their integration into the Husaynids' religio-political platform of societal integration which the beylic deemed as integral to effective control of the populace.

© KONINKLIJKE BRILL NV, LEIDEN, 2024 | DOI:10.1163/9789004516175_005

1 Historical Accounts of the Bori Compounds

Firsthand accounts written from the early through the late nineteenth century provide evidence of the formation of distinct Bori ethno-religious compounds in the Regency. Aḥmad b. al-Qāḍī b. Yūsuf b. Ibrāhīm al-Fulānī al-Timbuktāwī, while not the first to have paid attention to these compounds, may have been one the earliest observers to deeply probe their connection to the *Sūdān Tūnis*. During his stay in Tunis on his way to pilgrimage, al-Timbuktāwī observed that the religious lives of the Sūdānic West Africans revolved around a number of Bori compounds he termed *diyār*; he carefully documented ten of them, and as indicated earlier called upon Tunisian authorities to destroy them because they were used, as he charged, for idol worshiping.[1] Among his descriptions of these compounds, al-Timbuktāwī wrote that each compound (*dār*) was headed by an elderly woman (*ʿajūz*) known and revered by her liturgical appellation as priestess (*ʿarīfa*) and identified on the basis of her West African origin or ethnicity. According to al-Timbuktāwī, the western and central Sūdānic community considered Dār Kofa important because it housed the holiest of the Bori spirits (*Sulṭān al-Jinn wa-l-Ṣahrāʾ*). As such, Dār Kofa occupied a highly revered status in their communal and religious life. At the time of his sojourn in Tunis, there were up to seven auxiliary units of Dār Kofa named after towns and cities in western and central Sūdān such as Dār Kano, Dār Nufe, Dār Zamfara, Dār Gwari, Dār Zakzak (Zaria) Dār Bambara and Dār Songhay.[2]

Writings dating from the early 1860s and the late 1890s by the Tunisian historian, Muḥammad al-Ḥachāʾishī, reveal that the character of these compounds evolved due to the changing political and economic situation of the central and western Sūdānic community resulting from the abolition of slavery in 1846. As al-Ḥachāʾishī has shown, while the auxiliary units of Dār Kofa, previously documented by al-Timbuktāwī, continued to exist side by side with the main establishment, in the post-abolition era additional compounds grew out of them. These new satellite units of the compounds were headed by a new class of Bori priestesses. These priestesses were very popular and influential among the diverse freed slaves from west and central Sūdān. Each new priestess controlled her own compound and had networks of Bori adherents and private clients. In this sense, the additional compounds they oversaw, given their gender and new status as freed slaves, differed from the ethnically centered

1 Aḥmad b. al-Qāḍī b. Yūsuf b. Ibrāhīm al-Fulānī al-Timbuktāwī, *Hatk al-Sitr ʿAmmā ʿAlayhi Sūdān Tūnis min al-Kufr*, Tunis: MS No. 21183, Bibliotheque Nationale de Tunisie, 1813.

2 al-Timbuktāwī, *Hatk al-Sitr*, p. 7, folio A.

compounds al-Timbuktāwī documented at the turn of the nineteenth century.[3] According to al-Ḥachā'ishī, the most important feature of the compounds controlled by the new class of Bori priestess was in their individual rather than communal character. Among this category of the compounds, al-Ḥachā'ishī's report included Dār 'Arīfat Bāghirmī (the compound of the Bāghirmi priestess), Dār 'Arīfat Wadai (compound of the Wadai priestess), and Dār 'Arīfat Dār Fur (compound of the Dār Fur priestess).[4] Although al-Ḥachā'ishī did not explain the reason for the association with the powerful new priestesses, it is clear that these newfound Bori compounds reflected the adjustment of the cult's adepts to the legal, social, and economic changes that came about as a result of abolition of slavery in 1846. Abolition and emancipation fostered self-reliance and a tendency towards private economic gains. After the abolition of slavery in 1846, freed slaves adjusted to these changes by organizing private and public performance of Bori ritual ceremonies. The priestesses who controlled these compounds used their influential positions to compete against each other for fame and Bori enterprise at private functions, including circumcision ceremonies.

Almost a hundred years after al-Timbuktāwī brought the Bori compounds to the attention of the Tunisian authorities, and nearly three decades after al-Ḥachā'ishī's account of them, A.J.N. Tremearne, who assiduously studied Bori beliefs in northern Nigeria and conducted a comparative study of the practice in North Africa, also provided useful accounts of the Bori compounds in Tunis.[5] Like al-Timbuktāwī, Tremearne noted the Bori-centered compound as being the most important characteristic of the West African community in Tunis. Using the structure of Bori compounds in Northern Nigeria, Tremearne described Dār Kofa in Hausa as a community house (*gidan jamā'at*), thus attesting to its central status as a communal space for the central and western Sūdānic community in Tunis.[6]

Although the physical imprints of many of the Bori compounds have long disappeared, oral interviews conducted with descendants of the central and western Sūdānic community of Tunis, and especially those associated with surviving units of the Bori compounds, provided the chance for respondents to

---

3 Muḥammad b. 'Uthmān al-Ḥachā'ishī, *Al-'Ādāt wa-l-taqālīd al-Tūnīsiyya: al-hadiyya wa al-fawā'id al-'ilmiya fī-l-'ādāt al-Tūnīsiyah* (Tunis, 1994), 300–301.

4 Muḥammad b. 'Uthmān al-Ḥachā'ishī, *Al-Rihla al-Saḥrāwiyya 'abra arā·dī·Tarābulus wa-bilād al-Tawāriq: Voyage au pays des Senoussia à travers la Tripolitaine et les pays Touareg*, Librairie maritime et coloniale (Tunis, c. 1988., 1903), p. 174.

5 Major A.J.N. Tremearne, *The Ban of the Bori* (London: Frank Cass, 1968), 23.

6 Tremearne, *The Ban of the Bori*, 12.

reminisce about their role in fostering solidarity and mutual support among the Sūdānic community of Tunis and their descendants to this day.[7] The annual visitation (*zīyārāt*) ceremonies to the shrines (*zāwiyas*) of Sīdī al-Saʿad al-ʿAbīd and Sīdī Marzūq, both located on the outskirts of Tunis, which are conducted by Stambāli adepts, still rotate along the lines of the fourteen Bori compounds (*diyār*) as has been the case since the eighteenth century.[8]

2 Origins and Developments of the Bori Compounds

As indicated in Map 4 below, Dār Kofa, the oldest of the surviving compounds or *diyār*, located in the western suburb between Bāb Djazīra and Bāb Djedīd in the Medina, was mentioned by contemporaneous sources as early as the first quarter of the eighteenth century. The author of *al-Mansūkhāt al-Sabaʿī*, for instance, attributes the origins of Dār Kofa to the political climate that split the early ruling class of the Ḥusaynid dynasty into the Ḥusayniyya faction (loyal to Ḥusayn ibn ʿAlī, the founder of the Ḥusaynid dynasty) and the Bāshīyya faction (loyal to ʿAlī Bey I, a cousin and heir apparent to Ḥusayn ibn ʿAlī).

While the extent to which the civil war crisis triggered the emergence of Dār Kofa and the associated private clubhouses (*nawādī*) had been briefly mentioned in the private reports of al-Sabaʿī, the impact of the civil war on the evolution of these clubhouses needs to be further explained and contextualized. Most historians of pre-colonial Tunisia stress the ramifications of the above-mentioned civil war that divided the Ḥusaynid ruling class into two rival factions as a defining feature of the early Ḥusaynid dynasty.[9] It unquestionably caused intense political instability. Thomas Shaw, a well-known British clergyman who visited Tunis from Algiers during the height of the civil war, for instance, attested in 1727 to the impact the conflict had on the economy and on daily life. When writing later about his tour of Tunis, Shaw complained

---

7 I am grateful to Abdelmejid Bournaouis of Dār Bornu (Sidi El-Bechir) for the interviews conducted about the history of Bori-Stambali adepts in Tunisia. Abdelmajid Bornaoui, Sīdī El-Bechīr, Tunis, July 19, 2001.

8 Interviews. Hamadī Bīdāīi, Sīdī AbdelSalem Lasmar, August 23, 2000; Habib Al-Juinī, Bab El-Djedid, Tunis, July 11, 2001; and Zohra Trabelsī, Bab Swouika, Tunis, July 12, 2001.

9 On the Ḥusaynid succession crisis, see Mohamed-Hédi Chérif, “Pouvoir beylical et contrôle de l’espace dans la Tunisie du xviii siècle et les débuts du xix siècle,” *Annuaire de l’Afrique du Nord* 22 (1983) pp. 41–61. See also Jamil Abun-Nasr, *A History of the Maghrib* (Cambridge: Cambridge University Press, 1987), 179–180.

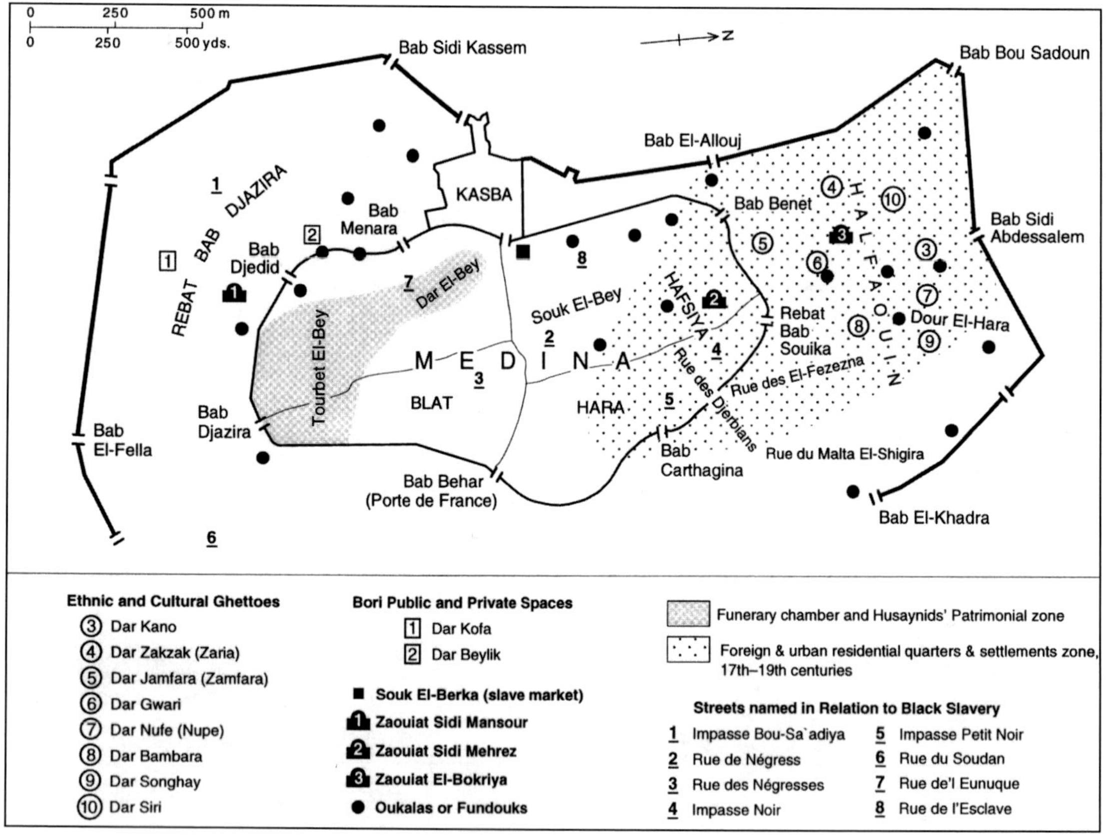

MAP 4 Distribution of Bori Religious and Communal *Diyār* (Households) in Tunis

that during his stay in the Regency, the civil war had deprived him of the requisite security to conduct his observations.[10]

In addition to the civil war's impact on economic and daily life, it was directly responsible for the import of the elite Black slave guards that ʿAlī Bey I imported from central Sūdān. As stated earlier, this was not without historical precedent. With the Islamization of North Africa in the eighth century, Black slaves from the Sahel region of West Africa, then called *bilād al-Sūdān*, were brought to Tunisia for various social, political and economic ends. Towards the end of the tenth century, the Aghlabids in the year 369/980, for instance, imported Black slaves for military purpose. The Zirids, successors of the Fatimids, who disbanded and killed the Blacks who had served the Aghlabids to undo their political legacy, also used Black soldiers from the *bilād al-Sūdān* to serve their own military and political needs. ʿAlī Bey I tapped into this existing tradition and commissioned the import of Black slaves directly from central Sūdān between the years 1738 to 1739.

The context of ʿAlī Bey's importation of the above slave corps from central Sūdān is worth exploring at length. Following the death of Ḥusayn b. ʿAlī and the defeat of his faction, ʿAlī Bey I became the heir apparent to the throne. However, his ascension did not go uncontested. In addition to Ḥusayn b. ʿAlī's faction, the Janissaries were still part of the Military Council (*Dīwān al-ʿAskar*) which ʿAlī Bey I now presided over. Most of these Janissaries maintained strong ties with the Turkish junta in neighbouring Algiers and had, in fact, been the direct cause of the downfall of the Muradite dynasty in 1702. During the height of the Ḥusaynid dynasty's succession crisis, some of the Janissaries had allied with Ḥusayn b. ʿAlī against ʿAlī Bey's camp. Therefore, in order to counterbalance any unforeseen threats from the Janissaries, and to rebuff their attempts to destabilize his regime, ʿAlī Bey sought recourse in a number of military measures. First, like ʿUthmān Dey in the early 1008s/1600s, he enlisted the *Zwāwa* corps, which Uthman Dey had previously recruited from the Kabyle tribe from Algeria.[11] Moreover, ʿAlī Bey I also imported black slave soldiers from central Sūdān to serve as his private palace guards. ʿAbd al-Majīd al-Sabaʾī's private papers document the immediate context of the Bey's importation of Black slaves:

> And in the year 1150–1151/1738–1739 … the prince ʿAlī Bey authorized the recruitment of *ḥurras* (palace guards) of the *Sūdān* (Blacks) in lieu of the

10 Thomas Shaw, *Travels or Observations Relating to Several Parts of Barbary and the Levant* (Oxford, 1738), 308–309.

11 Abun-Nasr, *A History of the Maghrib* p. 174.

> Turkish and the Arabs guards. This was due to the Arabs' lack of trustworthiness and his [ʿAlī Bey's] fear of their constant intrigues and plots. As for the Turks, because the prince was well aware of their desires to accumulate all sorts of powers into their own hands, he alienated them. And this is the main reason why ʿAlī Bey authorized the recruitment of the *Sūdān* as his palace guards and imported a great quantity of them into Tunis. He also facilitated their settlements and built hostelries for them and permitted them to establish their own clubhouses. Each one of these clubhouses was called *Kofa*, and only the *Sūdān* assemble in it and conduct their own matters.[12]

Ibn Abi Diyaf also referred to these little known *ḥurras* in his *Itḥāf*, stating that they were designated as *bawwāba*, meaning palace guards. According to Abi Diyāf, ʿAlī Bey I modeled the *bawwāba* along the lines of the famous enslaved soldiers (*ʿabīd al-Bukhārī*) which Mawlay Ismail had instituted in Morocco. Similar to the *ʿabīd al-Bukhārī* of Morocco, Abi Diyāf reported that ʿAlī Bey I embellished the *bawwāba* regiments with privileges by allotting them special uniforms to distinguish them from other military corps.[13]

Both Abi Diyāf and al-Sabaʿī are remarkably precise about the context in which the *bawwāba* were introduced into Tunis. Still, neither of these authors offers much information about the size of the regiments or the region of West Africa from which they were imported. Their regional origins, however, can be inferred from the very clubhouses that al-Sabaʿī's papers refer to as *kofa*, which literally refers to a gate in Hausa. As M.G. Smith, who has meticulously examined Hausaland's mode of political and economic organization in the pre-jihad period, has shown, the term *kofa*, apparently following a Bornu-Hausa political and administrative tradition, means a guard or intermediary of the king. Since the political climate culminated in the importation of the *bawwāba*, it is therefore likely that these Black corps may have been imported from central Sūdān, particularly from Bornu or Hausaland. As previously stated, diplomatic and political ties between rulers of Tunis and central Sūdān during Hafsid rule in the sixteenth century continued well into the late eighteenth century. Miss Tully, sister of the British Consul in Tripoli, who visited Tunisia in 1780, reported the sensational visit of a "Black Borno Prince" and his entourage to Tunis. According to Tully, the prince was an emissary of the king of Bornu,

12 Abdelmajid Al-Sabaʿī, *Mansūkhāt "Private Papers"*, Tunis; cf. Rached Limam, *Siyāsat Hammuda Bāsha fī Tunis* (Tunis: Manshūrāt al-Jāmiʿa al-Tūnīsiyya, 1980), 241.

13 See Aḥmad Ibn Abī Diyaf, *Ithaf ahl al-Zaman*, vol. II, 122.

and was in Tunis to promote the state's commercial and diplomatic interests.[14] Throughout the late eighteenth century until the eve of the prohibition of the Ghadames slave trade to Tunisia in 1841, both the Bornu and Hausaland regions of central Sūdān were the main sources of slaves entering the Regency of Tunis.[15]

Besides their regional origins, additional demographic clues about the nature of the *bawwāba* may also be inferred from their very occupation as slave guards. Because of the nature of this occupation, one is also left with the impression that they might have been similar in demographic characteristics such as age, marital status and cultural background. That is, they were young and unmarried, all being employed as palace guards. Quantitatively, we do not know the size and the number of this corps. Nonetheless, their qualitative impact on the religious and cultural developments associated with the West African community is one that needs to be recognized.

3 The Bori Compounds and the Caravan Slave Trade

Extant research suggests that between 1782 and 1841 most of the slaves entering Tunis were drawn overwhelmingly from central Sūdān, particularly Hausaland. Quantitatively, those drawn from the Niger Bend area in the western Sūdān followed slaves who were imported from Hausaland and Bornu. Then, between the early 1830s and 1841, the areas from which slaves were imported into Tunis expanded to include other parts of central Sūdān such as Dār Fur and Sennar. Before the 1830s, these areas, although occasionally supplying slaves to Tunis, had not been a regular source of slaves.[16]

The scale and the change in the source areas of slaves procured to Tunis during the period between the early 1830s and 1841 affected the size and character of the compounds. The most pronounced impact of the slave trade on the Bori compounds can be delineated in the physical character and public nature of these compounds. As indicated above, while Dār Kofa and its primary units were originally built as clubhouses, the Bori compounds that flourished after 1782 took the form of the local Tunisian structure of a *dār*, and corresponded

14 Miss Tully, *Narrative of a Ten Years' Residence at Tripoli in Africa: From the Original Correspondence in the Possession of the Family of the Late Richard Tully, Esq.*, 2nd ed. (London, 1817), 208.

15 Chater, *Dépendance et mutations précoloniales*, 174.

16 Ibid., 138–139.

to a Hausa concept of *gida*. Literally, both *dār* and *gida* mean a house with which successive members of particular family can identify with. In both cases, a *dār* or *gida* could have a broader meaning, including the affiliation of extended biological or cultural members even if they do not physically reside in the compound.

The slave trade altered the function of the Bori compounds. For example, whereas al-Sabaʿī's report indicates that during the eighteenth century the compounds were private clubhouses where the palace guards practiced the customs they brought from central Sūdān, it is clear from subsequent sources that by the turn of the nineteenth century they were no longer private clubhouses but had become public and communal centers or spaces. Al-Timbuktāwī who stayed in Tunis during the peak of the slave trade reported one of the most noticeable changes in the Bori compounds by describing the importance accorded to Dār Kofa by the Bori adepts. He equated their gatherings in this compound with the Muslim pilgrimage to the *Kaʿba*, thus clearly delineating the revered status Dār Kofa had attained by the time of his stay in Tunis. In admonishing Ḥammūda Pāsha to destroy this compound, the following passage from *Hatk al-Sitr* reveals the true picture of Dār Kofa at the height of the slave trade:

> At the head of the pantheon is Sarkin Gida. This deity is housed in Dār Kofa, where they [the slaves] all assemble every *Shaʿbān*, just as Muslims assemble at the Kaʿaba during the holy month of the pilgrimage. The pantheon also includes a *mattamore*, believed to be inhabited by a snake … And in this very pantheon are found images, musical instruments, banners, and numerous other paraphernalia. The chief priestess (*ʿarīfa*) of that pantheon is known to be always quarrelling with everyone whom she hears pronounce the Two Testimonies of Faith.[17]

Al-Timbuktāwī went on to add:

> This communal house of Dār Kofa was originally a religious endowment (*ḥabus*), dedicated to a freed female slave called Kofa.[18] … There are, moreover, several other houses, such as Dār Beylik, Dār Nufe, Dār Zakzak, Dār Kano, and Dār Sarā'.[19]

17 Al-Timbuktāwī, *Ḥatk al-Sitr*, p. 5, Folio A.
18 Ibid., p. 5, Folio A.
19 Ibid., p. 6, Folio B.

After urging Ḥammūda Pāsha to ban Bori practice in the country, al-Timbuktāwī went on to admonish him to destroy all the compounds associated with the Bori and wrote:

> When you realize this, O prince, it is altogether your legal duty to seize Dār Kofa and either convert it to a mosque, as the Prophet, blessings and peace of Allah be upon him, would do with all churches when the territories of the polytheists were conquered, or build a madrasa for the pursuit of sacred knowledge, or a hostelry for the believing soldiers who strive in jihad for the sake of Allah. For it is unlawful to preserve such a house for the worship of idols. It is also incumbent upon you to take all the idols from Dār Kofa, and from all the other houses, and burn them, and demolish all of their mattamores.[20]

Apart from Dār Kofa, which was undisputedly one of the biggest of the Bori compounds that was previously occupied by ʿAlī Bey's palace guards, it is not entirely clear whether or not the remaining compounds that al-Timbuktāwī enumerated were the same units that had once been part of Dār Kofa. What is clear, however, is that his stay in Tunis coincided with the peak of the Tunisian slave trade. This was the period during which the prime inhabitants of the ethnically identified units of Dār Kofa were brought to Tunis, and from the same cultural zone of central Sūdān where the palace guards (*bawwāba*) originated. While al-Sabaʿī's private papers did not explicitly reveal the religion that the palace guards practiced in their private clubhouses, because they originated from Hausaland it can be surmised that this religion was none other than Bori, which was the predominant form of indigenous African religious belief in this region. After the advent of the Sokoto caliphate's jihad in central Sūdān, the rulers of the caliphate attempted to ban Bori and persecuted its leaders. In the aftermath of the consolidation of the jihad in 1804, slaves entering Tunis came from this very region where Bori had been prevalent and where its adepts had been persecuted, leading to their enslavement. According to Abdullahi Mahadi, there is every reason to believe that the vast majority of enslaved Africans sold across the Sahara from this period were drawn from the masu-Bori or Bori practitioners. Mahadi asserts that Bori adepts were targeted by the leaders of Sokoto caliphate's puritanical campaigns as infidels and thus were subjected to enslavement.[21] Like their counterparts who were for-

20 Ibid., p. 18, Folio B.

21 Abdullahi Mahadi, "The Aftermath of the Jihad as a Factor in the Volume of the trans-

cibly shipped to the Americas, these enslaved West Africans from central Sūdān sent across the Sahara to the Muslim destinations of the slave trade did not abandon their religious beliefs or cosmology. Such was the case for Bori practice in Tunisia.

Other evidential changes reflected in the gender characteristics of the Bori compounds can be attributed to the acute gender imbalance in the slave trade particularly in the period after its peak after the 1780s. As pointed out earlier, the palace guards, who constituted the nucleus of the Bori compounds' inhabitants during their formative period, were mostly unmarried men. After the peak of the slave trade, which lasted from the late 1780s through the late nineteenth century, the gender composition of these compounds shifted markedly in favor of women. The scanty statistical inferences from the existing sources confirm that during the peak of the trade, female slaves outnumbered their male counterparts by two to one if not more.[22] Whether the palace guards were displaced after the defeat and ousting of ʿAlī Bey I by his Ḥusayniyya rivals or not, it is clear that by the turn of the nineteenth century, the manning of these Bori compounds was no longer associated with them. Accordingly, almost all the contemporaneous accounts from the late 1780s through the late 1860s have attested that female spiritual patrons dominated the compounds. Thus ss outlined in Figure 1 below, changes in gender composition of the slave trade corresponding to the increase volume of the slave trade not only led to expansion of the Bori compounds but also it altered their manning and operation in favor of women outnumbering male slaves.

The increased influx of slaves and the expansion of the source areas of slaves entering Tunis after the 1830s influenced the ethnic composition of the Bori compounds. After 1782, Hausa slaves were more numerous than those of Bornu origin and this was reflected in the structure, organization and manning of the compounds. Of the ten compounds al-Timbuktāwī reported in Tunis, slaves who came from the Hausaland cities of Kano, Katsina, Zamfara, Gwari, and Nupe occupied two thirds of them, compared to only one compound identified with Bornu. Nonetheless, the compound affiliated with Bornu was denoted as the largest of the ethnic compounds, and as such was called Dār Jamāʿat because it was the main community house. Other ethnically-based compounds that al-Timbuktāwī noted were those of the Bambara and Songhay from the

Saharan Slave Trade in the Nineteenth Century," in Elizabeth Savage (ed.), *The Human Commodity: Perspectives on the trans-Saharan Trade* (London: Frank Cass, 1992), 111–128.

22 See Louis Frank, *Histoire de Tunis; précédée d'une description de cette regence* (Paris: Firmin Didot Freres, 1851), 194.

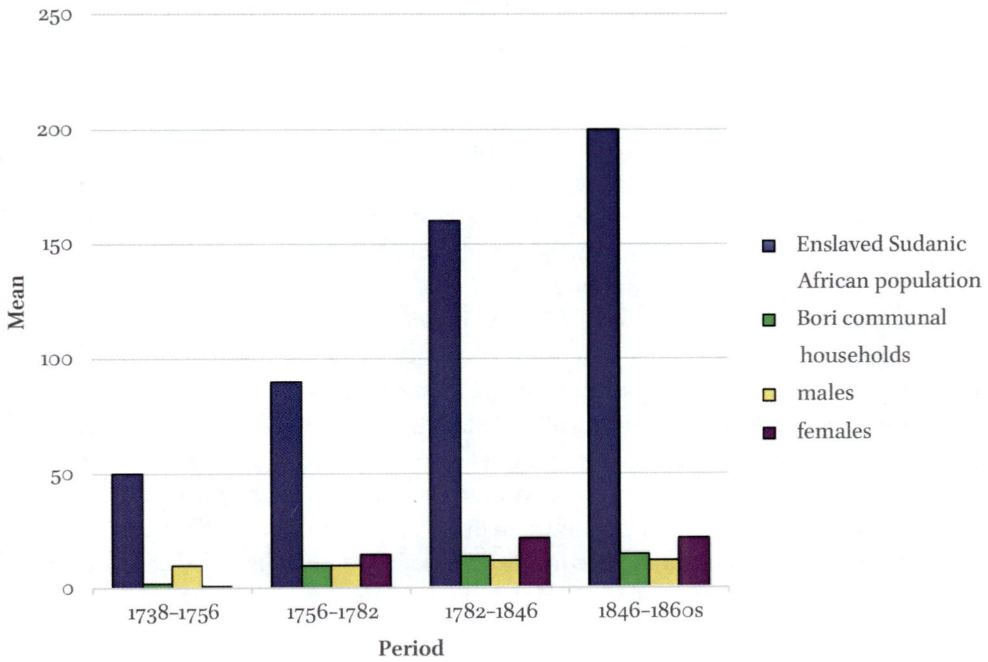

FIGURE 1 Ratio of the Bori households to gender and the volume of the slave trade

Niger Bend area. Although the Niger Bend was not a cultural zone where Bori was prevalent, a similar spirit possession cult known as the Holey cult did exist in that area. However, even if other possession cults from Sahelian Africa influenced practices in Tunisia, al-Timbuktāwī nevertheless identified them as Bori.[23]

4 The Locales of the Bori Compounds

In Tunis, the location and the geographical concentration of Dār Kofa, its auxiliary units, and the Bori compounds that developed after the peak of the slave trade and were characterized by ethnic affiliations differed. Whereas Dār Kofa and its auxiliary units were located in the western suburb of the Medina metro-

23 Ismael M. Montana, "Aḥmad Ibn al-Qadi al-Timbuktāwī on the Bori Ceremonies of Sudan-Tunis," in Paul E. Lovejoy (ed.), *Slavery on the Frontiers of Islam*, (Princeton: Markus Wiener Publishers, 2003), 161.

polis around the Ḥusaynid's ruling class zone of influence, the Bori compounds named after townships of central Sūdān remained in the same metropolis, but were clustered around the northern edge of the Medina.[24] As indicated in Map 4, many of these compounds were spread out between Ḥalfāouin and Bāb Sīdī ʿAbdelsalām in the north. This area was known for its heavy concentration of minority groups such as Jews and *barrāniyya* (foreign migrants). The famous *ḥāra* (Jewish quarter) is located in the same neighborhood. Many of the *barrāniyya* (foreign migrants) from neighboring countries such Algeria and Morocco also dwelt in this neighborhood.[25]

While the concentration of Dār Kofa and its auxiliary clubhouses in the western suburb was the result of the occupation of the *bawwāba*; being palace guards for the royal households of the Ḥusaynid ruling class during the time of ʿAlī Bey I, the concentration of the ethnically characterized Bori compounds in the northern edge of the Medina reflects a different process and pattern of settlement. To be sure, the slave trade and economic developments under Ḥammūda Pāsha attracted such settlements. Nicholas Hopkins offers additional clues about the geographical concentration of the ethnically based compounds in the Ḥalfāouin and Bāb Sīdī ʿAbdelsalām neighborhood. According to Hopkins, Sīdī al-Maḥrez, an eleventh-century marabout whose mosque and tomb is located at the heart of this neighborhood, played a key role in the concentration of the ethnically-based Bori compounds in this neighborhood. Following the Hilālī invasion of Tunis in the early part of the eleventh century, Sīdī al-Maḥrez was credited with rebuilding and protecting the soul of Tunis and is therefore depicted in popular parlance as *Sultān al-Medina* (patron and protector of Tunis). During his lifetime, Sīdī al-Maḥrez was also renowned for protecting minority groups including Jews, Black slaves and the *barrāniyya* (foreign migrants). After his death, many of these groups continued to live in proximity to his tomb because of the protection and comforts that they continue to seek through his intercession.[26]

The concentration of the ethnically-based compounds in the northern edge of the Medina was also augmented by transnational migrations. Many of the West Africans who dwelt in Ḥalfāouin and Bāb Sīdī ʿAbdelsalām came to Tunis

24 On the Medina, See P. Devey, "The Hafsia-Quarter Medina of Tunis, Tunisia," *Architectural Review*, (1983), 99–100, and J. Abdelkafi, *La Médina de Tunis: Espace historique* (Tunis: Alif, 1989).

25 J.S. Woodford, *The City of Tunis: Evolution of an Urban System* (Cambridgeshire: Middle East & North African Studies Press Ltd, 1990), 102–104.

26 N.S. Hopkins, "Traditional Tunis and Its Transformation," *Annals of the New York Academy of Sciences* 220 (1974), 427–463.

after the abolition of slavery. Many of them were voluntary migrants, such as the *mālamai* (sing. *mālam*) who were traditional Muslim teachers transiting either to the Muslim pilgrimage (*ḥajj*) or in quest of Islamic education in North Africa. Others simply migrated to Tunis because of the religious tolerance that the Ḥusaynid authorities accorded to Bori practitioners there. Because of the social organization of the West Africans, it was easy for newcomers from central and western Sūdān to assimilate into the existing Bori communities with similar ethnic or cultural affinities.

5 Conclusion

This chapter has sought to provide a historical and chronological framework to examine the Bori compounds in the city of Tunis and how they evolved from their nucleus origins associated with professional palace guards to become a complex ethno-religious communal space. How did these compounds reflect the political, economic and socio-religious climates in Husaynid Tunisia? In this chapter, the evolution and developments of the Bori compounds has been mapped out according to three interrelated yet distinct stages. In the first stage, the rise of the Bori compounds was closely associated with the political instability that engulfed the early phase of the Husaynid dynasty, founded in 1704. During this period, the nexus of the Bori compounds was originally built to serve as a clubhouse—a site of social gatherings and worship, frequented mainly by the male Black slave soldiers whom ʿAlī I imported from central Sūdān to serve as his palace guards (*bawwāba*). The second stage of the history of the Bori compounds coincided with the reign of Ḥammūda Pāsha, during which the caravan slave trade to Tunisia boomed. One of the main outcomes of the increased importation of slaves during the Pāsha's era was the change in physical character of Bori compounds from private clubhouses to communal centers. What is even more startling is the extent to which changes in the features and structure of these compounds correspond not only to the height of the caravan slave trade, but also the extent to which the ethnic characterization of these compounds mirrored the townships and geographical areas of central Sūdān from which the enslaved West Africans were drawn. Lastly, as seen in al-Ḥachāʾishī's account, the period following abolition of slavery in 1846 was no less important in shaping the physical features and functions of the Bori compounds. At the time al-Timbuktāwī was in Tunis, a key characteristic of these compounds was that they revealed an ethnic consciousness of the West and Central Sūdānic community. They were also centered on a number of Bori priestesses who were revered and only referred to as *ʿajūz* (old lady, pl. *ajāʾiz*).

After 1846, it appears that the entrepreneurial spirits of the newly minted Bori priestesses conferred an individualistic character on these compounds. During this period, there was shift from identifying the compounds with *ʿajāʾiz* to associating them with the new Bori priestesses who competed for clients based on their fame and geographical place of origin.

The chapter has shown how the locations and changes in the nucleus units of the Bori communal compounds established under the aegis of the Ḥusaynid Dynasty from the beginning of the eighteenth century reflected not only the regional origins of their occupants (the *bawwāba* or *kofafi*) from central Sūdān, but also the broader political developments that ushered in the early Ḥusaynid dynasty. In the aftermath of the instability that divided Tunis into *Ḥusayniyya* and *Bashiyya* factions until 1841, shifts in the character, size, gender ratio, location and concentration of the compounds reflected the economic developments that augmented the volume of slaves entering Tunis from the same cultural region where the first occupants of the compounds had originated. Then, between 1846 and the late 1880s, these compounds mirrored the changes in legal and socio-economic status brought about by the eventual abolition of slavery in 1846.

Thus, while the rise and evolution of these compounds in Tunisia serves as a comparative example of transfer, persistence and survival of ancestral West African cultures and family values that enslaved people carried across the Sahara to the Maghribi milieu, this was no exception. Rather it was indicative of a larger pattern of transfer, survival and retention strategies common to enslaved Africans forcibly transported out of their original "homelands" to the various destinations of the slave trade in the Maghrib and beyond.[27]

---

27 On the question of the survival and retention of culture in North Africa and the Ottoman Middle East, see Ehud R. Toledano, *As If Silent and Absent: Bonds of Enslavement in the Islamic Middle East*, New Haven and London: Yale University Press, 2007, especially chapter 5; Chouki El Hamel, "Constructing A Diasporic Identity: Tracing the Origins of Gnawa Spiritual Group in Morocco," *Journal of African History* 49 no. 2, (2008), 241–260; and John Hunwick, "The Religious Practices of Black Slaves in the Mediterranean Islamic World," in Paul E. Lovejoy (ed.), *Slavery on the Frontiers of Islam*, (Princeton: Markus Wiener Publishers, 2004), 149–171.

Epilogue

When he addressed *Hatk al-Sitr* to Ḥammūda Pāsha, the ruler of Tunis, al-Timbuktāwī's primary goal was to impress upon Tunisian political and religious authorities to ban the Hausa Bori possession cult rampant in the Regency. After pinning what he condemned as sedition (*fitna*) to a disctinct community among the Blacks of Tunisia (*Wusfān*)—which he isolated, labelled *Sūdān Tūnis*, and charged with unbelief (*kufr*)—the *shaykh* implored Ḥammūda Pāsha to impress upon Tunisian religious authorities the obligation to excommunicate, persecute, and even execute them should they refuse to repent or discontinue their infidel religious practices. Despite al-Timbuktāwī's eloquent description of the uncountable acts of polytheism (*shirk*) the *Sūdān Tūnis* community were spreading among the people of Tunisia, to date we have no known evidence suggesting that the Tunisian political and religious authorities heeded his admonition to ban the cult or excommunicate its adherents, let alone prosecute them. The closest attempt to banning the cult reportedly occurred during the early years of Tunisian independence under the late Tunsian President Habib Bourguiba (in power from 1957–1987) and his Neo-Dustur Party that deemed popular Islamic religious practices as backward and unsuitable for the image of the progressive state Bourguiba sought to foster. Along with the closure and curbing the activities of popular religious brotherhoods, in 1958 Bourguiba shut down the mausoleum (*zāwiya*) of Sīdī Saʿad which al-Timbuktāwī reported as having served as annual pilgrimage site for the Sūdānic West African community since the early eighteenth century.[1] Within a decade after its closure, the *zāwiya* of Sīdī Saʿad was reopened through the efforts of the same Bourguiba regime to integrate the Bori-Stambali ethno-religious performance as part of Tunisian national culture.[2]

In presenting this complete English translation of *Hatk al-Sitr* with the accompanying thematic chapters, the goal is to make the text of this treatise accessible by contextualizing it within its broader religious and intellectual environments—particularly the effects of the late eighteenth- and nineteenth-century militant jihad movements in western and central Sūdān—in order to

1 Ismael M. Montana, "The Stambali of Husyanid Tunisia: From Possession Cult to Ethno-Religious and National Culture," in *African Communities in Asia and the Mediterranean: Identities Between Integration and Conflict*, ed. Ehud R. Toledano (Trenton NJ.: Africa World Press, 2012), 181.

2 Richard C. Jankowsky, *Stambeli: Music, Trance, and Alterity in Tunisia* (Chicago: University of Chicago Press, 2010), 66.

© KONINKLIJKE BRILL NV, LEIDEN, 2024 | DOI:10.1163/9789004516175_006

understand al-Timbuktāwī's attitude and intollerence towards religious deviance. I have therefore sought to directly and indirectly highlight the links between *Hatk al-Sitr* and the radical Islamic religious changes occuring in western and central Sūdān on the eve of al-Timbuktāwī's pilgrimage and sojourn in the Maghrib. In fact, al-Timbuktāwī's theological iterations on such issues as religious innovation (*bidʿa*), anathemetization (*takfīr*), and enslavement (*istirqāq al-ʿabīd*), his critique of the Wahhābi position on intercession (*tawassul*), and his harsh condemnation of the polytheism of the enslaved Sudanic Africans (*shirk al-ʿabīd*) in the Maghribi milieu were rooted in the goals and teachings of the pan-Fulde militant jihad movements of Uthman Dan Fodio and Ahmadu Lobbo in central and western Sūdān. Only four years prior to al-Timbuktāwī's sojourn in the Maghrib, Dan Fodio, after defeating the Hausa city states in Hausaland in the central Sūdān, formally established the Sokoto Caliphate in 1804. Following the establishment of the caliphate, Dan Fodio was at the height of denouncing the same deviant religious practices that made *Sūdān Tūnis* the subject of al-Timbuktāwī's condemnation in the Maghrib. For his part, prior to launching his holy wars in the 1810s and establishing his theocratic state of the Caliphate of Hamdullahi in 1818, Aḥmadu Lobbo—who was himself heavily influenced by Dan Fodio—exhibited the most influence on al-Timbuktāwī's intollence of religious innovation (*bidʿa*).

Aside from addressing how the reverberations of these pan-Fulde Islamic jihad movements shaped al-Timbuktāwī's attitude towards the Bori cult, this book also sought to spell out the distinguishing characteristics of those he labeled *Sūdān Tūnis*. Situating this distinct ethno-religious community in their specific cultural and historical context is critical to understanding the depth of the reverberation of the western and central Sūdānic militant jihad movements in the Maghrib. While there has been a tendency to lump together popular religious practices dominated by people of African descent under the generalized categorization of "*religion des esclaves*" or slave religion, with little regard to their differring historical timeframe or religious practices, mapping out the characteristics of al-Timbuktāwī's *Sūdān Tūnis* allows for an in-depth understanding of the intricate diversity of historical origins, geographical distribution, and cosmological outlook that characterized the heterogeneous Black (*Wusfān*) community in the Regency, and indeed throughout the Maghrib. As illustrated in Chapter Two, unlike the portion of *Wusfān* comprising the *Shwāshīn*, *Aḥrār*, and other pre-existing Black groups in the Regency, the genesis of the *Sūdān Tūnis* community can be traced back only to the third decade of the eighteenth century when the heir apparent to the throne of the Husaynid Dynasty, ʿAlī Bey I, fell out with his uncle, Ḥusayn Ibn ʿAlī (the first ruler of the Husaynid Dynasty) over the succession crisis. To safeguard his regime, after ousting and murdering Ḥusayn Ibn ʿAlī in 1835, ʿAli Bey I imported young unmarried men from central Sūdān for use as palace guards (*bawwāba*). As indicated earlier, ʿAli Bey I allowed them to establish clubhouses (*nawādī*) where they followed their own indigenous religious practices, which according to contemporary historical and later anthropological accounts could have been none other than the central Sudanic Hausa possession cult of Bori. In the period between 1780 and 1820, as regular trade between the Regency and central Sūdān expanded under the aegis of Ḥammūda Pāsha's economic reforms, enslaved Sūdānic Africans drawn from the very geographical and cultural regions where ʿAlī Bey I's palace guards originated culminated in widespread diffusion of Sūdānic West African religious, cultural, and social organizational practices in the urban centers of the Regency, mainly in Tunis, but also in Sousse, Sfax, and Kairouan.

As for al-Timbuktāwī's appeal to the Tunisian authorities to excomminucate, re-enslave or even execute members of the *Sūdān Tūnis* for spreading their deviant and infidel religious practices in the Regency, such an extreme position can only be comprehended if placed in the context of the aforementioned militant Islamic jihad movements. As a scholar and a religious judge (*qādī*) intolerant of religious innovation (*bidʿa*), al-Timbuktāwī's ethnic ancestry as Fulfulde and his impeccable intellectual pedigree, coupled with the timing of his pilgrimage, suggests that he must have been a member of the Grand Council of *ʿulamāʾ* upon whom Shehu Ahmadu Lobbo relied in his revolutionary jihad movement in the Niger Bend.

When he weighed in on the Wahhābi controversy and refuted the Wahhābi denounciation of visitation (*zīyārāt*) to the tombs of *awliyāʾ* (saints) and intercession and closeness to Allah (*tawassul*) as polytheism (*shirk*) in the strongest possible terms, al-Timbuktāwī, instead, drew the attention of the Tunisian *ʿulamāʾ* to *Sūdān Tūnis* as the real polytheists (*mushrikīn*) worthy of excommunication from the Islamic *umma* for engaging in major polytheistic acts (*shirk al-akbar*) by glorifying their Bori deities. In his eyes, this was very different from Tunisian Muslims seeking intercession (*tawassul*) through holy men considered *awliyāʾ*. Yet despite his advocacy for the re-enslavement of *Sūdān Tūnis* for returning to "the source of slavery" or unbelief (*kufr*), it remains to be proven if al-Timbuktāwī's plea made any impression on the Tunisian political or religious establishments despite Rached Limam's claims to contrary.[3] For instance, exactly thirty-six years following the publication of *Hatk al-Sitr*, Aḥmad Bey (r. 1250–1271/1835–1855), Ḥammūda Pāsha's successor, who was morally opposed

3 Rachad Limam, "Some Documents Concerning Slavery in Tunisia at the End of the 18th Century," *RHM* 8, no. 11 (1981), 355.

to slavery, issued a mass emancipation decree on 24th January, 1846, but was met with swift defiance from slave-owning establishments, including religious leaders who pointed to Islamic law (*sharīʿa*) to justify their position.[4] Faced with this reality, the bey instructed Aḥmad Ibn Abī Diyaf, the chief scribe (*kātib*) in his court (*dīwān*), to issue an edict to the Sharīʿa Council for Judicial Ordinance (*Majlis al-Sharʿī*) seeking their opinion to legitimize and justify the abolition decree in religious terms. In his petition (*istiftāʾ*) to the *Majlis*, the bey cited the inhumane treatment of the enslaved Sūdānic West Africans and concluded that because the majority were also drawn from territorries from the *bilād al-Sūdān* (land of the Blacks) where Islam had long been established, their religious status was uncertain. If so, their enslavement violated if not outrightly contradicted the original precept for servitude, which was the condition of unbelief.[5]

At the helm of the *Majlis* that received the bey's petition were the two highest-ranking members of the Tunisian religious establishment: Ibrāhīm al-Riyāḥī (1180–1266/1767–1850), the Grand Muft of the Mālikī school who represented indigenous Tunisians, comprising the majority of the population, and Muhammad Bayram III (1220–1277/1806–1861), the Grand Mufti of the Ḥanafī Rite, head of the *Majlis* and representitive of the Turkified minority rulling class and their auxiliary servants of the mamluk class. In his response to the Bey's petition, other than praising the decision as enlightened and guided by his just deeds, al-Riyāḥī was silent on the merit of the Bey's argument over the illegality of the enslavement of Sūdānic West Africans. Meanwhile, his Ḥanafī counterpart, Bayram III, not only overtly supported the Bey's arguments on the grounds that the religious status of the Sūdānic West Africans was uncertain but reached out to historical precedence and cited, not al-Timbuktāwī's *Hatk al-Sitr*, but Aḥmad Bābā's classic argument concerning a legal prohibition against the enslavement of fellow Muslims.[6] Bayram concluded his fatwa by contending that anyone who was not convinced by the Bey's argument should consult Aḥmad Bābā's classic response to the question of illegal enslavement in his *Miʿrāj al-Suʿūd*.[7]

Whether Bayram III was unaware of al-Timbuktāwī's treatise advocating for keeping the Sūdānic West Africans in slavery remains to be proven by

4 Ismael M. Montana, *The Abolition of Slavery in Ottoman Tunisia* (Gainesville: University Press of Florida, 2013), 115.

5 Aḥmad Ibn Abī Diyaf, *Itḥāf ahl al-Zamān bi Akhbār mulūk Tūnis wa ʿahdi al-Amān*, 7 vols, Tunis: al-Dār al-ʿArabiyya lil-Kitāb, 1999.

6 Ibid., 4:89.

7 Ibid., 4:89.

future research. What is clear, however, is that the vast majority of the enslaved Sūdānic West Africans who provoked al-Timbuktāwī's wrath originated from the territories controlled by the theocratic Islamic caliphates whose proclaimed goal was to establish an Islamic socio-cultural order in western and central Sūdān. And similarly to Aḥmad Bābā, who insisted centuries earlier that non-belief was the sole legitimate reason for enslavement in Islam, al-Timbuktāwī likewise justified the reenslavement of *Sūdān Tūnis* on the grounds that their syncretic and unorthodox religious practices involving the Bori possession cult was a great act of polytheism (*shirk*), tantamount to returning to the original state or source of slavery, which is unbelief (*kufr*).

Granted that the two Timbuktu scholars may have held, in principle, a shared opinion on the legal basis for enslavement in Islam as a means of punishment for unbelief, the historical context underlying their reasoning and the tenor of their positions, however, diferred markedly. First, Aḥmad Bābā's position has its genesis in a petition (*istiftā'*) prompting his response, *Miʿrāj al-Suʿūd*, in which he refuted the widely held claims rooted in the classical ideology of enslavement in the Islamic context. At the core of these claims were the series of theoretical questions that were presented to him in the form of a petition concerning the equation of Blackness with slavery as a punishment for unbelief. Although these questions were theoretical in nature, they had riveting implications in justifying the enslavement of Sūdānic Africans (*al-Sūdān*) in a manner that was similar to that of pro-slavery proponents justififying the trans-Atlantic slave trade by claiming that European slavers were only tapping into the existing institution of slavery in Africa. Similarly, as demand for Sūdānic Africans as slaves increased, slavers in the Maghrib and other parts of the Islamic Middle East from the classical era until abolition, like their counterparts in the trans-Atlantic context, justified the enslavement of Sūdānic Africans on the grounds that the Blacks (*al-Sūdān*) were eligible for enslavement under Islamic law. While such a claim can hardly be justified in the Qur'ān, it was neverless rooted in the ideology of enslavement in the Muslim social order. The celebrated Arab medieval historian Ibn Khaldun (d. 806/1406) in his famous book, *al-Muqaddima* (Prolegomena), which he wrote two centuries prior to Aḥmad Bābā's *Miʿrāj*, overtly expressed this prejudiced view when he propounded that God made the *bilād al-Sūdān* a natural source of slaves. According to Ibn Khaldun, "the Negro [*sic*] nations are, as a rule, submissive to slavery, because [Negroes] have little [that is essentially] human and have attributes that are quite similar to those of dumb animals."[8] For centuries and down to

8 Cf, John Alembillah Azumah, *The Legacy of Arab-Islam in Africa: A Quest for Inter-Religious Dialogue* (Oxford: Oneworld, 2001), 135.

Aḥmad Bābā's exile years in Fez, such prevailing misconceptions and attitudes toward Black Africans (*al-Sūdān*) shaped the minds of many in the Maghrib and the larger Islamic Middle East towads the *bilād al-Sūdān*, seeing it as a land of heathens inhabited by polytheists eligible for enslavement. One major implication of these misconceptions was that while the term *ʿabd* (pl. *ʿabīd*) in its etymology did not entail racial connotation or racialization of slavery in any shape or form, Sūdānic Africans nevertheless came to be perceived synonymously as *ʿabīd* (slaves), even though they were not the only racial category of enslaved individuals in the universe of *Dār al-Islām* (the Abode of Islam). When asked if the Blacks could ever be legally free, since they hailed from the *bilād al-Sūdān*, Aḥmad Bābā—after dividing the Sudanic lands into two, the land of Muslims and land of unbelievers—pushed enslavability to the outside or the margins of the frontiers of Muslims lands. To him, it was illegal to enslave people from within lands controlled by Muslims, and only polytheists who lived beyond the frontiers of *Dār al-Islām* at the time such as the Mossi, the Yoruba, Dagomba, the Kotokoli and others who lived outside kingdoms of Mali and Songhay, at the time, could be enslaved. Those who dwelt within the *Dār al-Islām* could only be enslaved if they had no treaty (*ʿuhd*) with Muslims and were captured in a just war.

Unlike Aḥmad Bābā, who was careful to restrict legal enslavement to the religious status of the land as opposed to the status of an individual, al-Timbuktāwī's position on this question was spurred by the practical developments of the Islamic jihad states that expanded enslavement activities within the Sūdānic space of *Dār al-Islām*. Whereas the theoretical questions posed to Aḥmad Bābā were also informed by the classical ideologogy of enslavement in the Islamic context, al-Timbuktāwī's advocacy for the reenslavement of *Sūdān Tūnis* was rather directly related to the contemporaneous debate on anathematization (*takfīr*) that allowed or justified the enslavement of individuals deemed to be engaged in un-Islamic and unorthodox practices contrary to the ideals set forth by leaderships of the Islamic jihad movements in western and the central Sūdān. As discussed before, a hallmark of these jihad movements was the reorganization of western and central Sūdānic lands into Islamic caliphates or spheres of *Dār al-Islām*. In the wake of the formal establishment of jihad states, the criteria for membership in these states centered on upholding strict adherence to Islam. The ruling establishments which sought to rid these states from all forms of religious innovations (*biʿda*), polytheism (*shirk*), and anathematization (*takfīr*) imposed an Islamic socio-cultural order on the subjugated territories. Communities that continued to practice un-Islamic and unorthodox forms of worhship were invariably deemed to be unbelievers (*kuffār*) and thus eligible for enslavement. In the Sokoto caliphate, for instance, the attitude of the jihad leadership had catasthrophic implications for the masses in the Hausa city states classified as *maguzawa* (fire worshippers), many of whom were enslaved on the pretext that they were unbelievers by descent (*kuffār bi-l-ʾaṣl*).

Thus, in *Hatk al-Sitr*, al-Timbuktāwī's attack on the *Sūdān Tūnis* displaced community as unbelievers (*kuffār*) and his call for their re-enslavement was not only contrary to the spirit of religious tolerance and accommodation that prevailed in the Maghrib, but to that of the pre-jihad period in western and central Sūdān. His radical and dogmatic worldview, no doubt, echoes the reverberations of the late eighteenth- and nineteenth-century jihad movements in the Maghrib, and calls for closer attention to their intellectual effects beyond the interior of Muslim Africa to the frontiers of the Islamic and the African diaspora worlds.

PART 2

Hatk al-Sitr

Text and Translation

fol. A

اللهم صل على سيدنا محمد
وءاله[1] وصحْبه و سلّم
بسم الله الرحمن الرحيم وصلى الله على سيدنا ومولانا محمد وءاله وصحبه وسلم

قال العبد الفقير المعترف بذنبه القليل العلم والتقوى الراجي الغفران والستر عند مولاه الكريم احمد بن القاضي ابي بكر بن يوسف بن ابراهيم التنبكتاوي افُقا الفُلّاني الفُوتِي قبيلة الدَّوجقي مولدا الجنَّاوِي قراءة سامحه اللّه من عيوب لسانه وبقية ذنوب اعضايه انه هو المجيب الداعي القريب السميع اللطيف ونسئل[2] اللّه ان يوفقنا بالقول والعمل وان يعيننا على الطاعة والقيام بحقوقه وان يدخلنا وءاباءنا[3] واشياخنا واحبابينا وكل من نظر الى كتابنا هذا بعين الرضى والصواب او حمله الى حاكم او اصلح ما فيه من الفسادْ او طالعه او نسخه ولو باجرة جنة الفردوس بلا حساب يا رب العالمين اَلحَمْدُ للّه الذي تفرد بالواحدانية[4] ولم يشاركه احد في صفاته ولا في افعاله سبحانه هو الذي لمْ يستحق ولا يستحق احد ان يعبد في السماء ولا في الارض سوى ذاته جل وعلا عن ما يقوله الكفار والمشركون في جنابه وتنزه ان يكون ما لا يريد في ملكه وملكوته وهو وهو[5] الذي خلق الملايكة والجان والانس وجميع خلقه وكل يسبح بحمده ويشهد بوحدانيته والصلاة والسلام الدايمان الاكملان الاطيبان على صفيه الذي ارسله لابطال الشرك والكفر واعتقادات اهْله وعلى ءاله

[1] هكذا جاءت في المصدر، والصواب "آله" [2] هكذا جاءت في الأصل، والصواب "نسأل" [3] هكذا جاءت في الأصل، والصواب "آباءنا" [4] هكذا جاءت في الأصل، والصواب بالوحدانية [5] هكذا جاءت مكررة في الأصل

In the Name of Allah, the Most Merciful and Compassionate
May Allah bless and give utter peace to our master and lord Muḥammad, his folk, and companions.

Prologue

Says the needy servant [of Allah], who confesses his sins, who has little knowledge or piety, who hopes for pardon and covering up [of his sins] from his Generous Lord, Ahmad b. al-Qāḍī Abī Bakr b. Yūsuf b. Ibrāhīm from Timbuktu—al Fulānī and native of Fūtā Tribe, born in al-Dawjaqa and studied [the Quran] in Jennī—may Allah overlook the defects of his tongue and remaining sins of his limbs. Surely, He is the One who responds to the supplicant, the Near, the All-hearing, the All-kind. And we ask Allah to grant us success in our words and deeds, assist us in obedience and observance of His commandments, and cause us, our fathers, teachers, and loved ones—and all who look at this book of ours with favor and approval, or present it to a ruler, or correct whatever mistakes there may be herein, or read it, or copy it even if for a fee—to enter paradise without any reckoning, O Lord of the Universe.

All praise be to Allah, who is singularized in His Oneness, and has no cosharer in His attributes and actions. Exalted is He, besides whose Essence, none in heaven or earth deserves to be worshipped. He is far above what the unbelievers (*kuffār*)[1] and the polytheists (*mushrikīn*)[2] say of His honor, in whose physical and spiritual kingdoms naught comes to pass save His will. [For] it is He who created the angels, jinn, mankind, and His entire creation, all extolling His praise and bearing witness to His Oneness.

May everlasting, perfect, and pure blessings and peace be upon His Chosen One—whom He sent to abolish polytheism (*shirk*), unbelief (*kufr*), and the beliefs of their adherents—and upon his folk, companions, and community (*umma*) who strove [to uphold] His religion and Sunna, made clear to us the path of salvation, and warned us against every devil and his wiles.

---

1 *Kāfir* (pl. *kuffār*), which means "obliterating or covering," is derived from *kufr*. *Kufr* implies concealing benefits received. *Kufr* also means ungratefulness. The adjective *kāfir* is derived from the verb *kafara*.

2 *Mushrik* (pl. *mushrikīn*) is derived from *shirk*, which literally means polytheism, i.e. the worship of others alongside Allah. It also implies attributing divinity to any other besides Allah. *Shirk* also implies associating partners with Allah, setting up a *nid* (rival) in worship with Allah, or believing that the source of power, harm, or blessing is from others besides Allah. See "shirk," *EI*, vol. IX.

وصحبه وامته الذي[1] جاهدوا على دينه وسنته وبينوا لنا طريقة السلامة
وحذرونا عن[2] اتباع كل شيطان وكيْده وبَعْد فلما رجعت من الحج
الى تونس حرسها اللّه بحفظه المنيع وابقاها في ايدي المومنين[3] بحرمة بكة والبقيع
fol. B وجدت فيها فتنه[4] لا يجوز لاحد ممَّن في قلبه رايحة من الايمان ان يسكت عنها
باتفاق اهل التَّاصِيل والتفريع. ووجدت اهل الفضل والصلاح والعلم فيها
ما اطلعوا عليها حقيقة الاطلاع لكون ذلك لم يكن لكفار افقههم من اليهود
والنصارى بصنيع. بل ذلك من فعل كفار بلدنا السودانية اذلهم اللّهُ
بما اذل به فرعون والسامري باسمه العليم السميع. وكان امير المومنين[5]
[بها] في الوقت الاعز الاكرم المنصور الموىد[6] الذي ازعج بنُو الاعادي مع بعد
محلهم بشدة هيبته واذل رقاب الجبابرة بقوة بطشه وتحير [ت] عقول اهل
الفساد والظلم بسرعة انتقامه وصارت اليهود والنصارى يرعدون تحت
ذمته كانهم اسارى ينتظرون اعظم عقوبة يفعل بهم تاج الملوك
السيف الهندي المشهود له بالخير العلم الاعلم ليث الكتايب المولى المعظم
امير الامراء ابو المكارم سيدنا واميرنا حمودة باشا بن الاعز الاكرم الاعظم
علي باشا ادام اللّه عزته بالتقوى والعدل ما دامت السموات فوق الارض
ونصره على اعداءِ الحق وايده الله بالاستقامة ولا زال اللّه يرفع عنْه
شر كل جبار عنيد وامنه اللّه من الفزع الاكْبر وختم لنا وله بحسن
الخاتمة. آمين (إنّه) ممَّن له بنصر الدين ولوع وشغف كبير في ابطال ما ليْس
في الدين بمشْروع فاردت أن اخبر بهذه الفتنة اهل الحكم الشرْعي
من قضاته ومفاتيه وان منعني بعض الناس عن ذلك وقالوا هذه
فتنة قديمة فان فتنة فرعون اقدم من هذه وان قالوا لي ايضا انت
تخاف عقوبته أيدك اللّه فقلت ان عاقبني بالجرم فذلك له والا فكيف
يعاقبني على اعانته في دين اللّه ولو كان يعاقب الناس على مثل هذا

[1] هكذا جاءت في الأصل، والصواب "الذين" [2] هكذا جاءت في الأصل، والصواب "حذرونا من" [3] هكذا جاءت في الأصل، والصواب "المؤمنين" [4] هكذا جاءت في الأصل، والصواب "فتنة" [5] هكذا جاءت في الأصل، والصواب "المؤمنين" [6] هكذا جاءت في الأصل، والصواب "المؤيد"

To commence: When I returned from hajj to Tunis, may Allah guard it with His insurmountable protection and preserve it in the hands of the believers by the sanctity of Mecca and Baqīʿ [SIC], I found therein sedition (*fitna*),[3] which is impermissible for anyone with the faintest inkling of faith to keep silent about, according to the consensus of the scholars of principal and ancillary sciences (*ahl al-taʾṣīl wa-l-tafrīʿ*). I found that the notables, upright, and scholars there had no knowledge whatsoever about this [sedition], because it was not the deed of the unbelievers of their land, the Jews or the Christians, but the behavior of the unbelievers of our native land, Sūdān, may Allah disgrace them by what He disgraced Pharaoh and Sāmirī, for the sake of His name(s), the Omniscient, the All-hearing.

The commander of the faithful (*amīr al-muʾminīn*) at the time was the mighty and generous, the victorious and triumphant, who struck legions of his enemies with fear, despite their distance, with the strength of his might, and humbled the tyrants by his valor, and stymied the minds of the corrupt and wrongdoers by the speed of his vengeance, and under whose custody, both the Jews and Christians would tremble, as if prisoners waiting for his stern punishment. He is the crown of all kings, the sword of India, attested to by his good deeds, the most knowledgeable, the lion of squadrons, the glorious lord, the prince of princes, the father of the nobles, our master and prince—Ḥammūda Pāsha, son of the generous and honorable ʿAlī Pāsha, may Allah preserve his honor through piety and justice for as long as the heavens endure over the earth, grant him victory against enemies of the truth, help him on the straight path, endow him with everlasting protection from every tyrannical and obstinate transgressor, save him from the Greatest Terror, and bestow unto us and him a good ending, and unto those who help the religion, the eager, the most desiring to abolish what is not legislated in the religion. Amen.

So, I set about informing the people of legal authority, judges (*quḍāt*) and muftis, of this sedition. But some people prevented me from doing so when they said: "This is an ancient practice and affliction, for the affliction of Pharaoh is far more ancient," and when they also said: "You are apprehensive of his [the *amīr*'s] punishment, may Allah strengthen you." So, my response was that If he punishes me because of a crime then that is his right; otherwise, why would he punish me for helping him establish the religion of Allah? If he were to punish

3 *Fitna* (pl. *fitan*) has various meanings. In the Holy Quran, *fitna* occurs under different meanings: temptation, sedition, affliction, seduction, discord, commotion, civil strife, impiety, and unbelief. But according to the author's usage of the term, *fitna* is used to condemn the religious beliefs and practices of the Blacks of Tunis, which, according to him, implies sedition.

لما صحَّ قول الخطباء فيه شهابك الساطع الذاب عن دينك المدافع
لان من لم يدفع الشرك عن الدين لا يجوز ان يقال فيه مثل هذا ثمَّ ان fol. A
عاقبني بقولي ربنا اللّه وحده ولا يستحق العبادة غيره فلست باول من
عذب في اللّه وتوكلت على اللّه وكفى به حسيبا وعليه فليتوكل
المومنون وَلمَّا عزمت على اخبارهم بذلك علمت انه لا يتم مقصودي
في ذلك الَّا بتصريحي لهم باوْصاف تلك الفتنة وذلك لا يتم الَّا بكلام كثير
مع غلبة العجمة على اللسان فالفت في ذلك رسالة سميتها
هتك الستر عمَّا عليه سودان تونس من الكفر وحصرتها في مقدمة
وابواب وخاتمة فَقُلْتُ مستعينا باللّه لا رب غيره وما توفيقي
الا به وهو الفتاح الوهَّاب **اَلْمُقَدِمَةٌ** اِعْلَمْ هدانا اللّه وإياك
انه ليس لنا ان نحكم بكفر العبيد جميعا بل انما نحكم بكفر من فعل
شيْئًا مما يقتضي الكفر او قال قولا مقتضيا له أو من صدق بئالهتهم[1]
او من جُعِل [2]رءيسا في دار صنمهم رجلا كان او امراة او من اعان على
بقاء هذه الفتنة بعد ثبوتها لانه رضي بالكفر والرِضى بالكفر كفر
ولعَمري قلَّ من سَلِم منهم من هذه الاوصاف واعْلَمْ ايضا ان للكفر
اسماء والكافر اسم لمن لا ايمان له فان اظهر الايمان من غير اعتراف
بنبوءة النبي صلى اللّه عليه وسلم خُصَّ باسم المنافق وان طرا كفره
بعد الايمان خص باسم المرتد لرجوعه عن الاسلام وان قال بالهين
او اكثر كهؤلاء العبيد خص باسم المشرك لاثباته الشريك في الالوهية
وان كان متديّنا ببعض الادْيان والكتب المنسوخة خص باسم الكتابي
كاليهودي والنصراني وان كان يقول بقدم الدهر واستناد الحوادث اليْه

[1] هكذا جاءت في الأصل، والصواب "بآلهتهم" [2] هكذا جاءت بالمصدر، والصواب "رئيسا"

people simply because of this, then the words of the sermonizers, describing him as having luminous and bright blaze in chasing away [evil] and defending his religion, would not hold true, for he who doesn't preserve the religion against polytheism would not deserve such glorification. Moreover, if he were to punish me for saying "our Lord is Allah alone, besides whom none deserves to be worshipped," then I would not be the first to be punished for the sake of Allah. For I trust in Allah, sufficient is He, and let all believers put their trust in Him.

When I made up my mind to notify them [judges and muftis] about this sedition, I realized that my intention could only be accomplished by providing them with a full description of its manners, which would not be achieved without resorting to loquacious expressions with my foreign tongue. So I wrote on this topic a treatise entitled *Hatk al-Sitr ʿammā ʿalayhi Sūdān Tūnis min al-Kufr* [Piercing the Veil: Being an Account of the Infidel Religion of the Blacks of Tunis], which I confined to an introduction, some chapters, and a conclusion.

Thus, I wrote [the following], seeking the help of Allah, besides whom there is no lord; for my success is only through Him, the Opener, the Bestower of Bounties.

Introduction

Realize, may Allah guide us all, that it is not our intention to judge all slaves (*ʿabīd*) to be unbelievers. Rather, we only disfavor those whose deeds are indicative of unbelief (*kufr*), or whose speech implies as such, or who believe in deities, or who have been appointed a leader in their pantheon, be they a man or woman, or who assist in continuing this sedition after it being established [as wrong] because they are content with such unbelief—for being content with unbelief is in itself unbelief. Upon my life, seldom indeed are those who are far from fitting this description!

Realize also that unbelief (*kufr*) has categories: an unbeliever (*kāfir*) is a person who has no faith; while someone who outwardly displays his faith without confessing to the prophecy of the Prophet, peace and blessings of Allah be upon him, is termed a hypocrite (*munāfiq*); or if he professes his unbelief after having faith, he is termed an apostate (*murtad*) for renouncing Islam; and if he professes two gods or more, like these slaves (*ʿabīd*), he is termed a polytheist (*mushrik*) for ascribing a partner in the divinity of Allah; and if he adheres to some religions of [divinely revealed but] abrogated books, he is considered one of "those believers of the book" (*kitābī*) such as a Jew or Christian; and he

خص باسْم الدَّهري وان لم يثبت الباري تعلى خص باسم المعطل الى غيْر
ذلك مما في كتب الايمة **اَلْبَابُ اَلْأَوَّلُ** في اثبات شركهم fol. B
اِعْلَمْ اختصنا اللّه واياك بحسن الخاتمة ان شرك العبيد ثابت بيْن
اهل ال تونس بالعلم القطعي وبالتواتر المفيد للعلم الضروري لانه قل منهم
من لم يشاهد افعالهم من ذبح وسجود وبخور وتوضية [كذا] مذبوح وغير ذلك
ممَّا نذكره ان شاء اللّه تعلى فيما ياتي فاعلموا يا اخواني ان اللّه تبارك
وتعلى متطلع علينا ولا يخفى عليه شيء من حركاتنا وسكناتنا وقدْ
فرض اللّه تبارك وتعلى على كل عضو من اعضاء ابن ءادم[1] فريضة يطالب
بها يوم القيامة وقد فرض اللّه على اللسان النطق بالشهادتين وقراءة
ام القرءان[2] في الصَّلاة واداء الشهادة ونحوها وقد ذم اللّه تبارك وتعلى
من كتم الشهادة وقال عز من قايل "وَمَنْ أَظْلَمُ مِمَّنْ كَتَمَ شَهَادَةً عنده
مِنْ اللَّهِ وَمَا اللّهِ بِغَافِلٍ عَمَّا تَعْمَلُونَ".[3] وقال أيضا "وَلَا تَكْتُمُوا اَلْشَهَادَةَ وَمَنْ
يَكْتُمُهَا فَإِنَّهُ آثِمٌ قَلْبُهُ وَاللّهُ بِمَا تَعْمَلُونَ عَلِيمٌ"[4] ويجب على كل من
عنده علم بهذه الفتنة ان يودي[5] شهادته بما علم والحاصل ان القيام
بهذه الفتنة واجب على كل مَن وَلِيَ شيئا من امور المسْلمين من امير
وقاض ومفتي وغيرهم امَّا بالتغيير واما بتبليغها الى من يغيرها
ولا يجوز لاحد السكوت عنها بعد علمها لان هذه ليست من الامور
التي يشترط فيها توفر شروط الامر بالمعروف لان هذا شرك والقيام

[1] هكذا جاءت في الأصل، والصواب "آدم" [2] هكذا جاءت في الأصل، والصواب "القرآن" [3] سورة البقرة، ١٤٠ (لا يوجد أي تشكيل أو همزات أو مد لهذه الآية الكريمة في المخطوط الأصلي) [4] سورة البقرة، ٢٨٣ (لا يوجد أي تشكيل أو همزات أو مد لهذه الآية الكريمة في المخطوط الأصلي) [5] هكذا جاءت في الأصل، والصواب "يؤدي"

who professes the eternality of time and ascribes the unfolding of events to it is termed a materialist (*dahrī*); and he who denies the Creator, the Most High, is termed a denier of Allah's attributes (*muʿaṭṭil*); and so forth, as detailed in the books of the scholars.

Chapter 1: An Account Establishing the Polytheism (*Shirk*) of the Slaves

Realize, may Allah bestow us all with His devine providence, that the polytheism of the slaves (*shirk al-ʿabīd*) is established among the people of Tunis by decisive knowledge and mass transmission that is necessarily known, because it is rare to find a person who does not witness their practices, such as offering sacrifices, prostration, incensing, and ritual cleansing, and other manners that will be discussed. So, realize, O my brothers, that Allah, the Blessed and Most High, witnesses our actions, and none of our motions and rest are hidden from Him. And Allah, the Blessed and Most High, has ordained every limb of man with an obligation that he will be questioned about on the Day of Judgement: [for example,] Allah has ordained upon one's tongue the utterance of the Two Testimonies of Faith ["that there is no god but Allah, and that Muhammad is His prophet and messenger"], the recitation of Sūrat al-Fātiḥa (*Umm al-Qurʾān*) in the daily prayers, giving the testimony (*shahāda*), and so forth. And Allah, the Blessed and Most High, has dispraised those who conceal the testimony, for the Mighty has said: "And who is more unjust than one who conceals a testimony he has from Allah? And Allah is not unaware of what you do."[4] And He says again: "And do not conceal testimony, for whoever conceals it—his heart is indeed sinful, and Allah is knowing of what you do."[5] It is incumbent, therefore, upon whosoever has knowledge about this sedition to testify what he knows.

In short, resisting this sedition is binding and compulsory upon whosoever is entrusted with any of the affairs of the Muslims, be they the prince (*amīr*), judge, mufti, and the like, either by preventing it or disclosing it to those capable of doing so. It is impermissible for anyone to remain silent about this sedition after witnessing it because it is not [merely] among matters that fulfill the conditions of commanding the good and forbidding the wrong (*al-amr bi-l-maʿrūf*), since this [sedition] is plain polytheism, and resisting polytheism

4 Quran 2:140.
5 Quran 2:283.

به جهاد والقيام بالجهاد واجب ولو ادى ذلك الى اتلاف نفسه وماله ولو كانت هذه مما يشترط فيها ذلك لادى الى سقوط الجهاد عن الناس جميعا بل انما يشترط من تلك الشروط في هذا الموضع العلم بالمعروف والمنكر واما ظن الافادة والامن من المنكر الاعظم فليسا بشرطين هنا لانه ما نقل عن احد ان شرط الجهاد مع الكفار ظن افادة اسْلامهم ولَيْس fol. A
لنا ايضا منكر اعظم من الشرك حتى نخاف وقوعه بتغيير الشرك واما قوْل بعض الضعفاء من امثالنا ان الامر بالمعروف ساقط في هذا الزمان فلا يخفى عليك ان هذا القول يودي[1] الى ذهاب الدين المحمدي به بالكلية ~~واستد~~ واستدلالهم ايضا بقوْله تعلي "يَا أَيُّهَا الذين آمنوا عليكم أَنْفُسَكُمْ لَا يَضُرُّكُمْ من ضَلَّ إِذَا اهْتَدَيْتُمْ"[2] الاية باطل ايضا ولو كان الامر كذلك لما جاز للنبي صلى الله عليه وسلم واصحابه مقاتلة اهل الشرك والضلال لانهم الذين نزلت فيهم هذه الاية بل يجب على كل مومن[3] ان يقوم بالدين بقدر حاله ثم اذا عجز بعد القيام لا يضره ضلال من ضل اذا اهتدى نسْئل[4] اللّه بجاه محمد المصطفى ان يعيننا وامراءنا وقضاتنا على القيام بحقوقه وحفظنا اللّه واياهم من شر كل شياطين الجن والانس ءامينْ

اَلْبَابُ الثَّانِي في ذكر بعض اسماء ءالهتهم اِعْلَمْ اجارنا اللّه واياك من الشرك الاكبر والاصْغر ان اصنام هؤلاء العبيد لا تنحصر بعدد انما اذكر ما امكن لي في ذلك من الصور والآلات والمطامير والدِيار التي فيها الصور والآلات والمطامير فَمنْ ذلك سلطان ءالهتهم **شَرْكِنْدَوَ**[5] وهو الذي في دار كوفة وهي الدار التي يجتمعون فيها في شعبان كاجْتماع

[1] هكذا جاءت في الأصل، والصواب "يؤدي" [2] سورة المائدة، 501 (لا يوجد أي تشكيل أو همزات أو مد لهذه الآية الكريمة في المخطوط الأصلي) [3] هكذا جاءت في الأصل، والصواب "مؤمن" [4] هكذا جاءت في الأصل، والصواب "نسأل" [5] كذا في كل المخطوطات. الصحيح هو "سَرْكِنْجِدَ"

is a [form of] jihad, and jihad is a legal obligation even if it destroys one and one's wealth. If this was among matters that are stipulated, then jihad would no longer be obligatory for anyone. Moreover, knowledge of what is right and what is wrong would certainly be stipulated in this case. As for the suppositions of causing benefit and remaining safe from great evil, those are not valid conditions here, because it is not reported by any authority that jihad is preconditioned on causing reconversion to Islam. However, it is not for us to contest the greatest form of polytheism, by openly resisting it, until we are certain of its occurrence.

As for the opinion of the weak-minded, from the likes of us, that commanding the right no longer applies in this age, it cannot be lost on you that such a statement is indeed far from the Muḥammadan religion. Likewise, their reasoning by the words of Allah, the Most High, "O you who have believed, upon you is [responsibility for] yourselves. Those who have gone astray will not harm you when you have been guided"[6] is also flawed, for if that were the case, it would not have been valid for the Prophet, peace and blessings of Allah be upon him and his companions, to combat the polytheists and the deviant, as they were the very people upon whom this noble verse was revealed. Therefore, it is incumbent upon every believer to defend this religion in his own capacity. If, after trying, he proves incapable, no hurt can come to him from those who have strayed, for he has been rightly guided. We ask Allah by the rank of Muḥammad, the Chosen One, to help us, our leaders, and our judges in upholding His rights, and may Allah protect us and them from the evil of every devil, of the jinn and mankind. Amen.

Chapter 2: The Names of Some of Their Deities

Realize, may Allah save us all from the greater and lesser polytheism, that the [number of] deities of these slaves are beyond measure, and so I shall confine my description to their sculptures, musical instruments, *mattamores*,[7] and temples where such things are housed.

At the head of the pantheon is Sarkin Gida.[8] This deity is housed in Dār Kofa,[9] where they [the slaves] all assemble every Shaʿbān, just as Muslims

6 Quran 5:105.

7 *Maṭāmīr* (sing. *maṭmūrā*) are "*mattamores*" or underground granaries.

8 See A.J.N. Tremearne, *The Ban of the Bori*, 20–106.

9 Tremearne mentions *Sarikin Kofa* (keeper of the Gate), which must have been connected to Dār Kofa; Tremearne, *The Ban of the Bori*, 298–299.

الناس في بيت اللّٰه الحرام في اشهر الحج وفيها ايْضا مطمور يزعمون انَّ
فيه حية ويزعمون ان شَرْكِندَوَ[١] هذا هو سلطان جن البلاد والصحراء
وفي تلك الدار صور وءالالات[٢] ورايات وامور لا تعد ولا تحصر وَعريفة
تلك الدار ما سمعت كلمتي الشهادة عند أحد أبدًا الا خاصمته، وَاصل
دار كوفة هذه حبس على معتقة اسمها كوفة وعندهم صنم ايضا
يقال له شَرْكِ كُوَارِ[٣] وهو دون الاول في الرتبة بزعمهم لان هذا سلطان fol. B
في بلده فقط وهو بمنزلة القايد مع باشا وهو في دار جماعة كُوَارِ
وبَعْد هذين الداريْن لهم عجايز يعبدونها ويسمون كل واحدة
منهن عجوزا وينسبونها الى الفلاَّن ~~وهو~~ ويقولون لها عجوز الفلانتي [كذا]
وهي في دار سُكَيْ[٤] ودار بَصْبَرَ وفي كل دار من هذين مطمور وءالة
لهْو يقال لها كَصْبَرَ[٥] [كذا] ويعبدون تلك الآلة ويذبحون لها ولا يمسها
احد منهم إلا على الوضوء الكامل كما قال الله تبارك وتعلى في حقِ
كتابه "لا يَمَسُّهُ إلَّا الْمُطَهَّرُونَ"[٦] ويزعمون أن كَصْبَرَ[٧] [كذا] هذه نزلت من السماء

[١] سَرْكِنْجِدَ [٢] هكذا جاءت في الأصل، والصواب "آلات" [٣] كذا في كل المخطوطات. الأصح هو "سَرْكِنْ كَوَارْ" [٤] دار سونغاي [٥] غُمْنبِرِ [٦] سورة الواقعة، 97 (لا يوجد أي تشكيل أو همزات أو مد لهذه الآية الكريمة في المخطوط الأصلي) [٧] غُمْنبِر

assemble at the Kaʿba during the holy month of the pilgrimage.[10] The pantheon also includes a *mattamore*, believed to be inhabited by a snake.[11] They maintain that Sarkin Gida is the chief jinn of the towns and the desert. And in this very pantheon are found images, musical instruments, banners, and numerous other paraphernalia. The chief priestess (*ʿarīfa*)[12] of that pantheon is known to be always quarrelling with everyone whom she hears pronounce the Two Testimonies of Faith. (This communal house of Dār Kofa was originally a religious endowment (*ḥabus*),[13] dedicated to a freed female slave called Kofa.) They also have a deity called Sarkin Kuri,[14] whom they hold as inferior to Sarkin Gida because the former is merely the patron of its own town; it is much like how a regional administrator (*qāʾid*)[15] is in relation to the Pāsha,[16] and it is housed in Dār Kuwari.[17]

Besides these two houses are, what they term, "old women," whom they worship, and are known only by ascription, such as "the old lady of so and so," and are found in Dār Sukay [Songhay] and Dār Bambara. In each of these two houses is a *mattamore* and a musical instrument known as *kambar* [gumbiri].[18] They worship this instrument, offering it sacrifices, which no one may touch except in a complete state of ritual ablution, just as Allah, the Blessed and Most High, has said regarding His book: "None touch it except the purified."[19] For they claim that *kambar* [gumbiri] descended from heaven and was with Bilāl, may

10 See A.J.N. Tremearne, *The Ban of the Bori; demons and demon-dancing in West and North Africa* (London: Heath, Cranton & Ouseley Ltd, 1914), 30; and A.J.N. Tremearne, "Bori Beliefs and Ceremonies," *Journal of the Royal Anthropological Institute* 45 (1915), 59.

11 Tremearne mentions a snake worshipped by the Bori practitioners in Tunis called "mai-ja-chikki", and they believed that this snake kills intruders. Tremearne, *The Ban of the Bori*, 271; "Bori Beliefs and Ceremonies," 64–65.

12 The *ʿarīfa'*, also known as *Sarawniyya* in northern Nigeria, was usually an old woman who commanded respect among the Bori adherents. See Tremearne, *The Ban of the Bori*, 273.

13 *Ḥabus*, a charitable or religious endowment, is also known as a *waqf*. A *ḥabus* could be a portion of land from other revenue-producing property that remains inalienable and whose revenues are set aside for pious grounds.

14 *Kuri* or *kure* are both *iskoki* (spirits in Hausa). In Tunis, Tremearne mentions an infant Bori spirit known as Sarikin Kuri. Tremearne, *The Ban of the Bori*, 420, 483.

15 *Qāʾid* literally means a leader or chief. In the Ottoman administrative hierarchy, the word refers to a government official usually responsible for the supervision of regional districts in the regency of Tunis.

16 An honorific title denoting a high-ranking administrator in the Ottoman administrative system.

17 See Tremearne, *The Ban of the Bori*, 371–483.

18 For a discussion of Bori musical instruments, see Tremearne, *The Ban of the Bori*, 280; and Tremearne, "Bori Beliefs and Ceremonies," op. cit.

19 Quran 56:79.

وانها كانت عند بلال رضي اللّه عنه اعوذ باللّه من هذه المقالة
التي لا يفوه بها من في قلبه رايحة الإيمان ولهم غير ذلك في غيْر
هذين الداريْن من الديار كدار بَيْليكِ وَنُفِ وَزَكْزَكْ وَكَنُ وَسِرَ.
ولهم ايضا عجايز ومطامير في كل دار من ديارهم وَفي دار جَنْفَرَ[1]
ءالة تسمَّى دُنْدُفَ[2] ويذبحون لها ويدهنونها بالدم وفي راس كل
خادم جان يُذبح له ويُسْجد له كما سياتي في الصفة ان شاء اللّه تعالى
والحاصل ان لكل دار جمعة مطمورا وءالة تعبد وهذا كله معلوم
مشاهد لا يمكن لاحد انكاره ومن انكر فليسل الرجال والرجال من الاحرار
والعبيد والكبار والصغار والا فليختبرهم باجتهاده لان هذا ليس من
التجسس انما التجسس طلب معرفة ما يفعله الانسان في بيته وحده
وهذا اجْتماع في كل جمعة وفي كل سنة بل في كل دار من ديار
المسْلمين الا ما قل وكيف يمكن انكار هَذَا ولا تجد احدا من هؤلاء العبيد
الا وهو يقر بذلك ويكفر بعضهم بعضا بذلك وَلا يمكن ايضا ان يقول احد
ان عبادة الصور والآلات والمطامير والجان ليس بشرك اذ القايل[كذا] بذلك نفى fol. A
الشرك جملة لان المراد بالطاغوت في قوله تعلى "وَمَنْ[3] يَّكْفُرْ بِالْطَاغُوتِ
وَيُؤمِنُ بِاللَّهِ فَقَدِ اسْتَمسَكَ بِالْعُرْوَةِ الْوُثْقَى لا انْفِصَامَ لَهَا وَاللّهُ سَمِيعٌ
عَلِيمٌ. اللّهُ وَلِيُّ الذين آمَنُوا يُخرِجُهُم مِنَ الظُّلُمَاتِ إِلَى النُّورِ والذين كَفَرُوا
أَولِيَاؤُهُمْ الطَّاغوتُ يُخْرِجُونَهُمْ مِّنَ النُّورِ إِلَى الظُّلُمَاتِ أُولِئِكَ أَصْحَابُ النار
هُمْ فيهَا خَالِدُونَ"[4] وَقوله تعلى "أَلَمْ تَرَ إِلَى الَّذِينَ أُوتُوا نَصِيبًا مِّنَ الكِتَابِ
يُؤْمِنُونَ بِالجِبْتِ والطَّاغُوتِ"[5] ~~وَيَقُولُونَ لِلَّذِينَ~~ وَقوله ايضا "والَّذِينَ كَفَرُوا
يُقَاتِلُونَ فِي سَبِيلِ الطَّاغُوتِ فَقَاتِلُوا أَوْلِيَاءَ الشَّيطَانِ إِنَّ كَيدَ الشَّيْطَانِ
كَانَ ضَعِيفًا"[6] وَقوله ايضا "والَّذِينَ اجتَنَبُو الطَّاغُوتَ أَنْ يَعْبُدُوهَا

---

[1] زَمْفَرَ [2] دَنْدُفُ [3] هكذا جاءت في الأصل، والصواب "فَمَنْ" [4] سورة البقرة، ٢٥٦–257 (لا يوجد أي تشكيل أو همزات أو مد لهذه الآيات الكريمة في المخطوط الأصلي) [5] سورة النساء، 15 [6] سورة النساء،
٦٧

Allah be pleased with him—I seek refuge in Allah from this belief, which no one with even an atom's weight of faith would ever utter. There are, moreover, several other houses, such as Dār Beylik, Dār Nufe, Dār Zakzak, Dār Kano, and Dār Sarā'. In each of these houses, they have old women and *mattamores*. In Dār Janfara [Zamfara], they have an instrument called Dan Dafu[20] to which they offer sacrifices and then paint in blood. [They also allege that] each of the slaves is possessed by a jinn, to which they must offer sacrifices and prostrate, as will be discussed, God willing.

In short, all these communal houses contain a number of *mattamores* and instruments that are worshipped. All of this is common knowledge, plain [to the people of Tunis], and undeniable. Whoever believes otherwise, let him ask any of the men, free or slaves, young or old, or else present to them his juristic reasoning as a test, and this is not spying, which is to pry into what people may do in their own home. Meanwhile, these [slaves] assemble every Friday and every year, nay, in every house of the Muslims save but a few. How on earth can you then deny this, when you find every one of these slaves living like this and leading each other into unbelief by these [acts]. Nor can anyone maintain that worshipping sculptures, instruments, *mattamores*, and jinn is anything but polytheism, since he who says so denies the very idea of polytheism, because what is meant by "idol" (*al-ṭāghūt*) in the [following] words of Allah, the Most High, is everything that is worshipped besides Allah, whether animals, inanimate objects, or images: "So whoever disbelieves in Ṭāghūt and believes in Allah has grasped the most trustworthy handhold with no breaks in it. And Allah is hearing and knowing. Allah is the ally of those who believe. He brings them out from the darkness into the light. And those who disbelieve—their allies are Ṭāghūt. They take them out of the light into darkness. Those are the dwellers of the fire; they will abide eternally therein";[21] "Have you not seen those who were given a portion of the Scripture, who believe in superstition and Ṭāghūt";[22] "Those who disbelieve fight in the cause of Ṭāghūt. So fight against the allies of Satan. Indeed, the plot of Satan has ever been weak";[23] "But those who avoided Ṭāghūt, lest they worship it, and turned to Allah in repentance, for them are good tidings."[24]

---

20 Dan Dafu or Dafau, also known as Sarikin Makadda, is the chief of the drummers who supervises the Bori musicians; Tremearne, *The Ban of the Bori*, 315–316. See also Fremont E. Besmer, *Horses, Musicians & Gods: The Hausa Cult of Possession-Trance* (South Hadley, Mass: Bergin & Garvey Publishers, 1983), 94.

21 Quran 2:256–257.

22 Quran 4:51.

23 Quran 4:76.

24 Quran 39:17.

وَأَنَابُوا إِلَى اللَّهِ لَهُمُ البُشْرَى"[1] كل ما عبد من دون اللّه سواء كان من حيوان او جمادات او صورة وقد ذكر اللّه تبارك وتعلى في حق التماثيل والصور قوله تعلى "مَا هَذِهِ التَّمَاثِيلُ الَّتِي أَنْتُمْ لَهَا عَاكِفُونَ"[2] وقوله ايْضا "وَقَالُوا لَا تَذَرُنَّ آلِهَتَكُمْ وَلَا تَذَرُنَّ وَدًّا وَلا سُوَاعًا وَلا يَغُوثَ وَيَعُوقَ وَنَسْرًا. وَقَدْ أَضَلُّوا كَثِيرًا ولا تَزِدِ الظَّالِمِينَ إلا ضَلالًا"[3] ولا يمكن ايْضا ان يقول احد ان سجودهم هذا ليس بعبادة لا[4] السجود لغير اللّه يقع بمجرد الايماءِ فضلا عن حكٍ[5] جبهته وانفه وفمه في الارض للصنم او للآلة او للصورة او للمطمورة او للجان اَمَا سمعت يا مسكين قصة برصيص العابد مع الشيطان والمعْلوم انه ما سجد بجبهته ولا بانفه ولا بفمه بل انَّمَا اَوْمَأَ ايماءً[6] فقط فكفر بذلك وقال عز من قايل في حقه "كَمَثَلِ الشَّيْطَانِ إِذْ قَالَ لِلإِنْسَانِ اكفُرْ فَلَمَّا كَفَرَ قَالَ إِنِّي بَرِيءٌ مِّنْكَ إِنِّي أَخَافُ اللَّهَ رَبَّ العَالَمِينَ. فَكَانَ عَاقِبَتَهُمَا أَنَّهُمَا فِي النَّارِ خَالِدَيْنِ فِيهَا وَذَلِكَ جَزَاءُ الظَّالِمِينَ"[7] واما قول بعضهم انما يعبدون الجان وذلك ليس بشرك فالقايل بذلك افترى الكذب fol. B وفضح نفسه بين الناس لانه علم الناس بكونه من جملة البهايم ويفرط بالكتاب والسنة والاجماع واين هذا مع قوْله عز من قايل "وَيَوْمَ نَحْشُرُهُمْ[8] جَمِيعاً ثُمَّ نَقُولُ[9] [لِلْمَلائِكَةِ] أَهَؤُلَاءِ إِيَّاكُمْ كَانُوا يَعْبُدُونَ. قَالُوا سُبْحَانَكَ أَنْتَ وَلِيُّنَا من دُونِهِمْ بَلْ كَانُوا يَعْبُدُونَ الجِنَّ أَكْثَرُهُمْ بِهِمْ مُّؤْمِنُونَ"[10] وقول بعضهم انَّما يعبدون مسْلمي الجان فهو على تقدير صحته اي دليل دل على اسلام ذلك الجان ومن اين وقع الاجتماع بين الجان وبين هؤلاء العبيد حتى ميَّزوا بين مسْلمي الجان وكفارهم وقدْ تعزر ذلك لعلماينا فضلا عن هؤلاء البهايم الذين لا يعرفون فرضا ولا سنة بل لا يعرفون اسماءهم سلمنا

[1] سورة الزمر، ١٧ [2] سورة الأنبياء، ٥٢ [3] سورة نوح، 32-٤٢ [4] هكذا جاءت في الأصل، والصواب "لأن" [5] هكذا جاءت في الأصل، والصواب حذف التنوين [6] هكذا جاءت في الأصل، والصواب "إيماءةً" [7] سورة الحشر، 61-١٧ [8] هكذا جاءت في الأصل، والصواب "يَحشُرُهُم" [9] هكذا جاءت في الأصل، والصواب "يَقُولُ" [10] سورة سبإ، 04-١٤

And Allah, the Blessed and Most High, has mentioned regarding idols and images: "What are these statues to which you are devoted?"[25] He also said, "And they [the unbelievers] said, 'Never leave your gods and never leave Wadd, nor Suwāʿ, nor Yagūth, nor Yaʿūq, nor Nasr.' And they have already misled many; And [my Lord], do not increase the wrongdoers except in error."[26]

Also no one can disavow that this prostration of theirs is not a [form of] worship because prostrating to anything besides Allah is nothing more than imitating [worship], let alone rubbing [their] forehead, nose, and mouth on the ground before these idols, instruments, images, *mattamores*, or jinn.

Have you not heard, O poor soul, the story of Barṣīṣ, the adorer of Satan? It is well known that he did not prostrate with his forehead, nose, or mouth, but merely gestured [thus] and became an unbeliever simply by that act. Allah, the Most Glorious, says in his matter: "[The hypocrites are like] the example of Satan when he says to man, 'Disbelieve.' But when he disbelieves, he [Satan] says, 'Indeed, I am disassociated from you. Indeed, I fear Allah, Lord of the Worlds.' So the outcome for both of them is that they will be in the fire, abiding eternally therein. And that is the recompense of the wrong-doers."[27]

As for those who avow that they are merely adoring the jinn and that is not polytheism, they have fabricated lies and exposed themselves to people, for they are beheld by mankind to be but beasts that neglect the Holy Book, the Sunna, and scholarly consensus (*ijmāʿ*). Those were mentioned by the Most Glorious: "One Day He will gather them all together, and say [to the angels], 'Did these [people] use to worship you?' They will say, 'Exalted are You! You [O Allah] are our benefactor not them. Rather, they used to worship the jinn; most of them were believers in them.'"[28]

Some also assert that they only worship Muslim jinn, and if so, what is the evidence that these jinn are really Muslims? And where did the jinn and these slaves meet, such that the latter could distinguish between Muslim and evil jinn? Such [a fact that Muslim jinn exist] has proven true for our learned scholars, to say nothing of these beasts who know not even a single obligatory act (*farḍ*), nor the recommended (*sunna*), let alone their own names. Let us

25 Quran 21:52.
26 Quran 71:23–24.
27 Quran 59:16–17.
28 Quran 34:40–41.

وجود الدليل على ذلك [[على ذلك]] لاكن [كذا] لا نسلم صحة عبادة الجان المسْلم
والا لجوزنا صحة عبادة الانبياء والملايكة والاولياء لان مسلمي الجان
ليسوا باعلا مرتبة من هؤلاء وان نقول ايضا بعدم شرك النصارى
وحينيذ بكفر صاحب هذا القول لتكذيبه الكتاب والسنة والاجماع امَّا الكتات[1]
فقوله تعلى "قُلْ يَا أَهْلَ الْكِتَابِ تَعَالَوا إلى كَلِمَةٍ سَوَاءٍ بَيْنَنَا وَبَيْنَكُمْ
أَن لَاَ نَعْبُدَ إِلاَّ اللّهَ وَلَا نُشْرِكُ بِهِ شَيئًا وَلا يَتَّخِذَ بَعْضُنا بَعْضًا أَرْبَابًا
مِنْ دُونِ اللَّهِ فَإِنْ تَوَلَّوْا فَقُولُوا اشْهَدُوا بِأَنَّا مُسْلِمُونَ".[2] واما السنة
ففي المسند وغيره ان معاذ رضي اللّه عنه لما رجع من الشام سجد للنبي
صلى اللّه عليه وسلم فقال ما هذا يا معاذ فقال يا رسول اللّه رايتهم
في الشام يسجدون لاساتذتهم ويذكرون ذلك عن انبيايهم فقال كذا
يا معاذ لو كنت امرا احدا ان يسجد لاحد لامرت المراة ان تسجد لزوْجها[3]
لعظم حقه عليْها يا معاذ ارايت لو مررت بقبري اكنت ساجدا[4] قال لا
قال لا تفعل ومثل هذا كثير من الآيات والاحاديث كقوله تعلى "اتَّخَذُوا fol. A
أَحْبَارَهُمْ وَرُهْبَانَهُمْ أَرْبَابًا من دُونِ اللَّهِ وَالْمَسِيحَ ابنَ مَرْيَمَ وَمَا أُمِرُوا إِلَّا
لِيَعْبُدُوا إِلهًا وَاحِدًا لاَ إِلهَ إِلَّا هُوَ سُبْحَانَهُ عَمَّا يُشْرِكُونَ"[5] وقوله ايضا "وإِذْ قَالَ
اللَّهُ يَا عِيسَى ابْنَ مَرِيَمَ ءأَنْتَ قُلْتَ للنَّاسِ اتَّخِذُونِي وَأُمِّيَ إِلَهيْنِ مِنْ
دُونِ اللَّهِ"[6] وحديث انقلاع الشجرة للنبي صلى اللّه عليه وسَلم[7] وَامَّا
الاجماع فلا سبيل للعلماء الى مخالفة ما ثبت في الكتاب والسنة وان لم
يصح العبادة للنبي وعيسى ابن مرْيم على نبينا وعليهما الصلاة والسلام

---

[1] هكذا جاءت في الأصل، والصواب "الكتاب" [2] سورة آل عمران، ٤٦ [3] كذا في هذا المخطوط. أما في المخطوط رقم ٣٦٥٩٠ والمخطوط رقم ٦٢٦٨١ فقد ورد "ببعلها" [4] مسند ابن ماجه، كتاب النكاح، 4: 3581 [5] سورة التوبة، ١٣ [6] سورة المائدة، ٦١١ [7] صحيح البخاري، ٣: ٤٣-٦٣

suppose that evidence exists for this [fact of having Muslim jinn], but we cannot accept worshiping them, otherwise, worshipping the prophets, angels, or even saints (*awliyā'*) would be valid, because the Muslim jinn are certainly not higher in rank than the latter group. Also, some say that the Christians are not polytheists, then those who utter such beliefs have left the pale [of Islam] for belying the Holy Book, the Sunna, and scholarly consensus.

As for the Book, it is the words of Allah, the Most High: "Say: 'O People of the Scripture, come to a word that is equitable between us and you—that we will worship none but Allah and associate no partners with Him, and that none of us shall take others as lords besides Allah.' If then they turn away, say: 'Bear witness that we are Muslims.'"[29]

As for the Sunna, it is reported in the *Musnad* [of Ibn Mājah] and other authoritative books [of hadith] that when Muʿādh, may Allah be pleased with him, returned from Damascus, he prostrated before the Prophet, may blessings and peace of Allah be upon him, and the Prophet astounded asked: "What is this, O Muʿādh?" He said: "Prophet of Allah, I saw them in Damascus prostrating themselves before theirs masters, mentioning this practice to be inherited from their prophets." So he [the Prophet] replied: "Do no such thing, Muʿādh! If I were to command anyone to prostrate before another, I would command a woman to prostrate before her husband, for the magnitude of his rights over her. Tell me, Muʿādh, if you were to pass by my grave, would you prostrate yourself before it?" He said: "No." The Prophet said: "Then do not do so [now]."[30] Examples of this sort abound in Quranic verses and hadith, such as the words of Allah, the Most High: "They have taken their scholars and monks as lords besides Allah, and [they have also taken as their lord] Christ, the son of Mary, while they were commanded to worship but one God, none has the right to be worshipped but He. Praise and glory be to Him";[31] "And [beware of the Day] when Allah will say: 'O Jesus, Son of Mary, did you say to the people, 'Take me and my mother as deities besides Allah'?'"[32] And the hadith of the tree which uprooted itself before the Prophet, blessings and peace of Allah be upon him.[33]

As for consensus, there are no means for scholars to oppose what has been firmly established in the Quran and Sunna. If it is not valid to prostrate before our Prophet or the prophet Jesus, Son of Mary, blessings and peace of Allah be

29 Quran 3:64.
30 *Musnad Ibn Mājah*, The Book of Wedding, chapter 4: 1853.
31 Quran 9:31.
32 Quran 5:116.
33 *Ṣaḥīḥ al-Bukhārī*, 3: 34–36.

وغيرهما فكيف يصح العبادة للجان فضلا للآلة والصور والمطامير
والمطمور لا يليق به العبادة بل انما يليق به ادِّخَارُ القمح والشعير
ونحوهما فيه تاللّه وباللّه وايم الله بيس[1] ما صنعتم يا يها [كذا] العبيد
اتعبدون ما تحفرون وتنحتون وتلعبون به وتعرضون عن العبادة
لمن خلقكم وما تعملون وصوركم فاحسن صوركم وقول بعضهم انَّ
اجابة الدعاء مجربة عند شَرْكِندَوَ وهو الصنم الذي في دار كوفة
جهل محض لان اللّه تبارك وتعالى يجيب الكافر والمومن [كذا] واجابته
~~للمومن~~ للكافر استدراج واجابته للمومن كرامة واعانة على الطاعة
الا ترى يا اخا الجهل والضلال اجابته لابليس اللعين ولولا الاجابة
التي زعموها عند الاصنام لما عبد كثير من كفار اهل الكتاب ومشركي
العرب الاصنامَ الا ترى يا احمق البشر ان قولك هذا هو قول المشركين
ولذلك الاستدراج قال خليل الرحمن عند قوله تعلى "وَاجْنُبْنِي وَبَنِيَّ
أَنْ نَعْبُدَ الأَصْنَامَ. رَبِّ إِنَّهُنَّ أَضْلَلْنَ كَثِيرًا من النَّاسِ فَمَنْ تَبِعَنِي فَإِنَّهُ مِنِّي"[2]
وَاعْلَمُوا يا ساداتي ان هذه الفتنة شرك محض لانهم لا يخلو امرهم امَّا ان
fol. B يقولوا ان هذه الصور والآلات والمطامير والجان نافعة لهم بدفع الضرر
عنهم وجلب الخير كما في زعمهم فيكون الامر واضحا لا يحتاج الى دليل
وامَّا ان يقولوا انهم يتوسلون بها الى اللّه فذلك قوله تعلى "مَا نَعْبُدُهُمْ
إِلَّا لِيُقَرِّبُونَا إِلَى اللَّهِ زُلْفَى"[3] وامَّا ان يقولوا ان هذه المذكورات لا ينفعون
ولا يضرون سواء قالوا مع ذلك انما افعالنا في هذا كله لطلب الفلوس
عند الناس اوْ لا فذلك قوله تعالى "هَلْ يَسْمَعُونَكُمْ إِذْ تَدْعُونَ. أَوْ يَنْفَعُو[4]
نَكُمْ أَوْ يَضُرُّونَ. قَالُوا بَلْ وَجَدْنَا آبَاءَنَا كَذَلِكَ يَفْعَلُونَ".[5] فان قال لي

[1] هكذا جاءت في الأصل، والصواب "بئس" [2] سورة إبراهيم، ٥٣–63 [3] سورة الزمر، ٣ [4] هكذا جاءت الكلمة في المصدر على سطرين [5] سورة الشعراء، 27–٤٧

upon them, or before others, then how can it be deemed correct to worship the jinn, let alone those instruments, images, or *mattamores*? Surely, *mattamores* are not to be worshipped, but instead used for storing wheat, barley, and the like! I utterly swear by Allah, evil indeed are the iniquities you have wrought, O slaves! Will you worship something you yourselves have carved and crafted and played with, turning away from He who created you and your handiwork, and who has bestowed upon you your forms in the most perfect of ways?

The belief by some of them that supplications are proven to be answered in the presence of Sarkin Gida—the idol held in Dār Kofa—is pure ignorance, because Allah, the Blessed and Most High, answers the supplications of unbelievers and believers alike. His answering the unbelievers is a form of delusion [to lead them further astray] (*istidrāj*), and answering the believers is a miraculous grace (*karāma*) and inspires them in obedience. Have you not considered—O you living in the depth of ignorance and misguidance—His answering the accursed Devil? Were it not for His answering of supplications, which they ascribed to their idols, most unbelievers of the People of the Book and the polytheists of the Arabs would not have worshipped them. Do you not see, O stupidest of mankind, that this statement of yours is the utterance of the polytheists? And it was because of this very same delusion (*istidrāj*) that the intimate friend of the Most Merciful [Abraham], upon him be peace, supplicated: "And keep me and my sons away from worshipping idols. My Lord, indeed they have led astray many among the people. So whoever follows me—then he is of me."[34]

A Refutation of the Wahhābis

And realize, O my masters, that this sedition is pure polytheism because (a) they [the slaves] persistently accept, in all their matters, that these images, instruments, *mattamores*, and jinn benefit them by warding off harm, and bringing about good, in which case the matter is clear without need for further proof; or (b) they believe that they are turning and begging to Allah through these [idols] (*tawassul*), which Allah, the Most High, mentions as saying: "We only worship them that they may bring us nearer to Allah in position";[35] or (c) they say that the above-mentioned practices neither harm nor benefit them. Whether this statement comes alone or followed by saying "we only do all these things to earn money from people," then Allah, the Most High, has answered them: "'Do they hear you when you supplicate? Or do they benefit you, or do they harm?' They said: 'But we found our fathers doing thus.'"[36]

---

34 Quran 14:35–36.

35 Quran 39:3.

36 Quran 26:72–74.

قايل استدلالك بقوله تعلى "مَا نَعْبُدُهُمْ إِلَّا لِيُقَرِّبُونَا إِلَى اللَّهِ زُلْفَى"[1] يدخل

فيه التوسل بالانبياء والملايكة والاوْلياء نقول له اعوذ باللّٰه

ان نقول مقالة الوهابين القايلين بكفر من توسل بهولاء[2] السادات

والفرق بينهما ظاهر لان الله تبارك وتعلى اثبت المعجزة للانبياء

والكرامة [و] للاولياء للملايكة وذلك ثابت لهم في حال حياتهم وبَعْد

مماتهم وهو تبارك وتعلى [[وهو تبارك وتعلى]] اكرم من ان يقطع معجزاتهم

وكراماتهم بالموت بل هم احياء عند ربهم وَأمَّا الصور والآلات

والمطامير فلو اثبت اللّٰه لهم الكرامة لما ابطل اللّٰه تبارك وتعلى حجة مشركي

العرب حين قال في حقهم "مَا نَعْبُدُهُمْ إِلَّا لِيُقَرِّبُونَا إِلَى اللَّهِ زُلْفَى" لان قصدهم

بعبادة الاصنام التوسل بها الى اللّٰه ولما جاز للنبي صلى اللّٰه عليه وسلم

محاربتهم لاجلها واما الجان فانهم ثبت الكرامة لمن اسلم منهم

وعمل صالحا لاكن [كذا] لا تصلح العبادة لمخلوق مع عدم معرفة فرق هؤلاء

بين مسلمين الجان وكفارهم لان العابد لا يستحق العبادة لان اللّٰه فرض

على الملايكة والجن والانس العبادة له كما قال جل وعلا "وَمَا خَلَقْتُ الجِنَّ

fol. A

وَالإِنْسَ إِلَّا لِيَعْبُدُون"[3] وقال في حق الملايكة "وَقَالُوا اتَّخَذَ الرَّحْمٰنُ وَلَدًا

سُبْحَانَهُ بَلْ عِبَادٌ مُكَرَمُونَ. لَا يَسْبِقُونَهُ بِالقَوْلِ وَهُمْ بِأَمْرِه يَعْمَلُونَ"[4] وكيف

نكفر المسلمين بالتوسل الشرعي مثل اللهم ارزقني كذا وكذا بجاه محمد اوْ

صحابي او ملك او ولي صلى اللّٰه عليه وعليْهم وسلم وتكفير الوهابي

---

[1] سورة الزمر، ٣   [2] هكذا جاءت في الأصل، والصواب "بهؤلاء"   [3] سورة الذّاريات، ٦٥   [4] سورة الأنبياء،

Now, if someone were to tell me, "Your use of the words of Allah, the Most High, 'We only worship them that they may bring us nearer to Allah in position' as evidence [of polytheism] includes asking Allah through the prophets, angels and saints (*awliyāʾ*)," I would respond that I seek refuge in Allah from the doctrine of the Wahhābis, who excommunicate anyone that asks Allah through these masters. The difference between these two matters is obvious because Allah, the Blessed and Most High, has established the existence of miracles (*muʿjizāt*, sing. *muʿjiza*) for the prophets, and preternatural phenomena (*karamāt*, sing. *karāma*) for the angels and saints. This is proven for them during their lives and even after their death. Allah, the Blessed and Most High, is too generous to end their miracles by death. Moreover, they [the prophets and saints] are alive in the presence of their Lord.

As for the images, instruments, and *mattamores*, if these were established as having preternatural phenomena, vouchsafed to them by Allah, the Blessed and Most High, He would not have rendered the evidence of the Arab polytheists to be falsehood when He mentioned their words: "We only worship them that they may bring us nearer to Allah in position"; for their intention in worshipping those idols was to turn to Allah through them. Nor would it have been lawful for the Prophet, blessings and peace of Allah be upon him, to combat them [the polytheists] because of their idols. As for the jinn, even if preternatural phenomena have been established for those of them who have embraced Islam, and who have only done righteous deeds, it is impermissible to worship a creature, not to mention that no one can tell whether they are really Muslim or not. Moreover, they themselves are obliged to worship [Allah] and do not deserve to be worshipped, for Allah has made it obligatory for the angels, jinn, and mankind to worship Him, as He, the Majestic and High, says: "I did not create the jinn and mankind except to worship Me."[37] And He said concerning the angels: "And they said: 'The Most Merciful has taken a son.' Exalted is He! Rather, they are [but] honored servants. They cannot precede Him in word, and they act by His command."[38]

So what right do we have to excommunicate Muslims because of their turning to Allah [through the prophets and saints] (*tawassul*), when it is legally permissible, for saying such things as: "O Lord! Provide me with such and such by the honor of Muhammad, blessings and peace of Allah be upon him, or the honor of one of his companions, or [a certain] angel or a saint"? The excommunication of people for this *tawassul* by the Wahhābis has no legal basis.

37 Quran 51:56.
38 Quran 21:26–27.

الناس بالتوسل [ليس] لهم فيه دليل شرعي وَقولهم جواز التوسل خاص بالحي الحاضر دون الميت والغايب يحتاج الى دليل شرعي يدل على خصوصيته بالحي الحاضر والظاهر عندي انهم خبطوا في هذه المسئلة خبْط عشوا [كذا] لانهم انما عللوا المنع في ذلك بجعل المتوسل واسطة بينه وبين ربه وذلك موجود في الحي الحاضر وان قالوا ان ذلك عبادة للميت وللغايب لان بعض الناس قد عبدوا موتاهم فذلك موجود في الحي الحاضر ايضا لان فرعون قد عبد في حال حياته وان قالوا ان التوسل بالحي قد ورد في الشرع دون الميت فنقول لهم ما نقل احد دليلا شرعيا على منع التوسل بالميت والغايب وان لم يرد المنع والجواز فليكن بدعة وان كان ذلك بدعة فما نقل عن احد من السلف الصالحين والخلف تكفير المومن بالبدعة ولنكتف بهذا في امر الوهابي ولنرجع الى ما هو المقْصود في هذا الكتاب وَقول بعضهم هذا لا يضر لانهم اعتقدوا فيها صوت خرج من الحمر الوحشية لان النبي صلى اللّه عليه وسلم ما ارسل الا لابطال الاعتقاد عن كل ما سوى اللّه وَقول بعضهم ايضا هذا لا يضر لانا لا نعرف اعتقادهم قول خرج من رجل ما علم شيْئا من الدين من يوم خرج من بطن امه لان الشرع لا يحكم عن الباطن بل انما يحكم على الظاهر ولولا ذلك لما قتل كثير من الاولياء والعلماء وَاعْلم يا يها[1] البليد ان الشرع لا يراعى الا القول والفعل وقد بان لك يا يها [كذا] اللبيب الماهر شرك هؤلاء العبيد وان قال لي قايل لاي شيء تسميهم العبيد وهم معتقون والمعتق حر قلت له لانهم رجعوا الى اصل الرِّق الذي هو الكفر غفر اللّه لنا ولكم سيئات اعمالنا ولا ردنا واياكم على اعقابنا بمحمد وءاله صلى اللّه عليه وعليهم وسلم. fol. B

[1] هكذا جاءت في المصدر، والصواب "يا أيها"

And their assertion that *tawassul* is only lawful through someone who is alive not dead, and who is present not absent, requires legal proof. What seems obvious to me is that they have proceeded haphazardly in this matter, because they justify this prohibition by restricting *tawassul* to he who makes it an intermediary between himself and his Lord, and this happens in the case of someone who is alive and present. If they claim that *tawassul* is a kind of worshipping the dead and absent because some people worshipped their dead, then that is equally applicable to the living and present, for Pharaoh was worshipped during his lifetime. If they maintain that making *tawassul* through the living is transmitted in the Sacred Law, to the exclusion of the dead, then our reply to them is that no one has transmitted any explicit legal proof for the prohibition of *tawassul* through the dead and absent. So if neither the prohibition nor the legal validity is transmitted, it would be a reprehensible innovation (*bidʿa*); and even if this were the case, then excommunicating a believer for committing an innovation is not something that has been transmitted from any of the righteous predecessors or those that came after. Let this be sufficient [discussion] on the question of the Wahhabis, and let us return to the [main] subject of this treatise.

∴

Some of them may argue that this [sedition] is not harmful if they merely believe in it, but such an opinion is [worth no more than] the braying of a wild ass, because the Prophet, blessings and peace of Allah be upon him, was only sent to abolish all beliefs other than in Allah. Others opine that "this is not harmful because we do not know anything about their religion," which is the utterance of someone who hasn't understood anything about the religion [of Islam] since the day he was born, because the Sacred Law does not judge the inward [states of people], but rather what is apparent [of their actions]. If the matter were otherwise, many of the saints and scholars would not have been murdered. Realize, O you of stupidity, that the Sacred Law considers only words and deeds. O skillful and intelligent, the polytheism of these slaves should now be plain to you. If someone were to say to me: "On what grounds do you term them [the Blacks of Tunis] 'slaves' when they are emancipated, and an emancipated person is free?" I would reply because they have returned to the source of slavery, which is unbelief. May Allah forgive us and you the evil of our deeds, and drive us not back to whence we came, by the honor of Muḥammad and his folk, blessings and peace of Allah be upon them all.

اَلْبَابُ الثَّالِثُ في ذِكْرِ صِفَةِ عِبَادَتِهِمْ

اِعْلَمْ اختصنا اللّه واياكم باحسن الاعمال ان صفة عبادتهم لا تنحصر ولا تعد ولاكن [كذا] اذكر منها بقدر علمي فاعلم ان اول ما رايت من ~~اول~~ عبادتهمْ اني كنت يوما جالسا في دار سُكَيْ[1] قبل الحج فاذا خادم دخلت عليَّ فلما وصلت الى البيت الذي فيه اصنامهم سجدت فلما رايتها تفعل ذلك تحير قلبي وقلت ما هذا وقال لي الناس هذه امهم اعْنِي العجوز التي يعبدونها واخذني في ذلك غم شديد وقالوا لي يوما قبل هذا اَمَا تزور امك فقلت اين هي فدلوني على موضع كانه قبر عليه ثياب وقلت في قلبي لعل هذا قبر امراة صالحة وفرحت بذلك وسرت حتى وقفت الى قرب ذلك الموضع وقرات ما تيسر من القرءان بنية الزيارة وانصرفت مسرورا ثمَّ التفت الي صاحبي ضاحكا وهو يعرف ما في الموضع من الفتنة وقال اتزور صنما قلت لا بل امراة صالحة وقال لا واللّه ما زرت الا صنما ثم اخبرني بحقيقة الامر ولمَّا رجعت من الحج جاءتني خادم وانا جالس في حانوت رجل من اهْل تنبكتُ وقالت لي هات الفلوس فقلت لها يا ابنتي ماذا تفعلين بالفلوس وقالت لي نريد ان نلعب عند العجوز تعني صنمهم فقلت لها لو كنتِ تمشين الى الجامع لاعطيتك الفلوس واما العجُوز فما اعْرفها ، فقالت نعم لانك تكبَّرت fol. A علينا ولولا تكبرك لعرفت العجوز لانهم كل من جاء من السودان ان لم يدخل معهم في عبادة ءالهتهم فلا بد لهم ان يخاصموه ويغضبوه ويحبسوه ان كان لهم حكم عليه انظر يا اخي الى هؤلاء القوْم ادعوهم الى الجامع وهم يدعونني الى الصنم كان هؤلاء هم الذين ذكرهم اللّه في كتابه حيث قال "وَيَقَوْمِ [كذا] مَا لِي أَدْعُوكُمْ إِلَى النَّجوةِ

---

[1] دار سونغاي

Chapter 3: Describing Their Worship

Realize, may Allah favor us all with the best of works, that the description of their worship is an inexhaustible subject, so I shall speak of only what I know. The first time I saw of their worship was when I was sitting one day at the Dār Sukay [Songhay] before going on hajj, when suddenly a slave woman entered and went to the room in which their idols were and prostrated. When I saw her do that I was perplexed, and I asked what was going on. People told me that the idol was their mother, namely, the old woman whom they worship. I was extremely troubled by this. One day before this incident they had said to me: "Will you not pay a visit to your mother?" And I said: "Where is she?" They directed me to a wrapped tomb, and I thought to myself that perhaps this is a tomb of a holy woman and was gladdened by that. I continued until I drew close to that place. There I recited some verses of the Quran with the intention of making the occasion of a visitation (*ziyāra*)[39] and went away happy. Then my companion turned to me laughing, for he was aware of the sedition that was in that place, and said, "Are you visiting an idol?" I retorted, "No. I am only visiting a holy woman." He said, "No, I swear by Allah. You visited nothing but an idol." Then he told me the true story.

When I came back from hajj, I was sitting in the shop of a man from Timbuktu when a slave woman came to me and said, "Give me some money." I said to her, "Young woman, what will you do with the money?" And she said, "I will go and play[40] at the place of the old woman," meaning their idol. I said to her, "If you were going to the mosque, I would give you money, but as for the old woman, I know her not." She said, "Yes [that is true], because you have been too haughty in her regard: were it not for this, you would have got to know her." For anyone who comes from the bilād al-Sūdān [the land of the blacks] and fails to join them in the worship of their gods will necessarily be shown hostility, hatred, and even imprisoned if it is within their jurisdiction.

Look, my brother, at these people: I call them to the mosque, and they are calling me to idols. They are like those whom Allah mentions in His book: "And O my people, how is it that I invite you to salvation while you invite me to

39 *Ziyāra* means visitation to a shrine of a saint or religious sanctuary (*mazār*). *Ziyāra* in this treatise refers specifically to the Bori pantheons. See Tremearne, *The Ban of the Bori*, 224–230; "Bori Beliefs and Ceremonies," 59–61.

40 "Play" here refers to the spectacle of the Bori ceremonies in the public arena, where Bori musicians entertained public gatherings. For a discussion of the Bori cult in a public setting, see Ferchioui, "The Possession Cults of Tunis," 1–40, and Juwaylī, *Mujtamaʿātun li-l-dhānira*.

وَتدْعُونَنَي إِلَى النَّارِ. تَدْعُونَنِي لأَكْفُرَ بِاللَّهِ وَأُشْرِكَ به مَا لَيْسَ لِي بِهِ عِلْمٌ وَأَنَا أَدْعُوكُمْ إِلَى العَزِيزِ الغَفَّارِ. لَا جَرَمَ أَنَّمَا تَدْعُونَنِي إِلَيْهِ لَيْسَ لَهُ دَعْوَةٌ فِي الدُّنْيَا وَلَا فِي الْآخِرَةِ وَأَنَّ مَرَدَّنَا إِلى اللَّهِ وَأَنَّ المُسْرِفِينَ هُمْ أَصْحَابُ النَّارِ. فَسَتَذْكُرُونَ مَا أَقُولُ لَكُمْ وَأُفَوِّضُ أَمْرِي إِلَى اللَّهِ إِنَّ اللَّهَ بَصِيرٌ بِالْعِبَادِ".[1] "أَفَغَيْرَ اللَّهِ تَأْمُرُونِّي أَعْبُدُ أَيُّهَا الجَاهِلُونَ"[2] ومن صفة عبادتهم ايضا انهم اذا ارادوا ان يعبدوا اصنامهم ياخذوا دجاجة حمراء او سوداء او بيضاء باختلاف اصنامهم ثم ياتون بحبوب الجلجلان ومعها غيرها من الحبوب ويبخرون الدجاجة ويوضئونها ويطعمونها بتلك الحبوب فان اكلت الحبوب زغرتوا ويكتفوا ايديهم من ورايهم ويسجدوا لآلهتهم ويزعمون ان ءالهتهم قد قبلت منهم الصدقة ورضيت بذلك وان [[~~ساءت~~]] لم تاكل ساءهم ذلك ويزعموا ان ءالهتهم ردت عليهم الصدقة وسخطت عليهم ويتذللوا لها ويقولوا يا ساداتنا ما لكم تسخطون علينا وما لكم لا تقبلون صدقتنا وان اكلت فعلوا كما تقدم من الصفة ثم يذبحونها بغير تسمية وربما ذبحوها من القفا ثم يشربون من دمها عند الذبح وان لم تاكل الدجاجة شيئا من الحبوب
بدلوا دجاجة اخرى ويزعموا ان ءالهتهم ما رضيت بتلك الصدقة وان جاء fol. B
مريض او صاحب حاجة عندهم لطلب صحة او قضاء حاجة يقولوا له هات دجاجة كذا وكذا ثم يفعلون له كما تقدم من الصفة ويدهنونه من الدم ان كان مريضا ثم يسجد المريض اوْ صاحب الحاجة لآلهتهم وان كان المسْئول خادما صاحبة جان فانه يسجد للجان الذين في راسها ثم يقولون له حاجتك تقضى ويامرونه بان يذبح لآلهتهم في كل سنة في مثل ذلك اليوم وياخذون ماله في كل سنة وربما افتقر لذلك ومن صفة عبادتهم ايضا انهم يذبحون للمطامير في راس كل سنة واما الزيارة ففي كل جمعة ويكون ذلك بذبح وبغيره وان ذبحوا للمطامير اكلوا من اللحم بقدر طاقتهم ثم

[1] سورة غافر، 14–٤٤ [2] سورة الزمر، ٤٦

hell? You invite me to disbelieve in Allah and associate with Him that of which I have no knowledge, and I invite you to the Exalted in Might, the Perpetual Forgiver. Assuredly, that to which you invite me has no [response to a] supplication in this world or in the hereafter; and indeed, our return is to Allah, and indeed, the transgressors will be the dwellers of the fire. And you will remember what I [now] say to you, and I entrust my affair to Allah. Indeed, Allah is seeing of [His] servants."[41] "Say [O Muḥammad]: 'Is it other than Allah that you order me to worship, O ignorant ones?' "[42]

Another aspect of their worship is that when they are worshipping their idols, they take a hen, either red, black, or white, according to each idol's characteristics, bring coriander seeds and other grains, burn incense around it and cleanse it, and then feed those grains to the hen. If it eats the grains they ululate and place their hands in a begging position behind them, prostrating to their gods, and believe that they have accepted their offering and are pleased with it. If, however, the hen does not eat the grains, they take it ill and believe that their gods have rejected their offering and are wroth with them. Then they humble themselves before them and say: "O our masters, why is it that you are angry with us? Why is it that you do not accept our offering?" If the hen then eats, they do as was described above. After this they slaughter it without invoking Allah's name; sometimes they slaughter it by cutting the nape of the neck. At the time of slaughtering, they drink its blood.[43] If the hen refuses to eat altogether, they bring another one and claim that their gods were not satisfied with that [first] offering.

If a sick person or one in need comes seeking health or the fulfilment of a need, they tell him to bring a hen of such and such type, then they do with it as was described above and rub the person over with the blood if he is sick. The sick or needy then prostrates to their gods. If the one in charge of the ceremony is a slave woman who is possessed by the jinn, the sick or needy prostrates to the jinn, who is in her head. Then they say to him: "Your requests are granted," and they order him to offer a sacrifice to their gods every year on the same day. And every year they take from him what he has [of financial means], and he may well grow poor as a result.

Another aspect of their worship is their sacrificial slaughter to the *mattamores* at the beginning of every year. They make pious devotions, in the occasion of their visitation every Friday, which also involve slaughtering and other practices. If they offer a sacrifice to the *mattamore*, they eat as much of

41 Quran 40:41–44.
42 Quran 39:64.
43 See Tremearne, *The Ban of the Bori*, 72, 199, and 261.

يردمون البقية من اللحم والعظام في المطامير ولا يكسرون شيئًا من العظام
ولا يدخل احد معهم في ذلك الموضع الا بالطهارة ومع ذلك لا ترى احدا منهم
راكعا اوساجدا ابدا الا لامريْن اما لرفع شيء من الارْض او سجود للصَّنم
ومن عبادتهم ايضا انهم يوقدون النار في تلك المطامير جميع اليل [كذا]
دايما لا جرم ان فيهم نوعا من السحر الا ترى انهم يطعنون بطونهم
وجباههم بالسكاكين عند عبادتهم للجان ويزعمون ان الحديد
لا يدخل في بطونهم وَلعمري لو جعلوا السكين في يدي لطعنت بها
في بطونهم حتى تخرج من ظهورهم وهذا نوع من السحر زايد على كفرهمْ
ومن عبادتهم ايضا انهم يذبحون للشياطين في ءاخر شعبان ويزعمون
انهم ان لم يذبحوا لهم فانهم يهربون عن رءوسهم [كذا] انظر هذا كله مع منعه
تبارك وتعالى عن اتخاذ الشياطين اولياء من دُونِهِ اللّه وقال عز من
قايل "يَا أَبَتِ لَا تَعْبُدِ الشَّيْطَانَ إِنَّ الشَّيْطَانَ كانَ للرَّحمَنِ عَصِيًّا"[١] وقال ايضا
fol. A "إِنَّ الشَّيْطَانَ لَكُمْ عَدُوٌّ فاتَّخِذُوهُ عَدُوًّا إِنَّمَا يَدْعُوا[٢] حِزْبَهُ لِيَكُونُوا
مِنْ أَصْحَابِ السَّعِيرِ"[٣] وقال ايْضا "يَا أَيُّهَا الذين آمَنُوا لَا تَتَّخِذُوا عَدُوِّي
وَعَدُوَّكُمْ أَوْلِيَاءَ" الاية[٤]، هذا كله وقع عليهم لتركهمْ ما فرض اللّه عليهم
من الصلوات الخمس وغيرها وذلك قوله تعلى "وَمَنْ يَعْشُ عَنْ ذِكْرِ
الرَّحمَنِ نُقَيِّضْ لَهُ شَيْطَانًا فَهُوَ لَهُ قَرِينٌ. وَإِنَّهُمْ لَيَصُدُّونَهُم عَنِ
السَّبِيلِ وَيَحْسَبُونَ أَنَّهُم مُّهْتَدُونَ. حَتَّى إِذَا جَاءَنَا قَالَ يَا لَيْتَ بَيْنِي
وَبَيْنَكَ بُعْدَ المَشْرِقَينِ فَبِئْسَ القَرينُ. وَلَنْ يَنْفَعَكُمُ اليَوْمَ إِذْ ظَلَّمْتُم
أَنَّكُمْ فِي العَذَابِ مُشْتَرِكُونَ"[٥] أفَأَنْتَ [كذا] ومن عبادتهم انهم يقولون
عند سجودهم كل من قال غير هذا يعنون بذلك ءالهتهمْ فهو
كاذب ويقولون عند سؤالهم لآلهتهم ان شاء من في السماء وشاء

[١] سورة مريم، 44 [٢] هكذا جاءت في الأصل، والصواب "يدعو" [٣] سورة فاطر، ٦ [٤] سورة الممتحنة، ١
[٥] سورة الزخرف، 63–93

the meat as they can, then they bury the rest of it in the *mattamore*, but without breaking any of the bones. No one may enter that place with them unless he is in a state of ritual purity—despite which, you never see any of them bowing or prostrating except for two reasons: to pick up something from the ground or to prostrate to an idol.[44]

In addition, they light fires in those *mattamores* for the entire night, undoubtedly for some kind of sorcery. Do you not see them practice mortification of the flesh, piercing their abdomens and foreheads with knives, when worshipping the jinn, and maintaining that the blade doesn't enter their abdomens? I swear by my life, were they to put a knife in my hand, I would plunge it into their abdomens until it came out of their backs. This is a form of sorcery that extends beyond their unbelief.

Another aspect of their worship involves making sacrificial slaughter to the devils at the end of Shaʿbān, asserting that if they did not do so, the jinn would flee from their heads. Look at all of this, which is in spite of Allah, the Most High, having forbidden the taking of devils as one's patrons without Him. He says [relating the words of Abraham]: "O my father, do not worship Satan. Indeed, Satan has ever been, to the Most Merciful, disobedient."[45] Allah also says: "Indeed, Satan is an enemy to you; so take him as an enemy. He only invites his party to be among the dwellers of the blaze."[46] And He says, "O you who have believed, do not take My enemies and your enemies as allies ..."[47] All this has befallen upon them because they abandoned the five [daily] prayers, and other acts, which Allah ordained upon them. And that is found in His saying, "And whoever is blinded from remembrance of the Most Merciful—We appoint for him a devil, and he is to him a companion. And Indeed, they (devils) hinder them from the Path (of Allah), but they think they are being guided aright! Till, when (such a one) comes to Us, he says (to his devil companion), 'Would that between me and you were the distance of East and West!' Ah! The worst companion (indeed)! When you have done wrong, it will avail you nothing, that Day, that you shall be partners in the punishment."[48]

Another aspect of their worship is that, when prostrating before their gods, they say that whoever holds an opinion contrary to theirs, namely, against their gods, is a liar. When asking their gods for something, they say: "If those who are

44 i.e., they never bow to Allah as part of their worship.
45 Quran 19:44.
46 Quran 35:6.
47 Quran 60:1.
48 Quran 43:36–39.

من في الارض ومرادهم من في الارض ءالهتهم والله اعلم بمرادهمْ
بمن في السماء ولا يختلف اثنان في كون هذا كفر صريح وكيف لا وقد
قال النبي المختار صلى الله عليه وسلم لمن قال له ما شاء اللّه وشيت[١]
اجعلتني نِدّاً بل ما شاء اللّه وحده وقال لاصحابه لا تقولوا ما شاء
اللّه وشاء محمد ولاكن [كذا] قولوا ما شاء اللّه ثم شاء محمد[٢] ومن عبادتهم
ايضا انهم يشربون الدماء عند ذبحهم لآلهتهم ويزعمون ان الجان
هم الذين يشربون ذلك الدم ولو لم يكن غير في هذه الفتنة غير
هذا الموجب غير هذا تغييرها لحرمة الدم الخارجة عند الذبح لقوله تعلى
"إِنَّمَا حَرَّمَ عَلَيْكُمُ المَيْتَةَ والدَّم وَلَحْمَ الخِنزِيرِ وَمَا أُهِلَّ [به] لِغَيْرِ اللَّهِ"[٣] يايها [كذا] المكلف
بتغيير هذا المنكر لا تسمع قول من يقول لك هذا امر قديم وهذا عمل
عبيد ما لك فيه حاجة وهذا لعب محض لان القايل بهذا اشد ضررا في الدين
fol. B من الشيطان ولا تتبع هذا القول واسمع قول اللّه عز وجل "يَا أَيُّهَا الذِينَ
آمَنُوا لَا تَتَّبِعُوا خُطُوَاتِ الشَّيْطَانِ ومَن يَتَّبِع خُطُوَاتِ الشَّيْطَانِ
فَإِنَّهُ يَأْمُرُ بِالفَحْشَاءِ والمُنكَرِ"[٤] وَلا يغرنكم يا اخواني قولهم الصالحين
لان ذلك تلبيس على المسلمين لان مرادهم بالصالحين بُورِي وذلك
اسم للجان الذين يعبدونهم وَلعمري ان هؤلاء زين لهم الشيطان
اعمالهم واعتقدوا ان اعمالهم من احسن الاعْمال كما قال اللّه تبارك
وتعلى في حقهم "أفَمَن زُيِّنَ لَهُ سُوءُ عَمَلِهِ فَرَآهُ حَسَنًا فَإِنَّ اللَّهَ يُضِلُّ
مَن يَشَاءُ وَيَهدِي مَن يَشَاءُ" الآية[٥] يا يها[٦] المنادي بتغيير هذا
المنكر فاعلم انك مسئول عنه يوم القيامة لقول النبي صلى اللّه عليه
وسلم كلكم راع وكلكم مسئول عن رعيته.[٧] وَواجب على كل مومن

[١] هكذا جاءت في الأصل، والصواب "وشئت" [٢] سنن إبن ماجه، ١: ٤٨٦-٥٨ [٣] سورة البقرة، ٣٧١
[٤] سورة النور، ١٢ [٥] سورة فاطر، 8 [٦] هكذا جاءت في الأصل، والصواب "يا أيها" [٧] صحيح البخاري، 11:

in heaven and those who are on earth will it," meaning by "those who are on earth" their gods. And Allah knows what they mean by "those who are in heaven." There is no question as to this practice constituting open unbelief (*kufr*). How can it be otherwise, for when someone addressed the Prophet, blessings and peace of Allah be upon him, with the words "Whatever Allah wills and you will," he replied, "Are you making me an equal with Allah? Instead say: 'Whatever Allah alone wills!'" He also said to his companions: "Do not say 'Whatever Allah and Muḥammad will,' but say: 'Whatever Allah wills, then Muḥammad wills.'"[49]

Another aspect of their worship involves drinking the blood [of the sacrificial animal] when making offerings to their gods, maintaining that it is, in fact, the jinn who drink that blood. Even if there was nothing more to their sedition than this, it would be enough to have it done away with, in view of the unlawfulness of consuming flowing blood from a sacrificial animal. For Allah, the Most High, says: "He has only forbidden you dead animals, blood, the flesh of swine, and that which has been dedicated to other than Allah."[50]

O you who are responsible for changing this evil, listen not to those who may tell you: "This is a time-honored custom, and the slaves have a right to do it. It is mere play!" For he who says this is more of a detriment to the religion than the Devil. Do not follow such speech but listen to the words of Allah, the Mighty and Majestic: "O you who have believed, do not follow the footsteps of Satan. And whoever follows the footsteps of Satan—indeed, he enjoins immorality and wrongdoing."[51] And do not, my brothers, let their use of the word "righteous" (*al-ṣāliḥīn*) fool you. For they are but confusing the Muslims, as what they mean by "righteous" is the Bori, which is a name of the jinn they worship. I swear upon my life, the Devil has decked out fair for their [slaves] deeds, and they think that they are doing the most excellent of works, as Allah, the Blessed and Most High, says about them: "Then is the one whom the evil of his deed has been made attractive so he considers it good [like one rightly guided]? For indeed, Allah sends astray whom He wills and guides whom He wills."[52]

O you calling for preventing this evil, realize that you shall be responsible for it on the Day of Judgement, for the Prophet, blessings and peace of Allah be upon him, has said: "Indeed, each of you is a guardian and every guardian

49 *Sunan Ibn-Maja*, 1: 684–685.

50 Quran 2:173.

51 Quran 24:21.

52 Quran 35:8.

منع ولده وزوجته وخادمه ومن تحت رعيته عن مشاهدة هذه
الفتنة فضلا عن الفعل به لانه مامور بحفظ ما رعاه عن الهلاك
في الكتاب والسنة والاجما ع اَمَّا الكتاب فقوله تعلى "يا أَيُّهَا
الذِينَ آمَنُوا قُوا أَنفُسَكُم وأَهلِيكُمْ نَارًا"[١] وَاَمَّا الحديث فللحديث
المتقدم وَاَمَّا الاجما ع فالعلماء متفقون على ذلك والسلطان
يسْئل عن جميع ما يحكم فيه والرجل يسْئل عن اهل بيته والعلماء
يسلون [كذا] عن ابلا غ المناكر للامراء لانفرادهم بمعرفة [الفرق] بين المعروف
والمنكر وصاروا رعاة لذلك ءاه على نفسي كيف لا يجب المبادرة الى
هذه الفتنة وهي فتنة يخاف وقوع عذابها على جميع من فعل ومن
لم يفعل لان عقوبة المعْصية اذا نزلت لا تختص بالفاعل فقط
كما قال تبارك وتعلى "وَاتَقُوا فِتْنَةً لَا تُصِيبَنَّ الذِينَ ظَلَمُوا مِنْكُمْ خَاصَّةً
وَاعْلَمُوا أَنَّ اللَّه شَدِيدُ العِقَابِ"[٢] ولو لم تكن اعمالهم هذه شركا على التقدير fol. A
الفاسد لوجب منعها لانها ذات ما يفعله كفار اهل السودان
وَمعلوم ضرورة ان المسلم يرتد بمجرد فعله ما يخص الكافر كلبس
الزنار مثلا ان اختص به وكيف لا يجب منع مشابهة الكفار وقد
مُنِعْنا من السجود في صلاة الجنازة لقطع حجة اعداء الدين يوم القيامة
ليلا[٣] يقولوا اذ يقال لهم لِمَ عبدتم الاصنام من دون اللّه انَّا
عبدناهم كما ان المسلمين كانوا يعبدون الموتى فرفع اللّه السجود
منها لذلك سدا للذريعة يا يها [كذا] العبيد على م[٤] تشركون باللّه
بعد ان قال اللّه تبارك وتعلى حكاية عن لقمان "يَا بُنَيَّ لَا تُشْرِكْ بِاللهِ

[١] سورة التحريم، 6 [٢] سورة الأنفال، ٥٢ [٣] هكذا جاءت في الأصل، والصواب "لئلا" [٤] هكذا جاءت في الأصل، والصواب "علام"

is responsible for his charge."[53] It is compulsory upon every believer to prevent his son, wife, servant, or anyone under his guardianship from observing—let alone taking part in—this sedition. For he is responsible for protecting those under his care from destruction, according to the Quran, Sunna, and scholarly consensus. As for the Quran, Allah, the Most High, says: "O you who have believed, protect yourselves and your families from a fire …"[54] As for evidence from hadith, then see the above-mentioned [hadith on guardianship]. As for consensus, the scholars are in complete agreement about this point: the ruler is responsible for all who are under his reign; the man is responsible for the members of his household; and the scholars are responsible for reporting social evils to the rulers because they alone are able to distinguish between the good and the wrong, and have become guardians thereof. Woe unto myself, how can this sedition be avoided when its punishment is feared to befall everyone—whether or not they practiced it! Because when punishment for sin descends, it doesn't single out the perpetrator alone, as Allah, the Blessed and Most High, says: "And fear a trial which will not strike those who have wronged among you exclusively, and know that Allah is severe in punishment."[55]

Even if we suppose that these practices do not amount to polytheism, but mere immorality, it would still be obligatory to prevent them, because they entirely resemble the practice of the unbelievers of the bilād al-Sūdān (the Land of the Blacks). Moreover, it is necessarily known of the religion that a Muslim may apostate simply by imitating practices that are specific to the unbelievers, such as wearing a monk's girdle (*zunnār*),[56] which is common to the unbelievers. Then why would it not be incumbent to prevent Muslim from resembling the unbelievers, when Allah has forbidden us from prostration in funeral prayers to disprove the opinion of the enemies of the religion who, when they will be asked on the Day of Judgement: "Why ever did you worship idols besides Allah?" cannot respond: "We did so just as the Muslims worshipped the dead." So Allah removed prostration from funeral prayers to block the means [to such arguments].

O you slaves, how on earth can you ascribe partners to Allah after He, the Blessed and Most High, has said, narrating the words of Luqmān: "O my son,

---

53 *Ṣaḥīḥ al-Bukhārī*, 11: 18.

54 Quran 66:6.

55 Quran 8:25.

56 *Zunnār* (pl. *zanānīr*) is a rope worn around the waist in Bori ceremonies. It is tied around the hip of a man or a woman with magic decorations and worn during religious performances, particularly during the trance-induced performance that takes places after midnight.

إِنَّ الشِّرْكَ لَظُلْمٌ عَظِيمٌ"[1] وقال ايضا "وَمَنْ يُشْرِكْ بِاللهِ فَكَأَنَّمَا خَرَّ مِنَ السَّمَاءِ فَتَخْطَفُهُ الطَّيْرُ أَوْ تَهْوِي بِهِ الرِّيحُ فِي مَكَانٍ سَحِيقٍ".[2] يا اخواني فاسمعوا قوْلي وكونوا كما قال اللّه تبارك وتعلى "إِنَّمَا كَانَ قَوْلَ الْمُؤْمِنِينَ إِذَا دُعُوا إِلَى اللَّهِ وَرَسُولِهِ لِيَحْكُمَ بَيْنَهُمْ أَنْ يَقُولُوا سَمِعْنَا وَأَطَعْنَا وَأُوْلَئِكَ هُمُ الْمُفْلِحُونَ"[3] انما هذه نصيحة لكم لان النصيحة من الدين لقول النبي صلى اللّه عليه وسلم إنما الدين النصيحة الحديث[4] ولاكن لا تسمعون قولي ولا يسمع قولي منكم الا من اراد اللّه به خيرا لقوله تبارك وتعلى "إِنَّكَ لَا تَهْدِي مَنْ أَحْبَبْت، وَلَكِنَّ اللَّهَ يَهْدِي مَنْ يَشَاءُ وَهُوَ أَعْلَمُ بِالْمُهْتَدِينَ"[5] ولعمري اذا ارايت هؤلاء العبيد ما تحسبهم الا مومنين مخلصين كلا بل قلوبهم خالية عن [كذا] الايمان كما قال علام الغيوب "وَإِذَا رَأَيْتَهُمْ تُعْجِبُكَ أَجْسَامُهُمْ وإِنْ يَقُولُوا تَسْمَعْ لِقَوْلِهِمْ كَأَنَّهُمْ خُشُبٌ مُسَنَّدَةٌ"[6] جعلنا اللّه واياكم من الذين
fol. B اراد اللّه بهم الخير بجاه سيد ولد عدنان صلى اللّه عليه وءاله وسلم تسْليما

خَاتِمَةٌ اعلم ختم اللّه لنا ولك بكلمتي الشهادة عند الموت ناطقين بها وان كل ما ذكرت لك من الصور والآلات والمطامير والجان لا يستحق العبادة بل ان هؤلاء ختم اللّه على سمعهم وعلى قلوبهم وجعل على ابْصارهم غشاوة ولولا ذلك لما عبدوا هذه المذكورات بل هي بالاهانة احق وبان تهجر اوفق ولذلك انشات اقول مهاونا لآلهتهم

[1] سورة لقمان، ٣١ [2] سورة الحج، ١٣ [3] سورة النور، ١٥ [4] سنن النسائي، كتاب البيعة: 7914 [5] سورة القصص، ٦٥ [6] سورة المنافقون، ٤

do not associate [anything] with Allah. Indeed, association [with Him] is great injustice"?[57] He also said: "And he who associates [anything] with Allah—it is as though he had fallen from the sky and was snatched by the birds or the wind carried him down into a remote place."[58]

O my brothers, take heed of my advice and be as Allah, the Blessed and Most High, has described: "The only statement of the [true] believers when they are called to Allah and His messenger to judge between them is that they say: 'We hear and we obey.' And such are the prosperous ones."[59] Verily, this is sincere advice for you, because advice is a part of the religion. For the Prophet, blessings and peace of Allah be upon him, said: "The religion itself is but sincere advice."[60] However, none of you shall heed my advice save those whom Allah wishes good for, in view of His having said: "Indeed, [O Muḥammad,] you do not guide whom you like, but Allah guides whom He wills. And He is most knowing of the [rightly] guided."[61]

I swear upon my life, when you behold these slaves, you would not perceive them save as true believers. Nay! Their hearts are bereft of faith, as the Knower of the Unseen has said: "And when you see them, their forms please you, and if they speak, you listen to their speech. [They are] as if they were pieces of wood propped up …"[62]

May Allah make us and you among those whom He wills good for, through the rank of my master [Muḥammad], the son of 'Adnān, all blessings and peace of Allah be upon him and his folk.

Conclusion

Realize, may Allah end our lives uttering the Two Testimonies of Faith, that all of what I have described to you, of sculptures, instruments, *mattamores*, and jinn, is not worthy of worship. Rather, Allah has set a seal upon their [slaves] ears and hearts, and veiled their eyes—otherwise, they would never have worshipped these things. These objects deserve to be disdained and abandoned, for which reason, I composed the following verses, disdaining their gods:

57 Quran 31:13.
58 Quran 22:31.
59 Quran 24:51.
60 *Sunan an-Nasa'i*, The Book of Bay'ah, 4197.
61 Quran 28:56.
62 Quran 63:4.

لرَبٍّ ينقى كل وقت من القذا * لقد ذل من بالعيب يوصف دايما
لقد هان معبود يلطخ بالدما * ويعطي حبوب الجلجلان واعظما
لقد صَغُر المعبود ليس مقره * سوى راس مخلوق أَعف وأَظلما

وَقولنا لرب ينقى الخ صفة للمطْمور وَقولنا يلطخ بالدما [كذا] صفة للآلات والصور التي يلطخونها بالدم وَكذلك قولنا ويعطى الخ وَقولنا واعظما صفة للمطمور ايضا لانهم يردمون العظام فيها وَقولنا لقد صغر المعبود الخ صفة للجان الذين يزعمون انهم في رءوسهم [كذا] ويعبدونهم يا يها الامير الاسعد اعلم انه ليس في بلاد المسْلمين كافة حبْس محبس للصنم وعدم ذلك في بلادك اوْلى واليق لكثرة مدح الناس لك وثنايهم [كذا] عليْك بالخير خصوصا على منابر المسلمين سدد اللّه امرنا وامرك فاعلم ايضا يا سيدي تاللّه وباللّه وايم اللّه ان تغييرك هذا المنكر اعظم لك اجرا من بناء الف مسجد والف مدرسة واعطايك كل يوم الف دينار للمساكين ومجاهدتك النصارى وكيف لا يكون هذا اعظم اجرا من بناء المساجد وما والاه وحفظ ايمان المسلم واجب اكد من غيره واما الجهاد في سبيل اللّه فهو وان كان من ادخال الايمان في قلوب الكفار وهو من اعظم العبادات لاكن حفظ الدار العامرة اهم من تعمير الخالية fol. A
ولا يخفى عليك ان هذا المنكر قد شاع وعمت به البلوى الا ترى يا اميرنا ان كثيرا من نساء المسْلمين دخلت معهم في هذا المنكر ولا يقدر ازواجهم[1] عليهن شيْئا لانه لا يخفى عليك ان رجال هذا الزمان تحت ايدي نسايهم هذا من اعظم الفتن ايضا وَلعل هؤلاء الرجال ما سمعوا الحديث لن يفلح قوم ولوا [عليهم] امراة[2] والا ترى ايضا يا سيدي ان ضعفاء الرجال دخل معهم في هذا المنكر ايضا يا سيدي اما رايت هؤلاء العبيد قد ضلوا واضلوا وهلكوا واهلكوا واكلوا اموال بلادك ظلما وزورا والا ترى انهم ياخذون اموالا لا تحصى ولا تعد في ايدي النساء لعبادة الجان والمساحقة ودخلت نساء المسلمين يسرقن اموال ازواجهم (كذا) لانفاقها

[1] هكذا جاءت في الأصل: والصواب "أزواجهن" [2] صحيح البخاري، كتاب المغازي: 28

A lord in constant need of cleaning from impurities,
Forever described as contemptible in its shame.
Despicably worshipped and sullied with blood,
Offered coriander seeds and bones.
How lowly the object of their worship,
Dwelling in the head of its creation—shameful and dark.

The verse "A lord in constant need" describes the *mattamore*, and "sullied with blood", the instruments and idols they stain with blood. Likewise, "Offered … bones" also describes the *mattamores*, which they fill with bones. The [final] verse on "How lowly the object" describes the jinn whom they worship and believe reside in their heads.

O most auspicious prince, know that there is not to be found in all the lands of Islam a *habous* dedicated to idols. How much more fitting is it, then, that such a thing should be absent from your land, since people praise and laud you for your good deeds, especially so from the pulpits of the Muslims, may Allah guide our matters and yours. Know also, my master, that, by Allah, doing away with this reprehensible business will bring greater [divine] reward than building a thousand mosques and a thousand schools, giving away a thousand dinars a day to the poor, and waging jihad against the Christians. And how should the matter be otherwise, when preserving the faith of Muslims is more obligatory than anything besides? As for Jihad for the sake of Allah, if it involves spreading true faith into the hearts of the unbelievers, then it is amongst the greatest acts of worship; however, preserving an inhabited house is worthier than populating an empty one. It cannot be lost on you that this evil practice has become rife and a widespread calamity.

Do you not see, O our prince, that many Muslim women have entered with them into this reprehensible practice, while their husbands stand idly by? For it is no secret that the men of this age are under the thumbs of their womenfolk, and this, too, is of the greatest seditions. Perhaps these men have not heard of the hadith: "A people governed by a woman shall never prosper."[63] And do you not also see, my master, that the weakest of these men enter into these evil practices with them?

My master, have you not seen how the behavior of these slaves leads them astray and causes others to be led astray, and will destroy them and others, and will devour the wealth of your land unjustly and falsely? Do you not see that they take uncountable sums of money at the hands of women for the worship of jinn and for acts of lesbianism? Muslim women have begun to steal money

63 *Ṣaḥīḥ al-Bukhārī*, On Military Expeditions, 82.

في لعب عبادة الاصنام والمساحقة والا ترى ان النساء قد استغنيْن
عن الرجال بالخدم والا ترى ان كل من اعتقت من الخدم اذا كانت
جميلة او صاحبة مال لا يقدر احد ان يتزوجها ولا يتزوجها اِلَّا بُورِي
حتى تاخذ الخدم مالها ان كان لها مال او يجعلْنها زوجة ان كانت
جميلة وَان ارادت ان تتزوج يقلن لها انكِ زوجتك [كذا] بُورِي وهو
الجان الذي في رءوسهن وَان ابت قولهنَّ فانهن يبلغن امرها او امْرَ
من اراد ان يتزوجها من الرجال لقيادهن ثم يامر القياد
بحبسهما واكل مالهما ملا اللّه بطونهم نارا هذا كله من اجل
هذه الفتنة اِيَّاكم يا اخواني ان تاكلوا ما ذبحوا لآلهتهم لانه جيفة
لانهم لا يسمون فيه اسم اللّه عند الذبح ولا يغرنكم قولهم بانهم يسمون
اللّه فيه لان صدقتهم للشيطَان والشيطان لا يقبل ما ذكر فيه اسْم اللّه
fol. B في زعمهم وهو موافق للعقل لان الشيطان عدو اللّه والعدو الكامل
في العداوة لا يقبل شيْئا مما فيه شان عدوه انظروا يا اخواني
ما صنعوا المسلمين (كذا) من الغرور كاليهود حيث اطعموهم الجيفة خيانة
وَمكرا كفانا اللّه من شرهم يا سيدنا ان لم تقم بتغيير هذا المنكر فلا
يقوم احد به في زمانك فضلا عن من بعْدك لانه قل ان يوجد
مثلك بعدك وَلذلك ندعوا لك بطول العمر في طاعة اللّه وطاعة
رسوله واذا عرفت هذا فَواجب عليك وجوبا فرضا يا يها الامير
ان تاخذ دار كوفة اما ان تبنيها جامعا كما كان النبي صلى اللّه عليْه
وسلم يفعل بكل كنيسة اذا فتح بلاد اهل الشرك او مدرسة
لطلب العلم او وكالة لعسكر المومنين الذين يجاهدون في سبيل اللّه.
لانه لا يصح ان يحبس دار وغيرها لعبادة الاصنام ليعبدوا ءالهتهم
فيها وواجب عليك ايضا ان تاخذ كل صنم من دار كوفة ومن كل دار
من ديار جماعتهم وتحرقها بالنار وَان تهد جميع المطامير التي في ديارهم
وَان تجعل مناديا ينادي في بلدك ان كل من رءا[1] الخدم يلعبن مجتمعات

[1] هكذا جاءت في الأصل، والصواب "رأى"

from their husbands to pay for such acts. Do you not see how women give up men for servants? Do you not see that every slave woman who is emancipated, if she is beautiful or wealthy, no one may marry her except the Bori, who is the jinn that resides in their heads? If she rejects what they say, they will report her case, or that of any man wishing to marry her, to their leaders, who will order them to be imprisoned and their fortune seized. May Allah fill their bellies with fire!

All of it is because of this sedition. O brethren, beware of eating what they have slaughtered to their gods, for it is a carcass, and they mention not the name of Allah when slaughtering—and let not their words to the contrary deceive you, for their "charity" is offered to the Devil, who, according to their belief, does not accept anything that has had the name of Allah recited over it. This makes perfect sense, because Satan is the enemy of Allah, and the deadly enemy does not accept anything related to his enemy.

Behold, our brothers, how vanity made Muslims no different from the Jews, when they fed them[64] carrion, out of treachery and cunning, may Allah protect us all from their evil.

O our lord, if you do not do away with this reprehensible evil, no one else will during your lifetime, let alone afterwards, since few like you would be found. Thus we pray for your life to be prolonged in obedience to Allah and His messenger. When you realize this, O prince, it is altogether your legal duty to seize Dār Kofa and either convert it to a mosque, as the Prophet, blessings and peace of Allah be upon him, would do with all churches when the territories of the polytheists were conquered, or build a madrasa for the pursuit of sacred knowledge, or a hostelry for the believing soldiers who strive in jihad for the sake of Allah. For it is unlawful to preserve such a house for the worship of idols. It is also incumbent upon you to take all the idols from Dār Kofa, and from all the other houses, and burn them, and demolish all of their *mattamores*. You should also send out a caller across your land to announce that whosoever sees slave women "playing" together in their communal houses (*diyār*), or in the house

64 The reference of "those fed carrion" is vague in the original manuscript.

في دار جماعتهم او دار رجل من رجال بلدك من غير عرس ونحوه ان يخبرك
لتاخذهن وتعذبهن عذابا لا يكدْن ان يسلمن منه لانهن غيْر
مامونات على الشرك عند اجتماعهن واجتماع النساء مذموم مطلقا
في الشرع وَان تقول ايضا ان كل من رءا خادما تصرع فلياخذها ~~وليحبس~~
وليحبسها بعد الضرب الشديد وان تابت بعد ذلك فنعم والا فليقتلها
وَان تمنعهم ان يخرجوا الى الحلاج وغيرها من مواضع عباداتهم وَان تجعل
لهم في ذلك حاكما مختصا عارفا بالكتاب والسنة هذا كله بعد ان تامرهم
الان بالتوبة فان امتنعوا فاقتلهم لانهم مرتدون والمرتد لا يقر على fol. A
دينه وان قالوا بانهم باقون على كفرهمْ الاول ولم تقم بينة او قرينة
تدل على كذبهم فاجبرهم على الاسلام الان لانهم مجوس فليس لهم كتاب
والمجوسي يجبر على الاسلام مطلقا بالتهديد والضرب وَان تامر اهل
مملكتك كلهم ان يغلقوا ابوابهم دون هؤلاء الشياطين لانهم فتنة
اعْظم من فتنة المسيح الدجال اَلَا ترى انهنَّ ادخلن الشرك على نساء
المومنين وضعفاء الرجال الى ان يظهر اسلامهن وحسن حالهن وَمِن
ادخالهن الشرك على نساء المومنين وضعفاء الرجال انهن ان توسل
احد من النساء والرجال المذكورين الى ءالهتهنَّ يقلن له لا بد لك ان تذبح
لآلهتنا في كل سنة وان لم تفعل فلا بد ان تقع عليك او [على] زوجك او ابنك
مصيبة وَانت يا سيدي تعرف ان النساء ناقصات العقل والدين[1]
والجهال كالبهايم فواجب عليك ايضا ان ترسل الى كل بلد من بلدانك
من سوسة وصفاقس وقيروان وغيرها ان يغيروا هذه الفتنة
اعاذنا اللّه واياك من السلب بعد العطاء وواجب على كل قاض ومفتي
ان يمنع هؤلاء العبيد في نكاح المسلمات ونكاح المسْلمين نسايهم بعد
ثبوت شركهم والقيام في ذلك واجب لتصريح كتاب اللّه على حرمة
ذلك لقوله تعلى "وَلَا تَنْكِحُوا الْمُشْرِكَاتِ حَتَّى يُؤْمِنَّ وَلأَمَةٌ مُّؤْمِنَةٌ خَيرٌ مِنْ
مُّشْرِكَةٍ وَلَوْ أَعْجَبَتْكُمْ وَلا تُنْكِحُوا الْمُشْرِكِينَ حَتَّى يُؤمِنُوا وَلَعَبْدٌ مُّؤْمِنٌ خَيْرٌ

[1] صحيح البخاري، ١: ٨٤

of any man—other than at weddings and the like—should inform you, so that you seize them and administer a painful chastisement from which they can scarcely recover, since they cannot be trusted not to perform acts of paganism during their assemblies, and, in any case, gathering of women is undisputedly condemned by the Sacred Law. You should also say that anyone who sees a slave woman fall possessed should take her and imprison her, after beating her soundly. If she repents thereafter, well and good, but if not, she is to be put to death. You should also forbid them from going out to the outskirts of Jilāz, and other such places of their worship, and you should appoint for this purpose an official who has knowledge of the Book and Sunna. All of this should be done after you have ordered them to repent. If they refuse, put them to death, for they are apostates and an apostate cannot be confirmed in his religion. If they say that they are following their original paganism and there exists no proof or circumstantial evidence that they are lying, force them into Islam now, for they are of the Majūs, who have no [divinely revealed] scripture, and the Majūsī is to be forced to Islam by threat and beating, unconditionally. You should order the people of your kingdom to close their doors to these devils, for they are far worse an affliction than the Antichrist. Do you not see that they have introduced polytheism to the believing [Muslim] women and to the weak-minded men? [They should be thus excluded] until they make their commitment to Islam manifest and become of good conduct.

Among their introducing polytheism to believing women and the weak-minded men is that if any of the former or latter pleads to their gods, they say to him: "You must sacrifice to our gods every year." If he refuses to do so, they say to him: "Some misfortune will befall you, your wife, or son."

As you know, my lord, women are lower minded and incomplete of religion,[65] and ignorant like the wild beasts. It is, therefore, incumbent upon you to send whoever is capable of doing away with this sedition in all the towns of your country, Sousse, Sfax, Kairouan, and others. May Allah protect us and you from being deprived after having been given. It is obligatory for every judge and mufti to ban these slaves from marrying Muslim women, and Muslim men from marrying [slave] women, after it is apparent that they are polytheists. Establishing these principles is imperative as their prohibition is manifested in the Book of Allah, in view of His, the Most High, having said: "And do not marry polytheist women until they believe. And a believing slave woman is better than a polytheist, even though she might please you. And do not marry polytheist men

65 *Ṣaḥīḥ al-Bukhārī*, The Book of Menses, 1:48.

مِّنْ مُّشْرِكٍ وَلَوْ أَعْجَبَكُمْ"[١] وقال ايضا "وَلا تُمْسِكُوا بِعِصَمِ الكَوَافِرِ"[٢] وقال ايضا
"لَنْ يَجْعَلَ اللَّهُ لِلكَافِرِينَ عَلَى المُؤْمِنِينَ سَبِيلًا"[٣] فواجب ايضا على كل
قاض ان يفسخ النكاح بينهم وبين المسلمات ان كن عندهم وكذلك العكس
fol. B وان يمنعهم من الشهادة والتزكية والجرح وغير ذلك من امور الدين وواجب
وان لا يصلي عليهم احد اذا ماتوا حتى يتوبوا الى اللّه تبارك وتعلى وواجب على كل
مفتي ايضا ان يفتي بان لا يعتق كل احد عبدا و خادما حيث علم انه
يدخل معهم في هذه الفتنة لانه لا يجوز لاحد ان يفعل شيئا مما يودي
الى خروج المسْلم من سواد المومنين الى سواد الكافرين يا يها
العلماء لا يجوز لكم السكوت عن هذه الفتنة بعد اطلاعكم عليها لانه
قد جاء في الحديث وانتم اعلم مني به اذا ظهرت الفتن وسكت العالم
فعليه لعنة الله[٤] اذا فهمتم هذا الحديث علمتم انه واجب على كل
عالم ان يتكلم في ذلك بالقول فيذكر الحكم فيها فان سُمِع منه ورُجع
اليه حصل المراد وان ترك قوله كان قد قام عذره عند اللّه وقام بما
وجب عليه ويسلم من الافات العظيمة التي عليها في عدم الكلام
فَانه قد ورد ان يوم القيامة يتعلق الرجل بالرجل وهو لا يعرفه
فيقول له ما لَك ما رايتك قط فيقول بل رايتني يوما على منكر فلم تغيره
عليَّ وبالكلام ينجوا من هذا الخطر والكلام ليس فيه مشقة واكثر
المناكر والبدع في زماننا هذا ليس على العالم مشقة ولا خوف علىَ في الكلام
فيها وَانما يترك الكلام من استانست نفسه بالعوايد الردية ولا
حول ولا قوة الا باللّه العلي العظيم انا للّه وانا اليه راجعون الحمد للّه
رب العالمين وَصلى اللّه على سيدنا محمد وعلى ءاله وصحبه وامته وسلم

[١] سورة البقرة، ١٢٢ [٢] سورة الممتحنة، ١٠ [٣] سورة النساء، ١٤١ [٤] مسند ابن حنبل، 2: 754

[to your women] until they believe. And a believing slave man is better than a polytheist, even though he might please you."[66] And He also says, "And hold not to marriage bonds with disbelieving women;"[67] and, "And never will Allah give the disbelievers over the believers a way [to overcome them]."[68]

Thus it is incumbent upon every judge and mufti to nullify any existing marriage contracts between them [the slaves] and Muslim women and vice versa; to prohibit them from giving legal testimony, standing as a reliable witness, and all other religious functions; never allow anyone to pray over their dead unless they repented to Allah, the Blessed and Most High; and to issue a fatwa that no one is to free a slave or slave woman if he knows that he or she will join them in this sedition, for it is unlawful for anyone to do something that will lead a Muslim to leave the pale of the commonality of believers for the commonality of unbelievers.

O learned scholars! It is unlawful for you to remain silent about this sedition after knowing the truth, for it is mentioned in the hadith—and you know better than I—"When sedition occurs and the scholar remains silent, the curse of Allah will be upon him."[69] If you comprehend this hadith, then you shall realize that it is incumbent upon every scholar to say something about this sedition and mention the legal ruling pertaining to it. If he [the slave] listens and repents, then the scholar's goal is accomplished, and if he ignores his advice, then the scholar would be excused by Allah for having done his duty, and remain safe from the great punishment that would otherwise befall him for remaining silent [on the matter]. It is related that on the Day of Judgement a man will hold another man whom he does not know tight; the latter will say: "What is the matter with you, I have never seen you before." The former will reply, "Nay, you saw me indeed one day when I was committing an evil act and you did not stop me." So by mere words alone, one can be saved from danger. And speech doesn't take much effort. Most of the evils and reprehensible innovations of our time are not difficult for the scholar to address, who need not fear speaking up about them. Indeed, only those who have accustomed themselves to vile habits have forsaken speech. There is no power or motion but through Allah. "Verily to Him do we belong, and to Him shall we all return." All praise be to Allah, Lord of the Universe, and may Allah's utter peace and security and blessings be upon our master Muḥammad, his folk, companions, and nation.

66 Quran 2:221.

67 Quran 60:10.

68 Quran 4:141.

69 *Musnad Ibn Ḥanbal*, 2:457.

تسليمًا قد كَمُل التاليف بعد العشاء ليلة الخميس الرابعة
والعشرين من شهر اللّه الاصب رجب وَكَانَ ابتداؤه في عشية يوم الاربعة
الثالث والعشرين في رجب المذكور في عام جكرش ارنا اللّه بَعْدها
fol. A بالخير والسلامة والعافية ءامين اللَّهمَّ اغفر لنا ولآباينا الى منتهى
الاسلام ولاشياخنا ولاحباينا وارزقنا واياهم علما مع العمل وحسن
الخاتمة وانصرنا وامراءنا على اعدايك اعداء الدين ولا تُشمت بنا اعداءنا
يا حي يا قيوم يا ذا الجلال والاكرام يا مجيب يا ارْحم الراحمين
سبحانك لا اله الا انت سبحانك اني كنت من الظالمين يا اللّه يا الله
يا الله بجاه محمد صلى اللّه وسلم عليه وعلى ءاله واخوانه من النبيين
والمرْسلين وعلى جميع الملايكة اجمعين الحمد للّه رب العالمين

نقلت هذه النسخة من خط يد المولف رحمه اللّه
تعلى ورضي ونفعنا به ءامين ووافق تمام
النسخ ضحى يوم [[~~الاحد~~]] الاثنين التاسع
عشر من شهر رجب الاصب
سنة ١٣٠١ ألف وثلاثماية وواحد
عرفنا اللّه خيرها ووقانا
شرها بجاه سيدنا
محمد وءاله
وتابعى
منواله
ءامين

وصلى الله على سيدنا ومولانا محمد وءاله وصحبه وسَلِّمْ تسليمًا
الحمدالله
كم حصرتني شدة بجيشها * وضاق صدري من لقاها وانزعج
حتى اذا ايست من زوالها * جاءتِ الالطافُ تسعى بالفرج
عن مولاي احمد الفاسي عن سيدنا محمد بن ناصر رحمهما الله

This work was completed after the evening prayer (*al-ʿishāʾ*) on Thursday 24 Rajab. It began in the evening of Wednesday 23 Rajab, 1223/1808. May Allah show us, after it, all goodness, safety, and well-being. Amen. O Allah, forgive us our sins and our forefathers of the Muslims, our teachers, and our loved ones; and grant us and them knowledge with practice and a goodly end. Grant us and our leaders victory over the enemies of the religion. And make not our enemies rejoice over our misfortunes, O Eternal Through Whom All Exists, O Possessor of Majesty and Magnanimity, O All-answering, O Most Merciful of the Merciful. Exalted are You. There is no Allah but You. Exalted are You. Verily I was of the wrongdoers! O Allah. O Allah. O Allah. By the grace of Muḥammad, blessings and peace of Allah be upon him, his brethren of the prophets and apostles, and by the grace of all angels and those brought nigh. And the close of our prayer is ever "All praise be to Allah, Lord of the Universe"; He suffices me and is the best to rely on. How excellent is the protector, and how excellent is the eternal bliss!

∴

This manuscript was copied from the handwriting of the author, may Allah, the Most High, have mercy on his soul. We beseech Allah to bless him and make this treatise beneficial to us. It was completed in the forenoon of Monday 19 Rajab, 1301/1884. May Allah guide us to the best of it and save us from its errors by the grace of our master Muhammad, his family, and all those who follow his path.

Amen.

How many a hardship held me tight in its claws?
Its mere meeting almost choked me to death.
When all hope to rid of it disappears,
Relief runs from nowhere and all pain clears.
By my Lord Ahmed Al-Fasi, from our Master Muhammad bin Nasser,
may Allah have mercy on their souls.

Glossary

ʿabīd (*sing ʿabd*) literally slaves, but generally denotes enslaved Blacks. The terms is also used colloquially to refer to people of sub-Saharan African descent in North Africa and the Middle East

ʿabīd al-Bukhārī slave soldiers composed of Sudanic Africans and Saharan Blacks established by the ʿAlawī ruler, Sultān Ismāʿīl (reigned 1672–1727)

adhān the Muslim call to prayer

ahl al-Kitāb the People of Book such as Jews, Christians, Zoroastrians, and Magians living under the sovereignty of the early Muslim rulers

ʾahrār (**sing** *hurr*) free Blacks

al-amr bi-l-maʿrūf commanding the good and forbidding the wrong

al-Jadal al-Wahhābiyya Wahhābi religious polemical debate

ʿajāʾiz (**sing.** *ʿajūz*) meaning old ladies, but referring to Bori priestess in Tunisia

ʿālim, See also *ʿulamāʾ* a religious scholar

al-musāḥaqa lesbianism

al-muwalladūn mixed race of Sūdānic descent

al-muwalladun al-ʿajām mixed race of Sūdānic descent who were non-native speakers of Arabic

al-ṣāliḥīn the righteous

al-Sūdān literally meaning, Blacks in reference to their Sūdānic African origins

amīr, **prince** ruler or a commander

amīr al-Muʾminīn Commander of the Faithful

ʿarāʾif (**sing.** *ʿarīfa*) *Bori priestess*

ardos Fulfulde clans

ʾaswad black

ʿatīq, (*pl. Maʿātīq*) freed slaves

ʾawliyāʾ (**sing.** *Wālī*) Muslim individuals who distinguished themselves during their lifetime as extraordinary pious and believed to be saints or have found such favor in the eyes of God and could perform miracles

barrāniyya foreign migrants

Bawwāba, (**sing.** *Bawwāb*) literally, doormen or gate keepers. The terms here refers to palace guards

Bash Agha a Chief eunuch, of Sudanic African origin, attached to the Beylical Court in the Bardo palace during the Husaynid Dynasty. Holders of this title also served as the governor over the enslaved Sudanic community of Tunisia during this period

Bey head of the Tunisian state under the Husaynid Dynasty

Beylik or Beylic an Ottoman providence

bidʿa a reprehensible religious innovation

Bilād al-Sūdān the Land of the Blacks

Bori (Hausa) a non-Islamic Hausa possession religious practice prevalent in West Africa, North Africa and parts of the Middle East

dahrī a materialist

Dandufu *Bori musical instrument*

Dār al-harb "abode of war," non-Islamic territory

Dār al-Islām *Islamdom, "abode of peace," an Islamic territory where Islamic law is enforced.*

Deyets the Algerian Turkish military general

Dhimmis "protected," referring "people of the Book" such as Jews, Christians, and Zoroastrians who are permitted to stay on their religious faith in Dār al-Islam.

Dina a Grand Council of the Islamic state in the Caliphate of Hamdallahi

Dīwān al-'Askar office of the Military Council

***Diyār*, (sing. *Dār*)** compound or households

Eyalet Ottoman province

farḍ a religious obligatory duty

fatwa a responsum, a legal opinion or ruling given in answer to a question by a Muslim Jurisconsult

fitna sedition or discord, also refers to the civil wars in early Islam

***Galadima* (Hausa)** deputy of the king

***gida* (Hausa)** a household or compound

***gidan jamā'at* (Hausa)** Bori community or public communal household

Gumbiri three-stringed lute with rectangular body decorated with cowrie shells for Bori ritual musical performance

ḥabus a religious endowment

ḥadīth the corpus of sayings which are believed to preserve the Prophetic tradition; an account of sayings and deeds, and is the second authority to Qur'an.

Hafsids An Almohad lineage which established an independent sultanate in Ifriqiyya

ḥajj the pilgrimage to Mecca which occurs in the month of *Dhul al-Hijja* annually and is the fifth pillar of Islam

ḥāra designation of a Jewish residential quarters in Tunisia

ibn al-qāḍī son of an Islamic religious judge

Ifriqiyya an area centered on modern Tunisia but including adjacent areas of modern Algeria and Libya

ijmā' consensus of the Muslim jurists on behalf of the Muslim community

***inna* (Hausa)** female Bori patron of the household

***iskoki* (Hausa)** Bori spirits

istidrāj delusion

istiftā' petition for a legal opinion from a Mufti (jurisconsult)

istirqāq al-'abīd Act of enslavement

Jihad literally means 'striving' or efforts for a self-discipline through the heart, hand, tongue or the sword. It also implies religious sanctioned warfare or campaign against non-believers.

Jilāz forest

Jinn *Muslim genies, refers to Bori spirits*

***karamāt* (sing. *Karāma*)** preternatural phenomena

***kasheka* (Hausa)** the deputy priestess

kātib the chief scribe

Ka'ba al-Musharraf the holiest place of Islam in Mecca

Kharja a procession to the *zāwiya* during the annual visitation season

Kitābī believers people of the book such as Jews, Christians or Zoroastrians

***kofāfi* (sing. *Kofa*)** meaning doormen.

kufr unbelief or infidelity

kuffār infidels or unbelievers who reject the message of Islam

kuffār bi-l-aṣālat pure non-believers

Medina city of Tunis

Maghrib Literally the sunset. The term is also used broadly to refer the lands of North Africa corresponding to modern Morocco, Tunisia, Libya and Algeria. It is also used to refer exclusively to Morocco

madrasa a school for pupil also a residential college where Islamic law and other religious subjects are taught

Majlis a council gathering of a ruler, prince or governor

***Magajiya* (*Hausa*)** female deputy to a queen. Use in Tunisia to designate the lower-level lieutenants and spokeswomen to the Bori priestesses

***Maguzawa* (Hausa)** literally fire worshippers. The term is applied to non-Muslim Hausa

Majus a Mgian, or Zoroastrian

***mālamai* (sing. *mālam*)** an Islamic religious scholar

Masu-Bori (Hausa) adepts of the non-Islamic Hausa possession religious practice

Mattamores *Granaries*

maʿātīq*, sing. *ʿatīq liberated slaves

munāfiq hypocrite

mushrikīn idolators

muʿaṭṭil a denier of Allah's attributes

mufti a religio-legal jurist who issues legal opinions (*fātāwā*)

***muʿjizāt* (sing. *muʿjiza*)** miracles

nawādī as clubhouses

Pāsha a high-ranking political and administrative title or position in Turkey and Ottoman northern Africa

Qādī "judge" trained in Islamic law in Muslim countries

Qādiriyya a Sufi order

qāʾid a regional administrator

qāʾid al-ʿabīd slave officials

***quḍāt* (sing., *qāḍī*)** judges trained in Islamic law

riqq slavery

***sarauniya* (Hausa)** a queen-mother in Hausa

***Sarkin Gida* (Hausa)** literally, a landlord. The term is, however, used by the Bori adepts in Tunis in reverence to their chief deity also referred to as the Holiest of the Bori deities

***Sarki* (Hausa)** kings or the ruling elites

Shahada Islamic profession of faith testifying that "There is no god but Allah and Muhammad is His Messenger."

Sharīfs guardians of the holy sites of Mecca and Medina

sharīʿa the religious law of Islam based on the Qurʾan, the Hadith, *ijma* (consensus of the jurists) and subsequent body of *fiqh*

shaykh term used as an honorific title as a head of a tribe or a Sufi order. The term also implies a learned scholar

Sha'abān the eight month of the Islamic calendar

shirk al-'abīd polytheism of the enslaved Sudanic Africans

Shirk a polytheistic religious practice

Shī'ī "party or faction" of Ali; those who believe that Prophet Muhammad designated Ali and his descendants as rightful descendants to be true leaders of the Islamic community after his death

***Shwāshīn* (*sing, Shūshān*)** freed slaves or free Blacks of enslaved descent

Sudānī A person of sub-Saharan African descent

Sūdān Tūnis Blacks of Tunis

Sufism Islamic mysticism

Sulṭān from "*sulṭat*" meaning authority refers to a ruler in a Muslim state with a more secular connotation than a caliph

Sulṭān al-Jinn wa-l-Ṣahrā' patron of the Jinn and the desert

Sultān al-Medina patron and protector of Tunis.

Sunna the saying, deeds and practice of the Prophet as preserved in the Hadith

'itq manumission

Takfīr anathematization or the action of declaring someone to be an unbeliever (*kāfir*)

ṭalaba pupil in madrassa setting in the *Bilād al-Sūdān*

ṭarīqas the popular Sufi religious brotherhoods

tawassul the Sufi practices of seeking the intercession of saints

tawḥīd the essential unity of God (absolute monotheism); Allah's absolute sovereignty over the universe

Torodbe a Muslim cleric

'uhd no treaty

***'ulamā'* (see also *'ālim*)** religious scholars

'ulamā' *al-sū'* vile Muslim scholars

umma the Universal Islamic community

'urūsh local principalities

walā' the clientele system of dependency or

wizārat al-kubrā the Office of the Prime Minister

wuḍū' ritual purification

***Wusfān* (sing. *Wasīf*),** literally meaning a servant, but commonly used in Tunisia and parts of the Middle East to refer Black population

Zakzak Zaria in northern Nigeria

zāwiya a Sufi lodge or mausoleum

ziyārāt visitation *to a zawiya*

zunnār a monk's girdle

Bibliography

Archives

Tunisian National Archives

Ahmad Bey to the Austrian consul, 24 Shawwal 1258/29 September 1842, Document 10 and 11, Dossier 421, Carton 230, Séries Historiques. Archives du Government Tunisienne.

Lettres des Caid de Sahel, Correspondences des Caids, Dossier 425-Carton 36. Archives du Government Tunisienne.

Lettres des Caid de Sahel, Correspondences des Caids, Dossier 425-Carton 36. Archives du Government Tunisienne.

The National Library (UK)

F.O. 100/29., 1845. Richardson, James, An Account of the Regency of Tunis. London [Unpublished]

Manuscripts

Aḥmadu Lobbo to al-Ḥāj Aḥmad ibn Abī Bakr al-Fūtī, SAVAMA-DCI/Hill Museum & Manuscript Library, (SAV BMH 34003).

al-Timbuktāwī, Aḥmad b. al-Qādī b. Yūsuf b. Ibrāhīm al-Fulānī, *Hatk al-Sitr ʿAmmā ʿAlayhi Sūdān Tūnis min al-Kufr*, Tunis: MS No. 21183, Bibliotheque Nationale de Tunisie, 1813.

al-Timbuktāwī, Aḥmad b. al-Qādī b. Yūsuf b. Ibrāhīm al-Fulānī, *Hatk al-Sitr ʿAmmā ʿAlayhi Sūdān Tūnis min al-Kufr*, Tunis: MS No. 09563, Bibliotheque Nationale de Tunisie, 1813.

al-Timbuktāwī, Aḥmad b. al-Qādī b. Yūsuf b. Ibrāhīm al-Fulānī, *Hatk al-Sitr ʿAmmā ʿAlayhi Sūdān Tūnis min al-Kufr*, Tunis: MS No. 18626, Bibliotheque Nationale de Tunisie, 1813.

al-Timbuktāwī, Aḥmad b. al-Qādī b. Yūsuf b. Ibrāhīm al-Fulānī, *Hatk al-Sitr ʿAmmā ʿAlayhi Sūdān Tūnis min al-Kufr*, Royal Library, Rabat: MS No. 6832, 1809.

Oral Interviews

Bīdālī, Hamadī Abdel Hamid and Abdelmajid, interview by the author. Sidi Abdel Salem, (Tunis), August 23, 2000.

Bornaoui, Abdelmajid, Sīdī El-Bechīr, Tunis, July 19, 2001.
Trabelsī, Zohra, Bab Swouika, Tunis, July 12, 2001.
Al-Juinī, Habib Bab El-Djedid, Tunis, July 11, 2001.

Websites

De-Constructing the Maghrib. A StoryMap: Demonstrating the Maghrib's Africanity (The Origins Debate on Race and Slavery in Morocco) https://storymaps.arcgis.com/stories/a227b874713745b0b86ca63ac515d597

Primary Sources

ʿAlī Pereejo, Muḥammad b., *L'inspiration de l'éternel. Éloge de Shékou Amadou, fondateur de l'empire peul du Macina*, ed. and trans. Georges Bohas, Abderrahim Saguer, and Bernard Salvaing, Brinon-sur-Sauldre: Grandvaux, 2011.
Amos, Perry, *Carthage and Tunis: Past and Present*, Providence, RI: Providence Press Company, 1869.
Bābā, Aḥmad, *Miʿrāj al-Suʾūd: Aḥmad Bābā's Replies on Slavery*, ed. John Hunwick and Fatima Harrak, Rabat: Institute of African Studies, 2000.
Bello, Muḥammad, *Infāq al-Maysūr fī taʾrīkh bilād al-Takrūr*, ed. Bahīja Shādhilī, Rabat: Publications of the Institute of African Studies, 1996.
al-Bukhārī, Abū ʿAbdallāh Muḥammad bin Ismāʿīl, *Al-Jāmiʿ al-Saḥīḥ: Saḥīḥ al-Bukhārī*, vol. 9, Cairo, n.d.
Dan Fodio, Usman, *Bayān wujūb al-hijra ʿalā l-ʿibād*, trans. F.H. El-Masri, Khartoum: Khartoum University Press & Oxford University Press, 1978.
El-Bekri, Description de l'Afrique septentrionale, ed. and trans. William Mac Guklin de Slane, Tangiers: Adolphe Jourdan, 1859 & 1913.
Frank, Louis, *Tunis: Descrition de cette régence*, in J.J. Marcel (ed.), *L'Univers pittoresque: Histoire et description de tous les people*, Paris, 1850.
al-Ḥachāʾishī, Muḥammad b. ʿUthmān, *Al-ʿAdāt wa al-taqālīd al-Tūnīsiyya: al-hadiya wa-l-fawāʾid al-ʿilmiya fī-l-ʿadāt al-Tūnīsiyya*, Tunis, 1994.
al-Ḥachāʾishī, Muḥammad b. ʿUthmān, *Al-Rihla al-Saḥrāwiyya ʿabra arādī Tarābulus wa-bilād al-Tawāriq*, Fr. trans. Muḥammad Lasram, *Voyage au pays des Senoussia à travers la Tripolitaine et les pays Touareg*, Librairie maritime et coloniale: Tunis, 1903.
Hallett, Robin, *The Penetration of Africa: European Exploration in North and West Africa to 1815*, New York: Praeger, 1965.
Hallett, Robin, *Records of the African association, 1788–1831*, London: T. Nelson, 1964.

Ibn Abī Diyaf, Aḥmad, *Itḥāf ahl al-Zamān bi Akhbār mulūk Tūnis wa ʿahdi al-Amān*, 7 vols, Tunis: al-Dār al-ʿArabiyya lil-Kitāb, 1999.

al-Idrīsī, Abū ʿAbdallāh Muḥammad b. Muḥammad al-Sharīf, *Nuzha al-mustāq fī ikhtirāq al-āfāq*, ed. and trans. R. Dozy and M.J. De Goeje, *Description de l'Afrique et de l'Espangne par Edrisi*, Leiden: Brill, 1866.

Pellissier de Reynaud, Henri Jean François Edmond, *Description de la Régence de Tunis, Exploration scientifique de l'Algérie pendant les années 1840, 1841, 1842*, vol. 16, Paris, 1853.

Rebillet, Commandant, *Relations commerciales de la Tunisie avec le Sahara et le Soudan*, Nancy: Imprimerie Berger-Levrault, 1895.

Robinson, Charles Henry, *Hausaland, or Fifteen hundred Miles Through the Central Soudan*, London: S. Low, Marston and Co., 1896.

al-Sabaʿī, Abdelmajid, Mansūkhāt "Private Papers", Tunis: CF: Rachad Limam, *Siyāsat Hammudah Bāsha fī Tunis, 1782–1814* (Tunis: Manshūrāt al-Jāmiʿa al-Tūnīsiyya, 1980)

al-Sarrāj, Mohammed al-Wazīr, *Al-Ḥulal al Sundusiyya fī-l-Akhbār al-Tūnīsiyya*, 5 vols., Tunis, 1970–1973.

Shaw, Thomas, *Travels or Observations Relating to Several Parts of Barbary and the Levant*, Oxford, 1738.

Tully, Miss, *Narrative of a Ten Years' Residence at Tripoli in Africa: From the Original Correspondence in the Possession of the Family of the Late Richard Tully, Esq.*, 2nd ed., London, 1817.

Secondary Sources

al-ʿAbbās, ʿAbd al-Muḥsin (ed.), *Handlist of manuscripts in the Centre de Documentation et de Recherches Historiques Ahmed Baba, Timbuktu*, London: Al-Furqan Islamic Heritage Foundation, 1995.

Abdelkafi, Jellal, *La Médina de Tunis: Espace historique*, Tunis: Alif, 1989.

Abun-Nasr, Jamil, "The Tunisian State in the Eighteenth Century," *Revue de l'Occident Musulman et de la Méditerranée* 33 (1982): 33–66.

Abun-Nasr, Jamil, *A History of the Maghrib*, Cambridge: Cambridge University Press, 1987.

Austen, Ralph A., and Dennis D. Cordell, "Trade, Transportation, and Expanding Economic Networks: Saharan Caravan Commerce in the Era of European expansion, 1500–1900," in Alusine Jalloh and Toyin Falola (eds.), *Black Business and Economic Power* (Rochester: University of Rochester Press, 2002), 80–113.

Austen, Ralph, "The Trans-Saharan Slave Trade: A Tentative Census," in Henry Gemery and J.S. Hogendorn (eds.), *The Uncommon Market: Essays in the Economic History of the Atlantic Slave Trade*, (New York: Academic Press, 1979), 23–76.

Austin, Allan D., *African Muslims in Antebellum America: Transatlantic Stories and Spiritual Struggles*, New York: Garland Publishers, 1997.

Ayoob, Mohammed, and Hasan Kosebalaban (eds.), *Religion and Politics in Saudi Arabia: Wahhabism and the State*, Boulder, CO: Lynne Rienner Publishers, 2009.

Aziza, Mohamed, *Formes traditionnelles du spectacle*, Tunis: Sociéte tunisienne de diffussion, 1975.

Azumah, John Alembillah, *The Legacy of Arab-Islam in Africa: A Quest for Inter-Religious Dialogue*, Oxford: One World, 2001.

Azzoubat, Jalloul, *Al-Qāḍī wa-l-Muftī Ismāʿīl Tamīmī wa-l-radd ʿalā Dalālāt al-Wahhābīyya*, Tunis, 2016.

Barcia, Manuel, "An Islamic Atlantic Revolution: Dan Fodio's Jihad and Slave Rebellion in Bahia and Cuba, 1804–1844," *Journal of African Diaspora, Archeology, and Heritage* 2, no. 1 (2013): 6–19.

Bédoucha, Geneviève, "Un noir destin: travail, status, rapport dépendence dans une oasis du sud-tunisiene," in Michel Cartier (ed.), *Le Travail et ses représentations: text rassemblés*, Paris: Édition des archives contemporaire, 1984.

Birk, J.S., *Across the Savanna to Mecca: The Overland Pilgrimage Route from West Africa to Mecca*, London: C. Hurst, 1978.

Boahen, Adu, "The Caravan Trade in Nineteenth Century," *Journal of African History* 3, no. 2 (1962): 249–359.

Brenner, Louis, "Muslim Thought in Eighteenth Century West Africa: The Case of Shaikh Uthmain b. Fudi" in Nehemiah Levtzion and John O. Voll (eds.), *Eighteenth Century Renewal and Reform Movements in Islam* (Syracuse, NY: Syracuse University Press, 1987), 39–68.

Brett, Michael, "Ifriqiyya as a Market for Saharan Trade from the Tenth to the twelve Century AD," *Journal of African History* 10, no. 3 (1969): 347–364.

Brett, Michael, "Population, Culture and Race in Egypt, the Sahara and North Africa" (paper presented at the Workshop on the Long-Distance Trade in Slaves Across the Sahara and the Black Sea in the 19th Century, [Unpublished], Bellagio: Italy, 10–16, December 1988: 1–7).

Brown, Carl L., "Color in Northern Africa," *Daedalus* 96 (1967): 464–482.

Brown, Carl L., "The Religious Establishment in Husaynid Tunisia," in Nikki R. Keddie (ed.), *Scholars, Saints, and Sufis: Muslim Religious Institutions in the Middle East since 1500*, Los Angeles and London: University of California Press, 1972.

Brown, Carl L., *The Tunisia of Ahmad Bey, 1837–1855*, Princeton: Prince University Press, 1974.

Brown, Jonathan A.C., *Slavery and Islam*, London: Oneworld Academic, 2019.

Brown, Jonathan A.C., *Islam & Blackness* London: Oneworld Academic, 2022.

Brown, William A., "The Caliphate of Hamdullahi, ca. 1818–1864: A Study in African History and Tradition," Ph.D. dissertation, University of Wisconsin-Madison, 1969.

Bunzel, Cole M. *Wahhābism: The History of a Militant Islamic Movement* (Princeton & Oxford, Princeton University Press 2023.

Burdet, Anita L.P., *The Expansion of Wahhabi Power in Arabia, 1798–1932: British Documentary Records*, Cambridge: Cambridge Archives Editions, 2013).

Burgard, Raymond, "Sesilasso en Tunisie: Voyage du prince de lacker-Muska en 1935," *Revue Tunisienne* 10, no. 2, (1932): 217–243.

Chanfi, Ahmad, *West African Ulama and Salafism in Mecca and Medina*, Leiden and Boston: Brill, 2015.

Chater, Khalifa, *Dépendance Et Mutations Précoloniales: La Régence De Tunis De 1815 À 1857*, Tunis: Publications de L'Université De Tunis, 1984.

Chater, Khalifa, "La traite au XIXe siècle d'après des sources tunisiennes," in André Martel (ed.), *Les arms et la Toge* (Montpellier: Centre d'Histoire et d'Etudes de Defense Nationale de Montpellier, 1997), 681–691.

Chater, Khalifa, "Esclavage et Commerce transsaherien au XIXe siécle dans las Règences de Tunis et Tripoli," *Cahier de la Mediterranée* 65 (Décembre) (2002).

Chérif, Mohamed-Hédi, "Hommes de religion et pouvoir dans la Tunisie de l'epoque Moderne," *Annales Economies Sociétés Civilizations*, 35, no. 3–4 (1980): 584.

Chérif, Mohamed-Hédi, "Pouvoir beylical et contrôle de l'espace dans la Tunisie du xviii siècle et les débuts du xix siècle," *Annuaire de l'Afrique du Nord* 22 (1983) pp. 41–61.

Clarke, Peter B., *West Africa and Islam: A Study of Religious Development from the 8th to the 20th Century*, London: Edward Arnold, 1982.

Cleaveland, Timothy, "Aḥmad Bābā al-Timbukti and his Islamic Critique of Racial Slavery in the Maghrib," *Journal of North African Studies*, 20 (1) (2015): 42–64.

Cook, Michael, "On the Origins of Wahhabism," *Journal of the Royal Asiatic Society of Great Britain and Ireland* 2 (1992): 191–202.

Cuco, Alex, *African Narratives of Orishas, Spirits and Other Deities*, Denver, CO: Outskirts Press, 2020

Curtin, Philip D. (ed.), *Africa Remembered*, Madison, WI: University of Wisconsin Press, 1967.

Curtis IV, Edward E., *The Call of Bilal: Islam in the African Diaspora*, Chapel Hill: The University of North Carolina Press, 2014.

Danmole, H.C., "Islam, Slavery and Society in Nineteenth Century Illorin, Nigeria," *Journal of the Pakistan Historical Society*, [Pakistan] 42, no. 4 (1994): 341–353.

Devey, P., "The Hafsia-Quarter Medina of Tunis, Tunisia," *Architectural Review*, (1983): 99–100,

Diouf, Sylviane A., "Devils or Sorcerers, Muslims or Studs: Manding in the Americas," in Paul E. Lovejoy and David V. Trotman (eds.), *Trans-Atlantic Dimension of Ethnicity in the African Diaspora* (New York: Continuum, 2003), 139–157.

Diouf, Sylviane A., "African Muslims in Bondage," in Joanne M. Braxton and Maria I. Diedrich (eds.), *Monuments of the Black Atlantic: Slavery and Memory* (Piscataway, NJ: Rutgers University, 2004), 77–90.

Dobronravin, Nikolay, "Literacy among Muslims in Nineteenth Century Trinidad and Brazil," in Behnaz Mirzai Asl, Ismael M. Montana and Paul E. Lovejoy (eds.), *Slavery, Islam and Diaspora* (Trenton NJ: Africa World Press, 2009), 217–236.

El Hamel, Chouki, "Constructing a Diasporic Identity: Tracing the Origins of the Gnawa Spiritual Group in Morocco," *Journal of African History* 49, no. 2 (2008): 241–260.

El Hamel, Chouki, *Black Morocco: A History of Slavery, Race, and Islam* (Cambridge: Cambridge University Press, 2013).

Ferchiou, S., "Stambali, La fête des 'autres gens': Présentation d'un film ethnologue," in Sophie Ferchiou (ed.), *L'Islam pluriel au Maghrib*, (Paris: CNRS Éditions, 1996), 339–346.

Fisher, Humphrey, "The Western and Central Sudan," in P.M. Holt, Ann K.S. Lambton, and Bernard Lewis (eds.), *The Cambridge History of Islam*, Vol. 2: *The Further Islamic Lands, Islamic Society and Civilization* (Cambridge: Cambridge University Press, 1970), 345.

Gomez, Michael, *African Dominion: A New History of Empire in Early and Medieval West Africa*, Princeton: Princeton University Press, 2018.

Gratien, Chris, "Race, Slavery, and Islamic Law in the Early Modern Atlantic: Ahmad Baba al-Tinbukti's treatise on enslavement," *Journal of North African Studies*, Vol. 18, No. 3 (May 2013): 454–468.

Green, Arnold, "The Sufi Orders in 19th-Century Tunisia: Sources and Prospects," *Revue D'Histoire Maghrebine*, 13–14 (1979).

Green, Arnold, "A Tunisian Reply to a Wahhabi Proclamation: Texts and Contexts," in Arnold H. Green (ed.), *Arabic and Islamic Studies: In Memory of Mohamed al-Nowaihi* (Cairo: The American University of Cairo Press, 1985), 155–177.

Green, Toby, *A Fistful of Shells: West Africa from the Rise of the Slave Trade to the Age of Revolution*, Chicago: University of Chicago Press, 2019.

Greenberg, Joseph, *Influence of Islam on Sudanese Religion*, Seattle: University of Washington Press, 1966.

Guy, Nicolas, *Dynamique sociale et appréhension du monde au sein d'une société Hausa*, Paris: Institut d'ethnologie, 1975.

Hall, Bruce, "The Question of 'Race' in the Pre-Colonial Southern Sahara," *Journal of North African Studies*, 10 (3–4) (2005): 339–367.

Hall, Bruce, *A History of Race in Muslim West Africa, 1600–1960*, New York: Cambridge University Press, 2011.

Hall, Stuart, *Representation: Cultural Representation and Signifying Practices, London Thousand Oaks, California: Sage in Association with the Open University, 1997.*

Hamdun, Said and Noel King, *Ibn Battuta in Black Africa, 1600–1960*, Princeton, NJ: Markus Wiener Publishers, 2011.

al-Ḥammāmī, ʿAbd al-Razzaq, "*ʿUlamāʾ Tūnis wa-l-Daʿwat al-Wahhābīyya*," *Ḥawliyyāt Jāmiʿat al-Tūnīssiyya* 30 (1989), 49–78.

Harrak, Fatima and Mohamed El-Mansour, *A Fulani Jihadist in the Maghreb: Admonition of Aḥmad Ibn Al-Qāḍī at-Timbuktī to the Rulers of Tunisia and Morocco*, Rabat: Institute of African Studies, 2000.

Heck, Paul L., "An Early Response to Wahhabism from Morocco: The Politics of Intercession," *Studia Islamica*, 107, no. 2 (2012), 235–254.

Hiskett, Mervyn, "Kitāb Al-Farq: A Work on the Habe Kingdoms Attributed to 'Uthmān Dan Fodio," *Bulletin of the School of Oriental and African Studies* 23, no. 3 (1960): 558–579.

Hiskett, Mervyn, "An Islamic Tradition of Reform in the Western Sudan from the Sixteenth to the Eighteenth Century," *Bulletin of the School of Oriental and African Studies* 25, nos. 1/3 (1962): 577–596.

Hiskett, Mervyn, *The Development of Islam in West Africa*, London: Longman, 1982.

Hopkins, J.F.P., and Nehemia Levtzion (ed. and trans.), *Corpus of Early Arabic Sources for West African History*, Cambridge: Cambridge University Press, 1981.

Hopkins, N.S., "Traditional Tunis and Its Transformation," *Annals of the New York Academy of Sciences* 220 (1974).

Hucks, Tracey E., *Yoruba traditions and African American religious nationalism*, Albuquerque: University of New Mexico Press, 2012.

Hunwick, John, *Sharia in Songhay: The Replies of al-Maghili to the Questions of Askia al-Hajj Muhammad*, Oxford: Oxford University Press, 1985.

Hunwick, John, "Songhay, Borno and the Hausa States, 1450–1600," in J.F. Ade Ajayi and Michael Crowder (eds.), *History of West Africa*, vol. 1, 3rd ed. (Cambridge: Cambridge University Press, 1985), 323–372.

Hunwick, John, "Islamic Law and Polemics Over Race and Slavery North and West Africa (16th–19th Century)," in Shaun E. Marmon (ed.), *Slavery in the Islamic Middle East* (Princeton, NJ: Markus Wiener Publishers, 1999), 43–68.

Hunwick, John, "Aḥmad Bābā on Slavery," *Sudanic Africa* 11 (2000): 131–139.

Hunwick, John, "The Religious Practices of Black Slaves in the Mediterranean Islamic World," in Paul Lovejoy (ed.), *Slavery on the Frontiers of Islam* (Princeton, NJ: Markus Wiener, 2004), 149–172.

Hunwick, John, *West Africa, Islam, and the Arab World*, Princeton, NJ: Markus Wiener, 2006.

Hunwick, John and Eve Troutt Powell, *The African Diaspora in the Mediterranean lands of Islam*, Princeton, NJ: Markus Wiener Publishers, 2002.

Ibn Abī Diyaf, Aḥmad, *Itḥāf ahl al-Zamān bi Akhbār mulūk Tūnis wa ʿahdi al-Amān*, 7 vols., Tunis: al-Dār al-ʿArabiyya lil-Kitāb, 1999.

Ibn Ramaḍān, Faraj, *Talāqqī al-Wahhābīyya fī Tūnis: maʿa wathāʾiq al-murāsalāt al-mutabādala*, Tūnis: Dār Muḥammad ʿAlī lil-Nashr, 2013.

Jankowsky, Richard C., *Stambeli: Music, Trance, and Alterity in Tunisia*, Chicago: University of Chicago Press, 2010.

Janson, Marloes, "Islam in Sub-Saharan Africa," in Martin Shanguhyia and Toyin Falola (eds.), *Palgrave Handbook of African Colonial and Postcolonial History* (New York: Palgrave Macmillan New, 2018), 951–977.

al-Juwayli, Muḥammad Hedi, *Mujtamaʿ ʿātun lil-dhākira, mujtamaʿ ʿātun lil-nisyān* [*Societies to be remembered; Societies to be forgotten*]: A Monograph on the Black Minority in Southern Tunisia, Tunis: Ceres, 1994.

Kane, Ousmane Oumar, "The Transformation of the Pilgrimage Tradition in West Africa," in Ousmane Oumar Kane (ed.) *Islamic Scholarship in Africa: New Directions and Global Contexts* (Woodbridge: James Currey, 2021), 90–110.

Kane, Ousmane Oumar (ed.), *Islamic Scholarship in Africa: New Directions and Global Contexts*, Woodbridge: James Currey, 2021.

Kani, Aḥmad M., *Diyāʿ al-siyāsāt wa-fatāwī-l-nawāzil mimmā huwa fī furūʿ al-dīn min al-masāʾil*, Cairo, 1988.

Larguèche, Abdelhamid, *L'abolition de l'esclavage en Tunisie à travers les archives, 1841–1846*, Collection Savoir, Tunis: Alif: Société Tunisienne d'étude du XVIIIème siècle, 1990.

Last, Murray, "Historical Metaphor in the Kano Chronicle," *History in* Africa 7, (1980): 161–179.

Last, Murray, "Reform in West Africa: the Jihad Movements of the Nineteenth Century," in J.F. Ade Ajayi and Michael Crowder (eds.), *History of West Africa*, Vol. II (Harlow: Longman Group Ltd., 1987), 1–47.

Last, Murray, "History as Religion: De-constructing the Magian "Muguzawa" of Nigerian Hausaland," in Jean-François Chrétien, Claude-Hélène Perrot, and Françoise Raison-Jourde (eds.), *L'invention religieuse en Afrique: Histoire et religion en Afrique noire* (Paris: Karthala, 1993), 45–57.

Last, Murray, and Muhammad A. al-Hajj, "Attempt at Defining a Muslim in 19th Century Hausaland and Bornu," *Journal of the Historical Society of Nigeria*, 3, no. 2 (1965), 231–240.

Lefebvre, Camille, "Hausa Diasporas and Slavery in Africa, the Atlantic, and the Muslim World," in *Oxford Research Encyclopedia of African History*, published online, 22 March 2022. https://doi.org/10.1093/acrefore/9780190277734.013.917.

Levtzion, Nehemiah, "Merchants vs. Scholars and Clerics: Differential and Complementary Roles," in Nehemia Levtzion and Humphrey J. Fisher (eds.), *Rural and Urban Islam in West Africa* (Boulder, CO: L. Rienner Publishers, 1987), 38–42.

Levtzion, Nehemiah, *Islam in West Africa: Religion, Society and Politics to 1800*, Brookfield, VT: Variorum, 1994.

Levtzion, Nehemiah and John O. Voll, "Introduction" in Nehemiah Levtzion and John O. Voll (eds.), *Eighteenth Century Renewal and Reform Movements in Islam*, eds. (Syracuse, NY: Syracuse University Press, 1987), 3–20.

Levtzion, Nehemiah and Randall L. Pouwels (eds.), *The History of Islam in Africa*, Athens, OH: Ohio University Press, 2000.

Limam, Rached, *Siyāsat Ḥammūda Bāsha fī Tunis* (Tunis: Manshūrāt al-Jamīʿa al-Tunisīyya, 1980).

Limam, Rached, "Some Documents Concerning Slavery in Tunisia at the End of the 18th Century," *RHM* 8, no. 11 (1981).

Lo, Mbaye and Carl W. Ernst, *I Cannot Write My Name: Islam, Arabic, and Slavery in Omar ibn Said's America*, Chapel Hill: The University of North Carolina Press, 2023.

Loftkrantz, Jennifer, "Intellectual Discourse in the Sokoto Caliphate: The Triumvirate's Opinions on the Issues of Ransoming, ca. 1810," *Journal of African Historical Studies*, 45, no. 3 (2012), 385–401.

Lovejoy, Paul E., "The Central Sudan and the Atlantic Slave Trade," in Robert W. Harms et al. (eds.), *Paths Towards the Past: African Historical Essays in Honor of Jan Vansina*, Atlanta: African Studies Association Press, 1994.

Lovejoy, Paul E., "Muslim Freedmen in the Atlantic World: Images of Manumission and Self-Redemption," in Paul E. Lovejoy (ed.), *Slavery on the Frontiers of Islam* (Princeton, NJ: Markus Wiener Publishers, 2004), 233–262.

Lovejoy, Paul E., "Slavery, the Bilad al-Sudan, and the Frontiers of the African Diaspora," in Paul E. Lovejoy (ed.), *Slavery on the Frontiers of Islam* (Princeton, NJ: Markus Wiener Publishers, 2004), 1–30.

Lovejoy, Paul E., *Slavery, Commerce and Production in the Sokoto Caliphate of West Africa* Lawrenceville: Africa World Press, 2005.

Lovejoy, Paul E., "The Context of Enslavement in West Africa," in Jane Landers and Barry Robinson (eds.), *Slaves, Subjects, and Subversives: Blacks in Colonial Latin America* (Albuquerque: University of New Mexico Press, 2006), 9–38.

Lovejoy, Paul E., *Jihad in West Africa During the Age of Revolution*, Athens: Ohio University Press, 2016.

Mahadi, Abdullahi, "The Aftermath of the Jihad in the Central Sudan as a Major Factor in the Volume of the Trans-Saharan Slave Trade in the Nineteenth Century," in Elizabeth Savage (ed.), *The Human Commodity: Perspectives on the Trans-Saharan Trade* (London: Frank Cass, 1992), 111–128.

Mamdani, Mahmood, "Introduction: Trans-African Slaveries: Thinking Historically," *Comparative Studies of South Asia, Africa and the Middle East* 38 (2), (2018): 185–210.

Mandaville, Peter G., (ed.), *Wahhabism and the World: Understanding Saudi Arabia's Global Influence on Islam*, New York, NY: Oxford University Press, 2022.

al-Mansour, Mohamed, "Al-Harraka al-Wahhābīyya wa rudud al-fiʿl al-Maghribiyya ʿinda Bidāyat al-Qarn al-Tāsiʿ Ashar," in *Al-Islām wa-l-Mujtamaʿ al-Maghribī fī al-Qarn al-Tāsiʾ ʿAshar* (Rabat, 1986), 175–191.

Martin, B.G., "Unbelief in the Western Sudan: Uthman Dan Fodio's Ta'lim al-Ikhwan," *Middle Eastern Studies* 4, no. 1 (1967): 50–97.

Martin, B.G., "Kanem, Bornu, and the Fezzan: Notes on the Political History of a Trade Route," *Journal of African History* 10, no. 1, (1969): 15–27.

Montana, Ismael M., "Aḥmad Ibn al-Qāḍī al-Timbuktāwī on the Bori Ceremonies of Sudan-Tunis," in Paul E. Lovejoy (ed.), *Slavery on the Frontiers of Islam* (Princeton, NJ: Markus Wiener Publishers, 2004), 173–198.

Montana, Ismael M., "The Trans-Saharan Slave Trade of Ottoman Tunisia, 1574 to 1782," *The Maghreb Review* 33, no. 2, (2008): 132–150.

Montana, Ismael M., "Bori Colonies in Tunis," in Behnaz Mirzai Asl, Ismael M. Montana and Paul E. Lovejoy (eds.), *Slavery, Islam and Diaspora* (Trenton NJ: Africa World Press, 2009), 155–167.

Montana, Ismael M., "Bori practice among enslaved West Africans of Ottoman Tunis: Unbelief (Kufr) or another dimension of the African diaspora?" *History of the Family: An International Quarterly* 16 (2011): 152–159.

Montana, Ismael M., "The Stambali of Husaynid Tunis: From Possession Cult to Ethno-Religious and National Culture," in Ehud R. Toledano (ed.), *African Communities in Asia and the Mediterranean: Identities Between Integration and Conflict* (Halle and New Jersey: Max Plank Institute and Africa World Press, 2011), 171–184.

Montana, Ismael M., *The Abolition of Slavery in Ottoman Tunisia* (Gainesville: University Press of Florida, 2013).

Montana, Ismael M., "European Capitalism and the Effects of Commercialization on Agriculture," *Labor History*, 58 (2), (2017), 201–215.

Montana, Ismael M., "The Forgotten Sudanic Palace Guards of Ali Bey I: Their Genesis, Functions, and Legacy in Ottoman Tunisia," *Comparative Studies of South Asia, Africa and the Middle East* 38, no. 2 (2018): 296–309.

Montana, Ismael M., "African Religion in the Maghreb and the Middle East," in *Oxford Encyclopedia of Slavery, the Slave Trade, and Diaspora in African History*, published online, 24 February 2022. https://doi.org/10.1093/acrefore/9780190277734.013.1166.

Montana, Ismael M., "Al-Timbuktāwī, Aḥmad b. al-Qāḍī," in Kate Fleet et al. (eds.), *The Encyclopedia of Islam Three* (Leiden & Boston: Brill, 2022), 148–150.

al-Naqar, ʿUmar, *The Pilgrimage Tradition in West Africa: An Historical Study with Special Reference to the Nineteenth Century*, Khartoum: Khartoum University Press, 1972.

Naylor, Paul, *From Rebels to Rulers: Writing Legitimacy in the Early Sokoto State*, London: James Currey, 2021.

Newbury, C.W, "North Africa and Western Sudan Trade in the Nineteenth Century: A Reevaluation," *Journal of African History* 8 no. 2, (1966): 233–246.

Nobili, Mauro, *Sultan, Caliph, and the Renewer of the Faith: Ahmad Lobbo, the Tarikh Al-Fattāsh and the Making of an Islamic State in West Africa*, Cambridge: Cambridge University Press, 2020.

Paden, John, *Religion and Political Culture in Kano*, Berkeley: University of California Press, 1973.

Pâques, Viviana, *L'arbre cosmique dans la pensée populaire et dans la vie quotidienne du nord-ouest Africain*, Paris: Institut d'Ethnologie, 1964.

Peters, M.F.E., *The Hajj: The Muslim Pilgrimage to Mecca and the Holy Places*, Princeton, Princeton University Press, 1994.

Reis, João José, *Slave Revolt in Brazil: The Muslim Uprising of 1835 in Bahia*, trans. Arthur Brakel, Baltimore: Johns Hopkins University, 1993.

Robinson, David, *Chiefs and Clerics: Abdul Bokar Kan and Futa Toro, 1853–1891*, Oxford: Clarendon Press, 1973.

Robinson, David, "Revolutions in the Western Sudan," in Nehemia Levtzion and R. Pouwels (eds.), *The History of Islam in Africa* (Athens, OH: Ohio University Press, 2000), 131–151.

Robinson, David, *Muslim Societies in African History: New Approaches to African History*, Cambridge: Cambridge University Press, 2004.

al-Rudaysī, Ḥamādī and Asmāʾ Nuwayra, *Al-Radd ʿalā al-Wahhābīyya fī-l-qarn al-tāsiʿ ʿashar: nuṣūṣ al-Gharb al-Islāmī namūdhajan*, Beirut: Dār al-Ṭalīʿa lil-Ṭibāʿa wa-l-Nashr, 2008.

Saad, Elias, *Social History of Timbuktu*, Cambridge: Cambridge University Press, 1983.

Salau, Mohammed Bashir, *Plantation Slavery in the Sokoto Caliphate: A Historical and Comparative Study*, Rochester: University of Rochester Press, 2018.

Sanneh, Lamin, *The Crown and the Turban: Muslims and West African Pluralism*, Boulder, CO: Westview Press, 1997.

Scaglioni, Marta, *Becoming the Abid: Lives and Social Origins in Southern Tunisia*, Milan: Ledizioni, 2020.

Smith, M.G., *Government in Kano, 1350–1950*, Boulder, CO: Westview Press, 1997.

Stewart, Charles C., "Frontiers Dispute and Problems of Legitimation: Sokoto-Masina Relations 1817–1837," *Journal of African History*, 17, no. 4 (1976), 499.

Takaki, Keiko, *The Stambali: A Black Ritual Group of Tunisia: The Slave Trade Background and Present Situation*, Tokyo: Monbusho Kagaku Kenkyuhi, 1992.

Temimi, Abdeljelil, "Les affinites culturelles la Tunisie, la Libye, le centre et l'ouest de l'afrique a l'epoque moderne," in Abdeljelil Temimi (ed.), *Etudes d'Histoire Arabo-Africaine* (Zaghouan: Cermodi, 1994), 27–39.

Temimi, Abdeljelil, "Pour une histoire sociale de la minorité africaine noire en Tunisie: Sources et perspectives," in Abdeljelil Temimi (ed.), *Études d'histoire arabo-africaine* (Zaghouan: Cermodi, 1994), 49–56.

al-Tlīlī, El-Ajīlī, "*Al-Wahhābiyya wa bilād al-Tūnisiyya zaman Ḥammūda Bāsha*," Tunis: Université de Tunis, 1983.

Toledano, Ehud R., "African Slaves on Ottoman Eastern Mediterranean: A Case of Cultural 'Creolization'?" in Eyüb Özel, Suha Ünsal, and Kudret Emirogli (eds.), *The Mediterranean World: The Idea, the Past and the Present* (Istanbul: Iletism Yayinlari, 2006), 107–124.

Toledano, Ehud R., *As If Silent and Absent: Bonds of Enslavement in the Islamic Middle East*, New Haven and London: Yale University Press, 2007.

Tremearne, A.J.N., "Bori Beliefs and Ceremonies," *Journal of the Royal Anthropological Institute* 45 (1915), 23–68.

Tremearne, A.J.N., *The Ban of the Bori; demons and demon-dancing in West and North Africa*, London: Heath, Cranton & Ouseley Ltd, 1914.

Trimingham, John Spencer, *Islam in West Africa*, Oxford: Oxford University Press, 1959.

Valensi, Lucette, "The Problem of Unbelief in Braudel's Mediterranean," in Gabriel Piterberg et al. (eds.), *Braudel Revisited: The Mediterranean World 1600–1800* (Toronto: University of Toronto Press, 2010), 17–34.

Valensi, Lucette, "Is Religion Always Relevant? The Case of Tunisia (First Half of the 19th century)," in Lothar Gall and Dietmar Willoweit (eds.), *Judaism, Christianity, and Islam in the Course of History: Exchange and Conflicts* (Berlin, Boston: De Gruyter Oldenbourg, 2011), 415–424.

Valentine, Simon Ross, *Force and fanaticism: Wahhabism in Saudi Arabia and Beyond*, London: Hurst & Company, 2015.

Walz, Terence and Kenneth M. Cuno, *Race and Slavery in the Islamic Middle East: Histories of Trans-Saharan Africans in Nineteenth-Century Egypt, Sudan, and the Ottoman Mediterranean*, Cairo & New York: The American University in Cairo Press, 2010.

Walz, Terence, "Sudanese, Habasha, Takarna, and Barabira: Trans-Saharan Africans in Cairo as Shown in the 1848 Census," in Terence Walz and Kenneth M. Cuno (eds.), *Race and Slavery in the Islamic Middle East: Histories of Trans-Saharan Africans in Nineteenth-Century Egypt, Sudan, and the Ottoman Mediterranean*, (Cairo & New York: The American University in Cairo Press, 2010), 52–53.

Warner-Lewis, Maureen, "Religious Constancy and Compromise Among Nineteenth Century Caribbean-Based African Muslims," in Behnaz A. Mirzai, Ismael M. Montana and Paul E. Lovejoy (eds.), *Slavery, Islam and Diaspora*, (Trenton, NJ: Africa World Press, 2009), 237–268.

Wilks, Ivor W., "Salih Bilali of Massina" in Philip D. Curtin (ed.), *Africa Remembered* (Madison, WI: University of Wisconsin Press, 1967), 145–151.

Woodford, J.S., *The City of Tunis: Evolution of an Urban System*, Cambridgeshire: Middle East & North African Studies Press Ltd, 1990.

Yusuf, Salahudeen, *A History of Islam, Scholarship and Revivalism in Western Sudan, Being an Annotated Translation with Introduction of 'Infāqul-Maisūr fī Tārikh Bilād al-Tukrūr of Sultan Muhammad Bello Bin Fodio*, Zaria: Tamaza, 2013.

Zawadowski, G., "Le rôle des negres parmi la population tunisienne," *En Terre d'Islam*, no. 2eme semestre (1942): 146–152.

Index

ʿabd 74, 100
ʿabīd 23, 25, 41, 50, 52, 55–56, 69, 72–78, 83, 86, 96, 100, 109, 111. (See also, kufr al-ʿabīd)
ʿabīd al-Bukhārī 25, 86
Abi Diyaf 20, 33–36, 86, 98
Abolition 60–61, 75, 80–82, 93, 94, 98–99
Acculturation 63, 69, 70, 78
Age of Revolutions x, 5–6
Aghlabids 56, 85
Aḥmad Bābā, al-Timbukti 9, 15–16, 20, 53, 98–100
Aḥmad Bey 35, 77, 97
ʿAlī Bey I 41, 51, 69–70, 83, 85–86, 89, 90, 92, 96, 97
al-Ḥachā'ishī 62–63, 71, 73, 75, 81–82, 93
al-Maḥjūb, Shaykh ʿUmar 34, 36–37
Anathematization (Takfīr) 5, 26, 29–30, 44, 46, 54, 76, 96, 100
al-Riyāḥī, Ibrāhīm 35, 98
al-Sabaʿī, al-Mansūkhāt 69–70, 83, 86, 88
al-Sarrāj, Mohammed al-Wazīr 71
al-Sūdān 52, 55, 74, 99, 100
al-Tamīmī, Shaykh Ismāʿīl 34, 36.
al-Timbuktāwī x, xi, 3–6, 9, 13–30, 37–46, 48–52, 54–58, 62–64, 66–70, 73–88, 89–93, 95–101
Ardos (Fulfulde elites and clans) 47

Bash Agha 72–74
Bayram III, Muhammad 98
Bey 69, 72, 77, 85, 98
Bey of Tunis 3, 42, 58, 77
Beylic 3, 70, 72, 77, 80
Beylical 68, 70–73
Beylik 70, 73
Bilād Sudān 6, 8–9, 14–16, 26, 30, 38, 52–59, 61, 65, 74, 76, 78, 85, 98–100. (See also 'aswad)
Bori compounds 39, 63–64, 66, 72–74, 80–81, 83, 87–94
Bori cult 3–5, 7, 25, 29–30, 38–41, 46, 51, 54–55, 58, 63, 69–70, 76, 78, 95–97, 99
Bori pantheon 39, 42, 65, 97
Bori practice 3, 10, 13, 41–42, 52, 59, 65, 71, 76, 78–79, 81, 83, 88–91, 93
Bori spirits 12, 40, 65
Bori x, xii, 3, 6–8, 10–14, 29, 39, 40, 42, 56, 60, 65–66, 68–70, 73, 135, 143
Bornu 9, 41, 59–60, 62, 71, 86, 87, 90.
Bourguiba, Habib 72, 95
Brown, Leon C. 35, 41–42, 69, 74

Caliphate of Hamdallāhi 13, 19, 96
Central Sudān xvii, 4–6, 8–11, 14, 15, 19, 26, 28, 29–30, 38, 39–43, 46, 49, 51–52, 54, 56, 57, 58–59, 64, 69, 73–74, 78, 81, 85–90, 92–97, 99–101
Clientage (walā') 57, 69, 75
Clubhouses (nawādī) 69–70, 73, 83, 86–89, 92, 93, 97
Commander of the Faithful (amīr al-Mu'minīn) 48, 107
Commanding the good (al-amr bi-l-maʿrūf) 40, 111
Consensus (ijmāʿ) 107, 119, 121, 137

Dan Fodio, Uthman 12–16, 29, 43–47, 96
Dandufu 26
Dār al-Islām 5–7, 17, 44, 46, 54, 100
Dār Bambara 81, 115
Dār Beylik 70, 73, 88, 117
Dār Gwari 81
Dār Jamāʿat 80–82, 90
Dar Janfara (Zamfara) 117
Dār Kano 81, 88, 117
Dār Kofa 39, 70, 73, 80–83, 87, 88–89, 91–92, 113, 115, 123, 143
Dār Nufe 81, 88, 117
Dār Sarāʿ 88, 117
Dār Songhay 81, 115
Dār Zakzak (Zaria) 70, 81, 88
Dār ʿArīfat Bāghirmī 82
Dār ʿArīfat Wadai 82
Dawjaqa 17, 105
deputy priestess (Kasheka) 65
Deyets 59
Dissension (fitna) x, 4, 28, 40, 50–51, 76, 95, 107
Diyār (Compounds) 39, 63, 80–81, 83, 84, 143

Emancipation 77, 82, 98
enslavement (istirqāq al-ʿabīd) 96

fatwa 39, 53, 76, 98, 147
Foreign migrants (Barrāniyya) 92
Frank, Louis 58–59, 61–62, 64, 72, 75–77
Freed slaves (Maʿātīq) 52, 55–56, 69, 74–78, 81, 82.
Fulfulde 17, 19, 43, 45, 47–48, 51, 97
Futa Jallon 17, 43
Futa Toro 12, 43

Galadima 73–74, 78
Gida 26, 80, 88. (See also gidade)
Gidan jamāʿat 80, 82
Grand Council (Dina) 48
Gumbiri 115

ḥadīth 28, 36, 121, 137, 141, 147
Hafsid 86
Ḥammūda Pāsha 3, 4, 17, 20, 25, 34–37, 39–41, 50, 58, 59, 62, 72, 73, 76, 88–89, 92–93, 95, 97, 107
Hatk al-Sitr 37–38, 48, 51–52, 74–75, 88, 95–98, 101, 103, 109
Hausaland 8, 10–12, 29, 43–48, 52, 58, 61, 86–87, 89–90, 96
Holey cult 91
Hussein Bey 77

Ibn ʿAbd al-Wahhāb, Muhammad 13, 31, 32, 34
Ibn Battuta 9
Idolators (Mushrikīn) 47, 51, 54, 97, 105
Ifriqiyya xii, 24, 28, 41, 56–57
Infidels (kuffār) 3, 12–13, 24, 32, 40, 44, 50, 52, 54, 76–78, 89, 100–101, 105
inna 73
iskoki 12, 115, (See also, Bori spirits)
Islamic scholars (ʿulamāʾ) 35, 41, 43, 71
islamization and Africanization 7, 9, 10, 14
Intercession (tawassul) 5, 14, 26, 29, 33, 36–38, 42, 46, 92, 96–97, 123, 125, 127

Jewish residential quarter (ḥāra) 8, 92
Jihad ix, x, 4–7, 12–17, 26, 29, 30, 32, 37, 40, 43–44, 46–52, 54, 57–59, 86, 89, 95–97, 100–101, 113, 141, 143
Jinn 38, 64–68, 105, 113, 115, 117, 119, 121, 123, 125, 131, 133, 135, 139, 141, 143
judge (al-qāḍī) ix, xi, 3, 17, 48, 81, 97, 105

Kano Chronicle 8
Kofa 39, 41, 70, 73, 80–83, 86–89, 91, 92, 113, 115, 123, 143
Kofāfi 41, 94, (See also, Kofa)
kufr al-ʿabīd 75

Lesbianism (al-musāḥaqa) 4, 141
Lovejoy, Paul x, xi, 5, 14

Madrasa 39, 89, 143
Magajiya 65
Maguzawa 11–12, 45, 51, 101
Magian (Majus) 39, 45, 51, 76, 145
Malam 62, 93
Mansa Musa 9–10
al-Maghīlī, Muḥammed b. ʿAbd al-Karīm 10, 161
Manumission (ʿatīq) 39, 71, 75–77
Mattamores 66, 89, 113, 117, 119, 123, 125, 131, 133, 139, 141, 143
Military Council (Dīwān al-ʿAskar) 85
Miss Tully 86
mixed race of Sūdānic descent (al-muwalladūn) 55
Moroccan Sultān, Mawlāy Sulaymān 25, 33–34
mufti 34, 37, 76, 98, 107, 109, 111, 145, 147
Muradids 52, 56

N'Dodjika 17

Old ladies (ʿajāʾiz, ajūz) 4, 14, 65, 81, 93, 94
Ottoman Empire x, 32, 34, 73

Palace Guards (Bawwāba) 25, 41, 70, 73, 85–89, 90, 92, 94, 97
Pāsha, Ḥammūda ix, 3–4, 17, 20, 25, 34, 36–37, 39, 40–41, 50, 58, 59, 62, 72–73, 76, 88, 89, 92–93, 95, 97, 107, 115
People of the Book (ahl al-Kitāb) 11, 23, 123
petition for a fatwa (istiftāʾ) 98–99
Pilgrimage (ḥajj) ix, x, 3, 5, 9, 18–20, 25, 30–31, 35, 37, 43, 44, 48–49, 80–81, 88, 93, 95–97, 107, 115, 129

Priestess (ʿarīfa, pl. arāʾif) 4, 15, 64–65, 73, 81–83, 188
procession (Kharja) 72

Qādiriyya 12, 35
qāʾid al-ʿabīd 72–73
Race 7, 15, 17, 55
Religious Endowment (ḥabus) 71, 88, 115
Religious Establishment 35, 55, 98
Religious innovation (bidʿa) x, 3–5, 13–14, 28–29, 31–33, 35–37, 43, 46, 50, 69, 79, 96–97, 100, 127, 147
Slavery (riqq) 74

Robinson, Henry Charles 61–63
Robinson, David 7–9, 11
Rumfa, Sultan Muhammad 10

Saints (ʾawliyāʾ) 14, 29, 31, 33, 37–38, 42, 69, 97, 121, 125, 127
sarauniya 64
Sarkin Gida 26, 64, 80, 88, 113, 115, 123. (See also, Sulṭān al-Jinn wa-l-Ṣahrā)
Scholars (ʿulamāʾ) 4, 11–12, 17, 19–20, 28, 29, 31, 33–37, 40, 43–44, 46, 48, 51, 76–78, 97
Scribe (Kātib) 98
Sharīfs 32
Sharīʿa 44–45, 48, 51, 98
Sharia Council (Majlis al-Sharʿī) 98
shaykh 13, 34–36, 40, 51–52, 76, 78, 95
Shaykh Aḥmadu Lobbo 13–14, 19, 29, 47–49, 96–97
Shaʿabān 70
Shikāyat al-Dīn x, 4, 17, 19, 20, 23, 24
Shirk 5, 13, 26, 29, 31, 33, 36, 38, 44, 51, 69, 79, 95, 97, 99–100, 105, 111
shirk al-ʿabīd 23, 75, 96, 111
Shīʿī 32
Shwāshīn 51, 55–56, 68–69, 78, 96 (See also, Shūshān)
Sīdī al-Maḥrez 92
Sīdī Marzūq 83
Sīdī Saʿad al-ʿAbīd 41, 69, 71–72, 78, 83, 95
Slave soldiers 25, 56, 85, 93
Sokoto Caliphate 4, 14, 16, 44–47, 51, 89, 96, 100
Sūdān Tūnis ix, xii, 3–4, 6, 21, 27, 38, 50–56, 57, 59, 61, 63–69, 71, 74, 77–78, 80–81, 95–97, 99–101, (See also kuffār Sūdān Tūnis)
Sufi Brotherhoods (ṭarīqas) 9, 35
Sufism 3, 28, 30, 31, 33, 63
Sulṭān 8, 10, 11
Sulṭān al-Jinn wa-l-Ṣahrāʾ 64, 81
Sultān al-Medina 92
Sultān of Gobir 12
Sultān, Mawlāy Sulaymān 33–34
Sunna 40, 105, 119, 121, 137
Syncretism 11, 48, 50, 56, 99

ṭalaba 44
tawḥīd 31, 36
Tijaniyya 35
Torodbe 12, 43
trans-Atlantic 5, 14, 65, 99
trans-Saharan 3, 7, 9, 10, 14, 28, 41, 57, 59, 62, 73
Tremearne, A.J.N. 42, 63–64, 70, 75, 82

Umma 21, 97, 105
Unbelief (Kufr) ix, 3–4, 6, 15, 21, 27, 29, 37, 38, 50, 52–54, 75, 79, 95, 97, 99, 105, 109, 135

Vile scholars (ʿulamāʾ al-sūʾ) 184
Visitation (Ziyārāt) 26, 31, 33, 36, 70, 71, 83, 97

Wahhābi controversy (al-Jadal al-Wahhābiyya) 13–14, 20, 26, 29, 30, 33–34, 37, 97
Wahhābi proclamation 3, 13–14, 20, 28, 29, 31–37, 50
Wahhabis 31–34, 36, 38, 40, 123, 125, 127
Western Sudān x, 3–5, 9, 10, 17, 19, 28, 43, 55, 60, 62, 81–82, 87, 93, 96
Wusfān 4–5, 50–52, 54–57, 63–64, 74–78, 95, 97

Zakzak 81, 88, 117
Zawiya 35, 71–72, 83, 95
Zirids 56, 85
Zoroastrians 11, 45, 51 (see also Magians)